MANAGING FOR PRODUCTIVITY IN THE HOSPITALITY INDUSTRY

MANAGING FOR PRODUCTIVITY IN THE HOSPITALITY INDUSTRY

ROBERT CHRISTIE MILL

VNR VAN NOSTRAND REINHOLD
New York

Copyright © 1989 by Van Nostrand Reinhold

Library of Congress Catalog Card Number 88-26114

ISBN 0-442-26451-8

Printed in the United States of America

Designed by Eve Sandler

Van Nostrand Reinhold
115 Fifth Avenue
New York, New York 10003

Van Nostrand Reinhold International Company Limited
11 New Fetter Lane
London EC4P 4EE, England

Van Nostrand Reinhold
480 La Trobe Street
Melbourne, Victoria 3000, Australia

Macmillan of Canada
Division of Canada Publishing Corporation
164 Commander Boulevard
Agincourt, Ontario M1S 3C7, Canada

16 15 14 13 12 11 10 9 8 7 6 5 4 3 2 1

Library of Congress Cataloging-in-Publication Data

Mill, Robert Christie.
    Productivity in the hospitality industry.

    Includes bibliographies and index.
    1. Hospitality industry—Labor productivity.
I. Title.
TX911.3.L27M55   1989   647'.94'0683   88-26114
ISBN 0-422-26451-8

This book is dedicated to Ruby and Bert, Bob and Jane.

CONTENTS

Preface

The subject of productivity, which has immediate bottom-line impact for both individual and corporate businesses, has gained nationwide attention in recent years, with good reason. Productivity in the United States has dropped steadily since World War II from an annual growth rate of 3.6 percent to a recent and continued actual decline, according to the Houston-based American Productivity Center. This general decline is mirrored in the hospitality industry, which for many years has been able to hide its poor productivity behind the dramatic increase in the size of the market. As the industry moves into the mature stage of its life cycle, however, deficiencies in productivity are showing up on the bottom line.

Future increases in profits will have to come from gains in productivity. There is much room for improvement: the National Restaurant Association estimates that the restaurant industry is only half as efficient as manufacturing industries; an earlier U.S. Department of Agriculture study of thirteen restaurants found that they were operating at between 74 percent and 78 percent efficiency.

Business school graduates are ill prepared concerning productivity, ongoing research by the accrediting agency for business colleges—the American Assembly of Collegiate Schools of Business—indicates. Responses from 160 randomly selected corporate personnel offices reveal the following:

> Fifty percent think recently hired M.B.A.'s have an inadequate knowledge of productivity.
>
> Sixty percent think bachelor-level graduates have an inadequate knowledge of productivity.
>
> Business students were rated only marginally better than other students.

The objectives of this book are twofold: to indicate how critical improved productivity is to improving the bottom line, and to show how productivity improvement programs can be designed and implemented.

The book takes a practical approach, dealing with the basic problem: "What is productivity and how do I, as a line manager, improve it within my operation?" Four key questions determine the book's structure.

1. Why should we be concerned about productivity and what can we do about it?

Chapter 1 reviews past attempts to define productivity and outlines their shortcomings. Many traditional measures of productivity have not been inflation-proof. For example, defining productivity as employee costs divided by sales means it could be increased as costs rise simply by raising menu prices or room rates. But this would not indicate whether employees were working harder or smarter.

We must be concerned about productivity because of the evidence suggesting it is on the decline. This is increasingly important to the hospitality industry, which can no longer count on a growing market. Because it is a labor-intensive industry, relatively little substitution of technology for people can occur without losing the whole meaning of the terms *hospitality* and *service*.

When we add to these concerns the fact that human resources traditionally have been undervalued in the hospitality industry, the scope of the problem becomes clear. The focus of this section is on the need to increase profitability by hiring, developing, and motivating productive employees.

2. How do we hire productive employees?

Chapter 2 expands on the realization that improved productivity begins by hiring employees who have the potential to be productive. Hiring productive employees means matching the characteristics of the future employee pool with the characteristics of the job.

This section explores the changing demographics and attitudes of the hospitality employee of the future. Increasingly we will see more women, minorities (largely Hispanic), the elderly, the handicapped, and part-time employees in the workplace. The employee of the future will also bring increased aspirations and a desire for more satisfaction on and from the job. The special problems and opportunities of each are explored in light of the characteristics of hospitality jobs.

3. How can workplaces and jobs be designed to maximize employee productivity?

Increased productivity can result from improved layout and design in the workplace. Chapter 3 details how to lay out facilities and specific work areas to maximize the use of utilities, equipment, and labor. Chapter 4 examines how tasks can be planned and employees scheduled to perform those tasks in the most productive way.

4. How can employees be motivated to be productive?

The last section is concerned with motivating insufficiently productive employees. Managers cannot directly motivate employees. Motivation comes from within each employee. Managers, however, can suggest a *company culture* that can produce productive employees. Company culture, the subject of chapter 5, is an expression by top management of "how we want to do things around here." How to identify and implement an appropriate culture is covered.

While the culture is the way management wants things to be, employees may perceive the workplace differently. The *organizational climate*—or "how it feels to work here"—is made up of six elements: clarity, standards, commitment, responsibility, recognition, and teamwork. Chapter 6 provides a model of organizational climate and guidelines on how to determine what roadblocks, if any, exist to prevent employees from becoming motivated and productive.

When employees perceive inadequate clarity, standards, or commitment, a program of *management by objectives* is called for. Chapter 7 examines this topic, which assumes that employees work toward objectives to which they are

FIGURE P-1 PROBLEM: HOW TO IMPROVE PRODUCTIVITY.

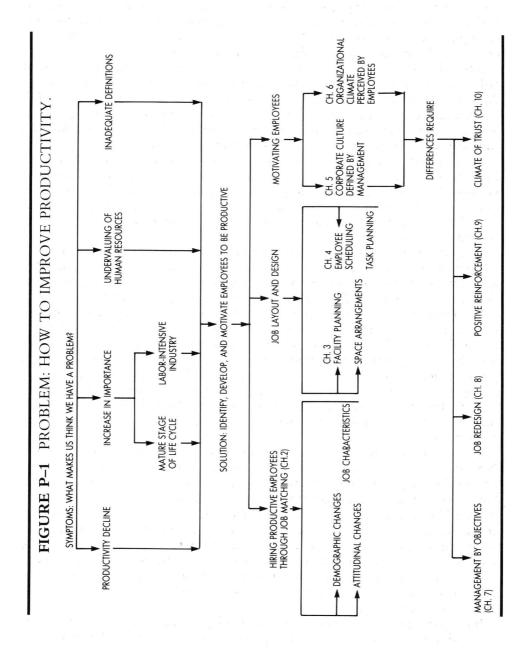

committed, and that such commitment comes from letting employees participate in the setting of the objectives.

Chapter 8 covers *job design*. When employees feel that they are being given insufficient responsibility, job redesign is desirable. Jobs may be enlarged or enriched. Job enlargement consists of adding more tasks; a dishwasher, for example, can begin busing tables four hours a day and washing dishes the other four hours instead of washing for the entire shift.

Job enrichment can be accomplished by adding some traditional management tasks to the employee's job. Typically, management plans the work, the employee does it, and management then determines if it has been done properly. Job enrichment seeks to make the employee responsible for some of the planning and/or control functions of the job. The assumption here is that in the long run, intrinsic rewards (the job itself) will motivate employees.

If recognition is seen as lacking, a strategy of *positive reinforcement* should be implemented. This consists of giving employees positive support when they do something right. Encouraging positive behavior will result in more of the same in the future. The focus is on extrinsic rewards; thus, chapter 9 deals with the roles of money and career advancement, in addition to other nonfinancial rewards, as motivators.

Chapter 10 considers the development of a *trusting relationship* between management and workers. When employees regard teamwork as a problem, management must take appropriate measures to establish a relationship of trust. Why and how this should be done are covered in this final chapter.

In summary, to ensure profitability in the future, the hospitality industry must improve its productivity. The responsibility for that task will fall heavily on the shoulders of management. Productivity can be increased by hiring people who have the potential to perform as desired. The layout and design of the physical facilities will determine to a great extent how much time employees can spend in productive activities—ones that increase output, minimize input, or both. Instituting techniques to simplify work can have the same effect. Once the employee knows how best to perform a particular task, improved scheduling can cut costs.

The major concern will be the motivation of the employee of the future. No amount of technical analysis and computer scheduling can overcome the key to the hospitality industry: the interaction between guest and employee. How can management ensure that guests are provided with the service they desire? Management must let the employees know what it stands for—the corporate culture. Differences between what management wants (culture) and what employees perceive (climate) can be resolved by letting employees know what is expected of them, redesigning jobs to cater to the increased expectations of employees, giving praise when it is justified, and creating an atmosphere of trust in which to work together. The result will be a more satisfied, more productive work force.

Implementation of the ideas and strategies contained in this book (fig. P–1) can enable management to meet the productivity challenge of the future.

1 | DEFINING PRODUCTIVITY

THE CHALLENGES OF PRODUCTIVITY

There is a widespread concern about decreasing U.S. productivity. Productivity—how efficiently resources are used to create outputs—has fallen in the United States since World War II, according to the American Productivity Center. From 1948 to 1965, productivity grew at an annual compound rate of 3.6 percent. From 1965 to 1973, the growth rate was 2.1 percent. The effect of the energy crisis was felt in an increase of only 0.2 percent between 1974 and 1975. The late seventies and eighties have actually seen a national decline in productivity.

Impact on the Hospitality Industry

Productivity in the hospitality industry is no better than the national trend; some would argue the prospects are far worse. If we consider productivity the relationship between the output of goods and services and the input of resources, the hospitality industry is not performing well. The National Restaurant Association, in fact, estimates that the restaurant industry is only half as productive as manufacturing industries.

Government figures indicate that in eating and drinking places, labor costs are outpacing sales and annual sales per employee are declining. From 1969 to 1980, sales per labor-hour decreased from $6.15 to $4.80 in constant dollars—more than a 20 percent decline. The problem is not that sales, even in constant dollars, have declined. In fact, from 1980 to 1985, sales in eating and drinking places increased an average of 2.7 percent after inflation. However, the industry required 4 percent more employee-hours to generate these sales. The result is a decline in productivity as measured by the ratio of output (in this case sales) to input (in this case employee-hours).

Life Cycle of the Hospitality Industry

There are several special factors that make the problem of productivity especially acute for the hospitality industry. The first of these is that the industry is in the mature stage of its life cycle. The idea of a life cycle is that products, services, and industries go through various stages of development. In the *introductory* stage the industry is rather new and appeals to a relatively small

1

number of people. In this stage of the hospitality industry, few people ate out, took vacations (which were for only the very affluent), or stayed in hotels.

The second stage is that of *growth,* which can be rapid. In travel and tourism, this began after World War II and increased dramatically in the sixties and seventies as a result of growing numbers of people and the amount of discretionary income they had. The impact was felt in foodservice in the seventies as a result of these and other factors.

The size of the market increased because of the baby boom. Income grew with the emergence of the two-career household. The number of such households has expanded to 55 percent of all families. Seventy percent of the women associated with the baby boom are in the labor force.

This means there are more people who have money to spend but lack the time to prepare food at home. The answer has been to eat out. Between 1972 and 1975, sales in eating and drinking places increased by 75 percent. In an era of growth, mistakes in operations can be disguised. Poor management can be covered up by the increase in sales from an expanding market.

There are limits, however, to the number of meals that can be eaten out and weekend vacations that can be taken. There are signs that a saturation point is approaching. The industry is moving toward—and fast food is already at—the *mature* stage of the life cycle.

In the previous stage, sales grow at an increasing rate. In the mature stage, sales are still rising—but at a decreasing rate. In this stage the industry cannot rely on more customers, guests, or tourists to fuel its profits. Growth in profits in the nineties will have to come from improving the effectiveness of the operation. This is the productivity challenge for the hospitality industry.

If no action is taken, the product, service, or industry moves into the *declining* stage of the life cycle. A decline in sales is experienced. Before this happens a new life cycle can be developed by identifying a new market for the product—for example, baby shampoo for adults who wash their hair every day—or a new time use for the product—as in the movement of fast-food operations into the breakfast business.

The hospitality industry can no longer rely on its previous years of growth to increase profits. As a maturing industry, its growth must come from increased productivity.

Nature of the Industry

A second challenge for the hospitality industry is that its nature makes productivity difficult to measure, much less improve. The hospitality industry provides a combination of products and services: a hamburger and quick service; a hotel room and a cheerful smile; a martini and a sympathetic ear. While we can measure the number of burgers sold, rooms cleaned, and drinks served, how do we quantify the intangible services?

A related problem is the labor-intensive nature of the industry. In delivering a service—in being hospitable—there is only so much substitution of machines for employees that can be made. In the hospitality industry, service is tied to people. This puts great pressure on managers to increase the productive use of employees rather than rely totally on technological innovation to produce a more productive operation.

Undervaluing of Human Resources

A third problem is that although employees are critical to increased productivity, we have traditionally placed little emphasis on employee development and training. Managers can understand the investment necessary in a machine and the value of a preventive maintenance program for that machine. They do not, however, regard money spent on an employee as an investment; rather it is seen as purely a cost. We have to realize that ROI means Return on Individual as well as Return on Investment. A 1982 study of high-quality managers by the American Hotel and Motel Association indicated that although managers considered the training and development of employees to be a significant problem, they admitted that few programs existed to take care of the situation. The problem, apparently, is not considered important enough for managers to do something about it.

TRADITIONAL DEFINITIONS OF PRODUCTIVITY

Productivity, as defined by the dictionary, is a quality or state yielding or furnishing results, benefits, or profits. Operationally it involves a relationship between the input of resources and the output of resulting goods and services. Resource input encompasses time, money, and materials. Input can be reduced by cutting down on the time taken to produce something, the cost to produce it, or the amount of material used. Output can be measured in terms of such things as meals served, customers served, and rooms cleaned. The role of management is to develop and organize a system that increases the value of the output faster than the cost of the input.

Traditional measures of productivity have focused on the effectiveness of the labor force. Typically they have been such things as:

Payroll ratio: payroll costs divided by sales

Sales per employee: sales divided by number of employees

Sales per hour: sales divided by the number of hours of operation

Sales per employee-hour: sales divided by departmental employee-hours

If productivity were defined as sales per employee, then it could be increased simply by raising, say, menu prices. A restaurant may be serving fewer customers, but the increase in prices could camouflage that—and inefficiencies in management as well.

Inflation-Proof Measures

The best measures of productivity are those that are inflation-proof and measure the performance of output. Productivity increases when more output results from the same or less input. For example, productivity could be measured as the number of customers, rooms occupied, or meals produced divided by the number of employee hours required. Alternatively, the number of employees per one hundred rooms could be used.

The U.S. Bureau of Labor Statistics defines productivity as output per employee-hour. It defines output as sales receipts adjusted for inflation and indexed to a base year to facilitate year-to-year comparisons. Input is the number of hours worked by all employees, both supervisory and nonsupervisory. The resulting ratios are productivity indices that are not affected by increases in prices or wages.

Contemporary Trends

Traditional views of how to increase productivity, focusing on such things as producing more with the same or fewer employee-hours, have been too narrow. Are employees more productive if they serve more meals per hour—but in a slipshod, surly manner? Is a restaurant more productive if convenience foods are used to reduce employee preparation time, but food costs are thereby increased to the point that contribution margin is less? A broader view of productivity must be taken.

The traditional focus has been on the producer's role in increasing output. How can we service more rooms, pour more drinks, serve more meals, process more guests at registration time? To this must be added an equal emphasis on satisfying the consumer of our products and services. If we register more guests but in a mechanical, impersonal way that may affect their return, are we being more, or less, productive?

While the U.S. economy has moved from a situation in which most of the working population was engaged in manufacturing to one in which services dominate, insufficient attention has been paid to the management of service productivity. In large part this is because service is so difficult to measure.

Professional managers realize that bottom-line results are achieved through the company's employees. An emphasis on efficient production that omits consideration of the role employees play is doomed to failure. Attention must also be paid to the quality of the work. Management must set performance standards of both quantity and quality and then manage employees in such a way that these standards are met.

A traditional method of increasing productivity has been to divide a job into specialized fragments and increase the efficiency of the pieces. The modern view sees work in holistic terms and seeks to humanize the job, to integrate employee and job to produce a satisfied employee who is performing productively. If jobs were less specialized and employees were better rounded by performing several jobs instead of just one, would the productivity of the whole increase? This is the modern view.

The values of employees are changing. They are becoming more demanding. While money is still important as a short-term motivator, many employees want more than a paycheck. They look for the job itself, where they might spend eight to twelve hours a day, to give them satisfaction. Management's task is to design jobs that can provide the enrichment employees are seeking.

A MODEL FOR IMPROVING PRODUCTIVITY

The task of management is to produce satisfied customers at a profit by planning, organizing, staffing, directing, and controlling the input at its disposal. This model is illustrated in figure 1–1.

Output

J. C. Penney is credited with saying: "If we satisfy our customers but fail to satisfy our business, we'll soon be out of business. If we get the profit but fail to satisfy our customers, we'll soon be out of customers."

It is important to introduce the idea of customer satisfaction into the profit equation for two reasons. First, it forces us to take more of a long-term view of our business. A guest may be attracted to a hotel, stay one night, and leave dissatisfied after paying the bill. The property has profited in the short run, but the guest will not return and will tell friends not to visit; the end result will be lost sales.

A second reason is that employees can relate to and get involved with customer satisfaction as an objective. It is harder for the average employee to relate to company profitability. While employees most likely know that the business must remain profitable for them to keep their jobs, they may not think they get their fair share of the profits. On the other hand, they, too, are customers: they, too, go out to dine, to drink, or to take a vacation. They

FIGURE 1–1 A MODEL FOR IMPROVING PRODUCTIVITY.

INPUT	PROCESS	OUTPUT
CAPITAL RESOURCES (MONEY, MACHINERY, MATERIALS, TOOLS)	PLANNED, ORGANIZED, STAFFED, DIRECTED,	
HUMAN RESOURCES	CONTROLLED BY MANAGEMENT	
INFORMATION RESOURCES		SATISFIED CUSTOMERS, AT A PROFIT

know what good service is when they demand it as customers. They can relate more to nonfinancial objectives, or output, than to pure profitability.

Input

There are three types of resources available to management. *Capital* is available in the form of money, machinery, materials, and tools. *Human resources* represent the people part of the equation. *Information* in its broadest sense refers to knowledge of new techniques, whether it is a new way to cook foods or advances in motivating employees.

Capital and human resources are subject to changes. For example, a $40,000-a-year chef might be replaced by a $15,000-a-year cook, standardized recipes, and commissary-produced convenience foods. Information resources determine the degree of substitutability to a great extent.

Process

It is management's responsibility to plan, organize, staff, direct, and control the input mixture to maximize output. The direction must come from top management but the effort, if it is to be successful, must involve the entire organization. The process involves a series of steps.

Define Output

The first step in the process of managing input to maximize output is to define the expected output clearly. Output is what we want to achieve. This involves setting specific standards and objectives in terms that are quantifiable and realistic and have a time frame. If standards and objectives are not formulated up front, there will be no way of knowing when or if the problems that exist have been solved.

As an example, we may wish to achieve a 98 percent positive rating on room inspections while expecting attendants to complete a room in twenty-five minutes.

Describe the Symptoms

"What seems to be the matter?" This question will elicit the factors that lead someone to believe problems exist. It may be that midweek business is down or wine sales have dropped off. At this point it is important to separate symptoms that can be observed from those that cannot. This has implications for the next step, symptom verification.

It is also useful at this stage to place symptoms into appropriate categories, such as those relating to sales, facilities, or personnel. A combination of an outsider and an insider is important in evaluating symptoms. An insider—

someone working on the property—has better knowledge of the operation's practices and procedures, physical layout, and employee characteristics. An outsider, on the other hand, can be more objective about the shortcomings of the property.

In our stated example, any of several things could bring the problem to our attention. It may be that labor costs for room attendants are higher than expected, or that the inspector's ratings are lower than the target, or that we have received a number of guests' complaints about the cleanliness of the rooms. Each or all of these items lead us to believe something is wrong.

Verify the Symptoms

Symptoms can be verified through personal observation and interviews. It is preferable that the problem solver observe and verify the symptoms firsthand. In our example, the manager might accompany the inspector on a tour of guest rooms, check the labor costs, and talk to several guests.

If the problem solver cannot verify symptoms firsthand, interviews may be in order. Such secondary information is less desirable than observation, however, because it is selective and filtered through the viewpoint and background of the original observer. If the manager relies on the opinion of the inspector instead of touring the rooms personally, improper weight might be placed on the inspector's interpretation of the standards. It may be that the inspector's standards are too high for the operation and this is causing the poor ratings.

Identify Trends

The purpose of trend analysis is to limit the area of investigation. This is accomplished by asking several questions: When? Who? Where? How much?

Concerning our example, ask:

When: Are the problems occurring only at certain times of the week (say, only on weekends) or of the year (during the slow summer months)? Let us assume the problems show up on weekends.

Who: Are certain attendants and inspectors involved? Perhaps they are the ones with insufficient training or experience. Our analysis might indicate that the problem seems to be with the employees who have been with us for more than three years.

Where: Is the problem confined to certain departments? Obviously we are primarily concerned here with housekeeping, although this problem has implications for the hotel as a whole. Closer examination might reveal a number of complaints dealing with the quality of the linens. This would extend our concern to the laundry. Guests also might be complaining about being shown to rooms that are not yet cleaned. This would bring in the front office.

How much: How much money are we over budget? Is it enough to get concerned about? How much time and effort should be spent on this? We might determine that we are sufficiently over budget that it is cause for concern.

Identify Critical Areas

A common tendency at this point is to limit the problem to a few critical areas. The problem of guest rooms that are not up to standard may involve the following critical areas:

Management philosophy	Quality of personnel
Organizational and departmental goals, standards	Hiring
	Promotion
Organizational structure	Scheduling
Supervision	Training
Employee relations	Turnover
Communications	Motivation
Job description	Layout and design
Performance standards	Maintenance
Image	Laundry
	Front office[1]

The problem may be that management has not expressed well enough how important clean guest rooms are, that the employees have not accepted the standards set, that housekeepers report to front-office managers who are not sufficiently skilled concerning room cleanliness, that too few employees are scheduled to get the work done, that poor-quality cleaning supplies are being purchased—and so on down the list.

The point here is to avoid limiting oneself to too few critical areas in attempting to identify the causes of a problem.

Identify Critical Principles

Critical principles are those specific standards or criteria within each critical area that apply to the problem at hand. In the area of scheduling, for example, the critical principles might be determined by asking:

- Are forecasts of needs considered as the basis for scheduling?
- Do schedules exist two weeks in advance?
- Are schedules posted?
- Are requests from employees for schedule changes considered?
- Are shifts and stations assigned on an equitable basis?
- Does the schedule provide for adequate staff within the budget?[2]

Make Comparisons

At this point comparisons can be made between the critical principles and the actual situation, in order to pinpoint the causes of the problem. As before, this is done through observation and interview.

In our example, we might identify as a departure from critical principles the fact that the assistant housekeeper is reluctant to cut the hours of veteran employees, although weekend business is much less than that during the week; employees might see this easier work as a reward for good service.

Suggest Solutions

Now solutions can be proposed to correct the deficiencies that have been found. We should be concerned that the proposed solutions will in fact correct the problems. It is important that the proposals are accepted by management and employees alike. This is necessary if any changes are truly to be implemented, rather than merely given lip service.

In our example, employees have to be told the importance of staying within the budget. Other incentives will have to be offered to them as rewards for their longevity. This may mean giving them more hours at the expense of newer employees; it may mean involving them in the process of setting standards; it may mean opening up promotional opportunities.

Bear in mind also that this involves only the scheduling and motivational aspects of the problem. Since this problem occurs only on weekends, it may be that supervision is lax and employees do not feel enough pressure to perform to weekday standards.

Test and Compare

It may be necessary to test the proposed solution before proper implementation can occur. This means thinking through the impact of the new procedure on other parts of the operation. The output in one situation may be the input in another. More hours for experienced employees, for example, means fewer hours for newer workers.

It should also be noted that solutions may have to be implemented in phases, over time. New procedures may have to be implemented. The cost of training everyone at once may be prohibitive; the operation also could not afford to have everyone away for training at the same time. The solution might be to implement the program first by instructing the training personnel, who in turn would train the employees shift by shift.

Then, comparisons must be made to determine how successfully implementing the solution has met the original objectives that were set. Further changes may have to be made. The key is to solve problems, not make them bearable.

Evaluation is ongoing. Each month, profit-and-loss statements allow for fine tuning of the operation. Yet the ultimate goal is surely to do things right the first time rather than constantly be involved in putting out fires.

SUMMARY

The subject of productivity is of increasing concern to hospitality operators as the industry matures. Despite difficulties in measuring the productivity of service employees in an industry that has consistently undervalued the efforts of its people, the task is proceeding.

Traditional measures of productivity have not been inflation-proof and are being replaced with more appropriate methods. Contemporary trends include adding customer satisfaction, service, quality, and a systems approach to customary considerations of productivity.

Deficiencies in productivity that are uncovered must be corrected. In the hospitality industry, the key to improved productivity lies in improving the output of the employees, both quantitatively and qualitatively.

When productivity problems are identified, the solutions can be approached through a systems model: defining the output, identifying and verifying symptoms, identifying trends, critical areas, and critical principles within these areas, making comparisons between what is and what should be, suggesting solutions, and comparing the results with the original objectives.

NOTES

[1]Kreck, Lothar A., *Operational Problem Solving for the Hotel and Restaurant Industry*, Boston, C.B.I. Publishing Company, 1978, 102.
[2]Ibid, 138–39.

SUGGESTED READINGS

Burley, Kenneth R., "5 Steps to Improving Productivity," *Foodservice Marketing*, August 1981, 22, 24, 26–27.
Kreck, Lothar A., *Operational Problem Solving for the Hotel and Restaurant Industry*, Boston, C.B.I. Publishing Company, 1978.
Labor Utilization and Operating Practices in Table Service Restaurants, Marketing Research Report no. 931, Agricultural Research Service, U.S. Department of Agriculture, September 1971.
"Measuring Productivity," *F.&B. Trends* 6, no. 3, issue 23, August 1982, 27–28.
Wooton, Leland M., and Jim L. Tarter, "The Productivity Audit: A Key Tool for Executives," *M.S.U. Business Topics*, Spring 1976, 31–41.
"The Year of Productivity," *F.&B. Trends* 6, no. 1, issue 21, March 1982, 2.

2 | HIRING PRODUCTIVE PEOPLE

THE CHANGING HOSPITALITY EMPLOYEE

Company hiring policies are limited by the type and number of employees available. It is important, therefore, to identify the major demographic trends that will affect future hiring practices.

> The slowing growth rate of the work force—21 percent in the 1970s, 12 percent in the 1980s—has led to predictions of labor shortages.

> Service industry employment is projected to increase but at a slower rate. Relative to national employment, 18.1 percent of all jobs were service jobs in 1969. By 1978 the figure was 20.3 percent. Projections for 1990 and 2000 are 22.3 percent and 23 percent, respectively.

> Foodservice alone employs over 7.5 million people. In 1976 over half of the foodservice labor force was under twenty-four years of age. The pool of workers sixteen to twenty-four years old will decline sharply through the 1990s.

> More than two-thirds of all labor force growth will come from increased participation by women in the workplace.

> Minority labor force growth will be twice that of the white labor force.

> The pressure of immigration, whether legal or illegal, will grow, particularly from Latin America.

In light of these trends, companies will have to turn to sources, some traditional, others less so, to meet their future employee needs.

WOMEN

More than five of every eight foodservice employees are now women. In 1973 about 10 percent of the members of Meeting Planners International were women; ten years later this had risen to 57 percent. Yet in all industries only 5 percent of all working women are managers, while 15 percent of all working men are managers. Much of the future growth in the labor force will come from women.

11

To benefit most fully from the assimilation of women into the hospitality industry, it is necessary to examine some of the difficulties women encounter and to develop policies that will attract and keep productive female employees.

One factor that encourages the stereotyping of women in the workplace is the perpetuation of certain myths:

- Turnover of women is higher.
- Absenteeism by women is higher.
- Women are not mobile.
- Women want jobs, not careers.
- Women cannot balance work and family demands.
- Women are too emotional.
- Women cannot get along with co-workers.
- Women lack the necessary personality traits, such as assertiveness and a willingness to take risks.

In fact, while the turnover rate of women is somewhat high, age and job level seem to be more important than sex in determining length of job tenure. More turnover occurs in lower-level positions and among younger employees. Women now tend to hold lower-level positions.

Absenteeism by women is almost equal to that of men. A recent Public Health Service survey indicates that women lose an average of 3.9 days of work a year, while the figure for men is 3.1 days.

Lack of mobility also tends to be related to age rather than sex. Men as well as women who are older are less likely to relocate.

There are projections that the future female employee will be attached to her work, considering it more a career than a short-term job. Attachment is measured by the extent to which an employee's involvement in the work is substantial and permanent. Historically, the patterns of participation of women in the labor force have differed from those of men. The men's pattern has been and continues to be a simple curve, with participation in the labor force rising steadily through their mid-twenties, leveling off until their mid-fifties, then falling gradually after age fifty-five and more steeply after age sixty-five. Women's participation rate curves have shown more of an M-shaped pattern. With an increasing proportion of women entering the work force through their early twenties, then leaving during their childbearing and child-rearing years, the participation rates have dropped until their late twenties, risen again until their mid-forties, then dropped once more, rapidly. Since 1950, however, participation rates for women of all ages between twenty and fifty-five have been rising—though they are still lower than those for men—and the M-like dip for young women has been flattening.

This suggests a new pattern for women consisting of high and continuing attachment to the workplace. Thus it appears that more women will be seeking careers rather than short-term jobs. This is in part reflected by the increasing percentage of women graduating from baccalaureate programs in hotel and restaurant management: in 1974 about 21 percent of all such graduates were women; in 1980 the figure was 38 percent. There is every indication this trend will continue.

The high, and increasing, participation of younger women in the work force indicates that they believe they can balance work outside the home with family demands.

As for the myth that women are too emotional, both men and women are subject to mood changes based on hormonal cycles. The principal differences are that the length of the male cycle is more variable and there are external signs of the female cycle. One female food and beverage manager responded in a survey:

"A woman must act professional, even more so than a man, to be respected. I have a bubbly personality and a good sense of humor, but I find it necessary sometimes to tone it down in order to be taken seriously."[1]

The survey also asked female food and beverage managers about their difficulties in dealing with peers, subordinates, purveyors, and customers. Most indicated the need to establish themselves with the males with whom they come into contact. But the major problem reported, interestingly, was in dealing with female colleagues who came for advice on personal problems, felt they would receive preferential treatment, or were jealous of another woman's career success. This situation will undoubtedly improve as more women enter the ranks of management.

One explanation for the lack of women in managerial positions is that female socialization practices encourage the development of personality traits and behavior patterns that are antithetical to those expected of managers. It is argued, for example, that women have a fear of success because of the perceived incompatibility between achievement and a sense of femininity. It is said that men see risk as an opportunity to win as well as lose, for example, while women view it primarily as a chance to fail; men are said to see what they are doing as a step toward future career goals, while women look toward their immediate situation for fulfillment.

Additional research suggests that the fear of success may be a response to situational factors rather than an internal motivational state. For example, playing team sports, now more prevalent among little boys than girls, teaches the key elements of management—strategy planning, working with others, competing.

The effect of socialization is seen in *The Managerial Women,* a study of twenty-five top female executives. All were firstborn children; most were close to their fathers, who encouraged them to be independent, self-reliant, and willing to take risks; team games were important to them as children; and all had a mentor—a male boss who encouraged and supported them.

Barriers to Promoting Women

There are a disproportionate number of male managers in the hospitality industry. With more females entering the supervisory as well as the hourly ranks, there will be more pressure on companies to promote women. There remain a number of barriers, however, to successful male-female business relationships. The most frequently given are:

Men fear women as peers because they are unable to free on-the-job sexual tensions.

Men have not been taught how to work with women as a co-worker.

Men fear that career women will exploit men's physical need of women.

Men do not trust or feel they understand women's emotions.

Men fear that a career woman without a family can devote herself totally to the job.

Men fear women because their wives do not like it.

Policies to Attract and Keep Women

Certain practices will ease the transition of women into the hospitality work force, especially into supervisory positions. The key is to move women initially into positions in which they will have the most chance of success. This means selecting or developing women who have expertise in their field clearly superior to the majority of people to be supervised; putting them at first into positions least affected by sexual stereotyping (not, for example, chief engineer); choosing positions in which expertise is a large and important component of authority; and providing visible support for a management program to develop women.

Visible support can be demonstrated in a number of ways. Most existing compensation programs are male-oriented. A reshaping in light of the particular needs of women would be helpful. Flexible work schedules, the provision of day-care centers, relocation counseling for employee and spouse, and medical benefits specifically for women are some of the demonstrable ways this could be accomplished. It has only been since 1978 that employers had to give equality of treatment to pregnant women, for example. Prior to 1978, many company health benefits specifically excluded pregnancy; women who became pregnant could not use accumulated sick leave. The law now requires that policies for pregnant employees be the same as policies for other temporarily disabled employees.

The Civil Rights Act of 1964 prohibited discrimination on the basis of race, color, religion, national origin, or sex. (Additional provisions have added handicap and age as protected classes.) In essence, this means that a person should be selected for, promoted to, or fired from a job based on job-related factors alone.

It is generally accepted by the courts that sexual harassment is a form of sex discrimination. Management must develop and implement clear policies on sexual harassment in order to create and maintain an atmosphere that will promote women's growth in the workplace.

Managers are responsible for harassment, both physical and verbal, by superiors, co-workers, and even nonworkers, such as suppliers or guests. Employers are responsible for the actions of supervisors even when they have no direct knowledge of those actions and even when company policy explicitly prohibits such actions. The manager may be held responsible unless immediate and appropriate action is taken.

To implement a preventive program, several actions are in order. Expected behavior of all employees should be spelled out in writing. The consequences of engaging in sexual harassment should be detailed, with more severe punishment for supervisors because of management's liability for their actions. Attitude training is a second step to sensitize employees to the problem. Part of this training should detail the rights and responsibilities of all employees. Third, a complaint mechanism and disciplinary procedure must be established and adhered to. Such a procedure would establish different sanctions for the various forms of harassment. Attempted seduction is obviously more serious than a verbal remark. Employees must know that they have a way to report any harassment without being subjected to discipline from an immediate supervisor.

There will be more women in positions of authority in the hospitality industry of the future. To encourage the introduction and promotion of women into the workplace, the myths and fears that prevent management from productively utilizing women must be recognized and addressed through policies, practices, and procedures designed to select, train, and promote women to be productive.

HISPANICS

Hispanics represent an increasingly important employee resource for the hospitality industry in certain geographic areas of the United States. The reason is that the number of Hispanics is growing, although the growth is concentrated geographically. The number of Hispanics in the United States grew, according to the Census Bureau, from 4.5 percent of the total population in 1970 to 6.4 percent in 1980. Although past growth has not been spectacular, demographers estimate that the Hispanic population is growing from 13.2 million in 1980 to 20.4 million in 1990, which will make this the country's largest minority. Nationwide, 16 percent of Hispanics work in service occupations, largely food-service and janitorial services. But their impact on the hospitality industry will be felt primarily in a few geographic areas. Nearly two-thirds of all Hispanics live in three states—California, Texas, and New York—in which one out of every five residents is Hispanic. Florida has close to one million Hispanics, making it their fourth most populous state. They are also heavily represented in terms of percentage of residents in New Mexico (36%), Arizona (16%), and Colorado (12%).

This potential group of employees, in fact, comprises three subgroups largely concentrated in three metropolitan areas. Mexican-Americans as a whole represent 60 percent of the country's Hispanics, and are largely concentrated in Los Angeles. This group is slightly younger than Hispanics in general; more than a third are younger than fifteen. They are very family oriented, with more than 80 percent of their households containing families, compared to 73 percent of all American households. Of all the subgroups, Mexican–Americans are most likely to know English, although one-third report not speaking it well. But only one in five speaks Spanish in the home.

Puerto Ricans, heavily concentrated in New York City, constitute the second largest Hispanic group. They are young and their population has a high growth rate. They are less likely to live in families than are Mexican–Americans; over 40 percent of Puerto Rican families in New York City, for example, are maintained by a women with no husband present. Yet two-thirds, compared to 55 percent of all Hispanics, said in a census survey that being masculine meant being a good provider for a wife and family.

Cubans are even more concentrated. Over half live in Miami, making up 25 percent of the city's population as well as 70 percent of all of the Hispanics in its metropolitan area. They are older, with a median age of forty-one, but like all Hispanics have a strong sense of family. Cubans also have a higher level of formal education.

Barriers to Hiring Hispanics

It is difficult to manage employees if a manager cannot communicate with them. Recent policies of the Equal Employment Opportunity Commission have stated that any rule totally prohibiting employees from speaking their own primary language is discriminatory; that an employer may require English to be spoken under very narrowly drawn rules, when it can be shown that this is justified by business needs; and that employers must clearly inform employees of the requirements of such rules and the consequences of violating them.

To facilitate communication, several companies teach English to employees in on-the-job classes, while some hotel and restaurant management programs require or encourage their students to study Spanish.

There exists a strong feeling among many Hispanics, however, that relationships between individuals are more important than norms of competitiveness, materialism, or achievement. The non-Hispanic manager may be limited in his or her ability to motivate because of an inability to establish a relationship.

Another problem affects Hispanic women. Although 50 percent of Hispanic women are in the labor force, there are cultural pressures on them. It is a very male-oriented, traditional society, and over half of all Hispanics express reservations about a married woman with children working outside the home. Problems would arise for female managers supervising employees with such an orientation.

An additional problem is that of illegal aliens. Under the Immigration Reform and Control Act of 1986, it is unlawful for any employer, regardless of the number of employees in the business, knowingly to hire any alien not authorized to work in the United States. If an employer learns that an already hired employee is unauthorized, it is illegal to continue to employ that person. Employers are required to verify the identity and work authorization of new employees. This can be done from such documents as a U.S. passport, a Certificate of Citizenship or Naturalization, an Alien Receipt Card, a Temporary Resident Card, an Employment Authorization Card, or an unexpired foreign passport with a visa allowing the bearer to work for a specified time.

Under the act, illegal aliens who can document that they entered the United States prior to January 1, 1982, and have resided here continuously could apply for temporary resident alien status, if they met the application deadline of May 7, 1988, for most workers.

Irrespective of legal issues, hiring illegal aliens involves issues of motivation and trust. The employer-employee relationship begins with a lie.

> Illegals live in a world of lies. They are not liars, but theirs is a world of lies. They have to live—to eat—and to eat they have to say things that others want to hear. If a boss asks if they are here legally, they say they are. But they know that the boss knows they are lying and the boss is lying when he acts like he believes him.[2]

Managers must ask themselves whether this is the best way to begin a business relationship.

Policies to Attract and Keep Hispanics

To produce productive employees, it is important to understand their underlying motivations. Although it is dangerous to generalize, several points can be made. Most Hispanics place a high value on the family. Because unemployment rates in Hispanic communities are so high, regular work is highly valued and important to the self-esteem and status of adult males as a way of contributing to the family. The concept of family loyalty is a great source of motivation. It also helps keep productivity high and absenteeism low, though turnover can be high among those family members who may work hard for several months, save money, and then leave the community to return to a family living elsewhere.

One catering company in Chicago attempts to bring the external motivating force of the family into the internal working environment by urging employees to bring family members in to visit the workplace. In this way employees feel that the family is in a sense assimilated into the workplace; the importance of the employee's work is heightened.

OLDER WORKERS

As the demand for jobs in the hospitality industry increases and the traditional pool of employees under twenty-five decreases, it is normal to consider age groups that will increase in number as sources of potential future employees. One such group is the older worker.

A recent study in the foodservice industry indicated that approximately 10 percent of employees and 13 percent of managers are over fifty years of age. Participation of those over fifty is highest in the institutional sector and lowest within fast-food units. These percentages are likely to increase as more of the U.S. population is found in the older age categories.

U.S. Census Bureau figures indicate that between 1982 and the year 2000 the population aged fifty-five to seventy-four is expected to increase 11.1 million, a jump of 31 percent. In 1982 about one in every five persons was fifty-five or older. This ratio will be one in four by 2010 and nearly one in three by 2030. As more customers appear in the older age brackets, the presence of older workers will be a marketing tool to appeal to that segment.

At least half of all working adults express a desire to continue working past the standard retirement age. This desire is aided by changes in Social Security that allow those between sixty-five and sixty-nine to earn more before benefits are affected. At present, seniors below the age of sixty-five can earn $6,000 before forfeiting $1 for every $2 over that amount. Employees between the ages of sixty-five and seventy can earn up to $8,160 before they are penalized. After the age of seventy there is no penalty. After 1990 the penalty will be reduced to $1 for every $3 over the allowed amount.

Barriers to Hiring the Older Worker

Recruitment of older employees is curtailed because of prejudice. Some of the persistent myths are:

- Older employees cannot work adequately.
- Older employees have too many health problems.
- Older employees are less productive and motivated.
- Older employees are more difficult to train.

There may indeed be performance slowdown in some older workers due to sensory and motor changes. This is an individual matter, however, and each person should be considered individually. Generally speaking, people age in a way consistent with the personalities they developed at an early age. Given a supportive climate, most people will choose to do things that give them a sense of self-esteem in a way consistent with their previously established values and concepts of life.

There is also a significant variation in health problems encountered with age. Overall, recent advances in medicine have resulted in healthier older people. As life expectancy continues to increase, older people actually have fewer serious illnesses per year than younger ones. Nearly all older people do have at least one chronic health problem, however. The most prominent are arthritis, hypertensive disease, hearing impairments, and heart conditions. Despite this, 80 percent of today's elderly conduct their lives with no restrictions caused by health problems.

Various studies have shown that major differences in productivity between younger and older employees are less likely than between different groups of younger workers. Some studies even suggest that the productivity of older employees is greater. Older employees have many characteristics that increase productivity. Older workers are more dependable, have lower absenteeism, are punctual, perform a high quality and quantity of work, show good judgment based on their past experience, interact well with others, and show greater motivation due to increased job satisfaction and less job-related stress. They also have fewer on-the-job accidents. One study of more than one million accidents from the early 1980s found that the accident rate for workers over the age of sixty-five was about half that of employees in their twenties.

Additionally they require less supervision. Foodservice managers rated older workers' performance highest in the areas of emotional maturity, quality of work, and guest relations, though lowest in adaptability and creativity.

Older workers have also been rated as above average during training. They rate highest in terms of quality of work, self-confidence, and volume of work, but lowest in ability to adjust to changes in work demands and flexibility to adapt to new tasks. Older workers may require more training initially. Once trained, however, they tend to remain longer than younger employees.

To be successful, training should follow certain principles, according to the American Association of Retired Persons. It should be directly related to the job for which the person is being trained. It should be given only for jobs that the employee has a real chance of getting upon completion of the training. Hands-on training is much more effective than passive learning. Older people learn better through self-paced and individualized instruction. Short-term training also seems to work better than longer-term programs.

Policies to Attract and Keep Older Workers

Older workers are difficult to reach for several reasons. First, if they have been out of the job market they probably will not be used to scanning newspapers for jobs. Second, they tend to think that job advertisements are for younger people even though age discrimination is unlawful. An outreach program is necessary. Employees close to retirement can be solicited regarding their interest in continuing full- or part-time work. Specialized organizations may be of assistance in contacting older potential employees. Examples are given at the end of this chapter.

Most national surveys indicate that older workers prefer part-time employment, phased retirement, and flexible work schedules. This finding was not supported, however, in a study of older workers in the foodservice industry. It does, however, appear that older people identify themselves with pictures of people eight to fifteen years younger than themselves. To attract the older employee, therefore, it is advisable to feature in job advertisements and literature pictures of employees younger than the age group being sought.

The major reason that seniors want to work is social interaction, followed by having a purpose in life. It is important, then, to stress opportunities to interact with others on the job. Let the seniors know that their experience is appreciated.

It is particularly important that the conditions of work and the benefits are clearly spelled out. While realizing that benefits for part-time employees will be less than for full-time workers, older employees are very concerned about health benefits to supplement their coverage in the event of illness. Because of the limit on earnings before Social Security is taxed, fringe benefits such as free or discounted meals and transportation are important in addition to health-insurance policies.

Three hospitality companies noted for their efforts with seniors are McDonald's, Kentucky Fried Chicken, and Marriott. The McDonald's McMasters program started in 1986 and at present operates in at least seventeen cities. Seniors are recruited in groups of six, eight, or ten. By coming in as a group they already have a source of support to turn to for any assistance. The trainees work one-on-one with a job coach—a McDonald's manager on leave for a year—and participate in fifteen to twenty hours of training a week. McDonald's specifically targets older employees to be salad makers, biscuit makers, hosts and hostesses, and even swing manager if the employee has previous experience.

Kentucky Fried Chicken developed the new position of part-time assistant manager to attract seniors who wanted stimulating part-time work and good fringe benefits. The managers receive medical and life insurance and paid vacations and holidays, in addition to a competitive salary.

The Marriott Corporation uses flexible work schedules, rotating shifts, and part-time positions to appeal to the older employee. In the company's fast-food restaurant the seniors work as host and problem solvers. After a training period of from one week to two months, they are assigned to a unit. For full-time employees, benefits include medical, life, and disability insurance, profit sharing, and stock purchases.

In summary, older workers represent a productive resource for hospitality companies. In an atmosphere that encourages the older employee, a company can gain by hiring dependable, productive employees who will also provide valuable role models for younger workers.

THE HANDICAPPED

A nontraditional source of employees that companies are increasingly turning to are the handicapped.

Under government programs a handicapped person is anyone who:

- Has a physical or mental impairment that substantially limits one or more activities
- Has a record of such an impairment
- Is regarded as having such an impairment

Disabled people include those who are visually or hearing impaired, stroke victims, arthritis sufferers, people with mental retardation, amputees, and those recovering from heart disease or accidents.

There are several good reasons for hiring the nation's estimated 35 million handicapped. There is some evidence that the turnover rate for handicapped employees is less. In an industry in which the cost of replacing an hourly employee can amount to one thousand dollars (according to the National Restaurant Association), the savings could be significant.

Handicapped employees also have a better safety record than others. This may be due to an awareness of their limitations; as a result, they take the time to be careful. Contrary to popular belief, hiring the handicapped does not raise insurance rates.

Handicapped employees are motivated by the opportunity they are being given to live a fuller life by contributing to society. Properly nurtured, the result is employees who come in on time and are strongly committed to their jobs.

Several economic programs are available to hospitality operators to reduce the cost of wages paid to handicapped employees. The On-The-Job Training Project, administered through the state offices of vocational rehabilitation, reimburses employers in part for wages paid to a handicapped employee and for consumable supplies used during training. Over a ten-year period, the project has trained more than fifteen thousand mentally handicapped people, 85 percent of whom have been retained by their employers.

A second program, the Federal Targeted Jobs Tax Credit, gives employers a tax credit of 50 percent of the first six thousand dollars in wages for one year. Job coaching by an on-the-job, agency-provided supervisor is available. The supervisor is there to train, to coach, and to ensure the job gets done even if the employee does not show up for work. In addition, Section 190 of the Tax Reform Act of 1986 provides for up to thirty-five thousand dollars in tax credits annually for site improvements that make privately owned, publicly used businesses more accessible to people with disabilities, customers as well as employees.

A final reason for hiring is compliance with affirmative action laws. To be covered by such protection, a person must be capable of performing a particular job with reasonable accommodation, if it is needed, to the person's disability. This may involve such things as adjusting work schedules to avoid rush-hour crowds, restructuring a job, or providing flexible leave policies. It does not apply if the employer can show it would create an undue hardship on the business.

Affirmative action is required by law for businesses that have contracts or subcontracts with the federal government. Although this laws has been on the books since 1973, over 90 percent of companies covered do not comply with it. Less than one in five offers reasonable accommodation, for example, for the physically handicapped. Tougher actions by the federal government are becoming more common.

It must be emphasized that it is against the law for any employer to discriminate against a handicapped person who can still perform the job to be done. Under the Rehabilitation Act of 1973, equal rights have been mandated for disabled people. In addition, the Education of All Handicapped Children Act guarantees an appropriate education for every disabled child. The result will be a better educated, organized, and employable group of disabled people in the future.

Barriers to Hiring the Handicapped

A number of potential problems arise for the operator desiring to employ the handicapped. There may be initial resentment and apprehension from existing employees. They may have little respect for a new employee, doubting his or her ability to do the job. This initial ignorance and lack of acceptance may not be an insurmountable problem, because the handicapped person is used to such a reaction from others and often anticipates initial resistance.

Another problem is the inability or reluctance of some handicapped individuals to work alone. To overcome this problem a manager may have to use fellow employees as role models so that individuals can imitate their behavior and learn more quickly. Another possibility involves having co-workers in the area give verbal cues to support a new individual so that he or she does not feel alone or unwanted.

A manager has more forms to fill out for handicapped individuals than for other employees during the first few months of development. Records have to be kept on the individual's advancement and on any problems that have occurred. These forms can also chart the progress of the employee and can help a manager decide the appropriate level of reinforcement necessary to maintain employee production. After the first few months of employment, the amount of paperwork should not exceed that for other employees.

However, the amount of time and effort spent on handicapped workers may build resentment within the company from other employees. A program to introduce colleagues to the handicapped worker should be initiated to explain the situation to everyone, leading to better understanding and communication.

Policies to Attract and Keep the Handicapped

The Friendly Restaurant Corporation is one company that has developed a systematic approach to employing the handicapped successfully. The four-step process involves:

- Identifying company needs
- Identifying community resources
- Establishing a mutual relationship
- Building the relationship and understanding the pitfalls

In terms of company needs, the mentally handicapped or restored individual may be perfectly satisfied to work the numerous routine, repetitive, mechanical, and tedious jobs that need to be done. These are the same jobs that are most victimized by high labor turnover. In the restaurant industry, the handicapped individual may be particularly suited to the duties of dishwasher, stock clerk, bus help, kitchen help, sorter, janitor, or truck help. The hotel industry can utilize the mentally handicapped in the housekeeping department in such jobs as porter, painter, office cleaner, janitor, laundry sorter, laundry folder, window washer, floor polisher, supplies stocker, and room attendant.

In 1981 the National Restaurant Association surveyed almost eight thousand association members about the extent to which the handicapped were employed in the foodservice industry. Replies from over fourteen hundred respondents indicated that almost half had employed mentally retarded and physically handicapped workers, while less than one-third had employed mentally or emotionally restored employees. The most important reason given for employing the handicapped was compassion for the less fortunate. However, focusing particularly on the mentally restored, respondents also felt handicapped employees were better than their co-workers in attendance, and most felt the quality of work, job tenure, and motivation to work were at least equal to that of their co-workers. If employees survived the first four weeks of adjusting to a new situation, they tended to stay for a long time. Most were employed in sanitation and food preparation.

A variety of community resources are available to the employer; a listing is included at the end of this chapter. Representatives of these organizations understand the feelings and attitudes of the general public. As such, they can work with management to dispel any anxieties. Typically, managers fear that the public might have negative perceptions of the employees and that there will be an adverse effect on business. There may be a fear of additional responsibility, together with a conscious or unconscious rejection of the disabled employee. The President's Committee on Employment of the Handicapped and West Virginia University together have created a computer-based information system on job-related limitations and how to adjust for them. Information can be requested at 1–800–JAN–PCEH.

A relationship between the employer and the agency can be developed by visiting the agency to meet with the clients, learn what they do, and determine if a job exists that matches their skills. In this way management is sensitized, or trained, as a first step before employees are introduced into the company.

Prior to the actual hiring of a handicapped person, the employer should evaluate that employee to decide what type of work is most suited to the individual's skill level and personality. The employer is concerned with four things:

1. The individual's intelligence level, aptitude, personality, and achievements.
2. The social skills of the individual: ease of interaction with others and compatibility with people.
3. Mental and physical limitations and medical care needed.
4. Vocational evaluation: past school experience, previous employment, and other job-related training.

The last step involves the building and nurturing of the relationship.

Upon hiring a handicapped employee, a hospitality operator needs to adapt orientation and training techniques to the individual's disability. The first step is to introduce the handicapped employee to co-workers. The new employee may need the manager's assistance to help overcome initial uncertainties in interacting with others and performing the required tasks. Next, the manager should familiarize the individual with the policies of the organization, terms of employment, and location of such things as the employee cafeteria, time clock, rest rooms, and so on. After these steps have been taken, the manager can proceed to demonstrate the tasks and duties the individual will be responsible for.

As an exception to the rule, the manager, rather than another employee, should exert direct influence over the handicapped employee's training. The reason is that many handicapped employees seem to adjust more rapidly to the uncertainties of employment when initially given the manager's full support and attention rather than haphazard employee-to-employee training. Naturally the amount of time the manager can give to training will be limited, but as much emphasis should be placed on this activity as time will allow.

Initially the manager may have to make special concessions to a handicapped employee until a transition has been made into the workplace. For example, the manager may have to accommodate the needs of the individual with such things as flexible scheduling, special training, or even special transportation arrangements. Once acclimated, handicapped employees expect to be treated like all others and are able to conform to the rules and regulations of the organization.

In motivating the mentally handicapped, a continuous schedule of positive reinforcement may be necessary to develop new behavior. Money may not work as well as other incentives because a mentally handicapped person might not have a realistic conception of its worth. It has been found that meals, drinks, and verbal praise may be more effective as positive reinforcement for the mentally handicapped.

PART-TIME EMPLOYEES

Another avenue to combat the shortage of qualified full-time employees is the use of part-time workers. Although no reliable estimates are available as to the numbers of part-time workers in the hospitality industry, it is generally accepted that the numbers are significant—and likely to grow. One reason is that they are not usually paid benefits. This can mean a difference of one-third of the wage bill.

Barriers to Hiring Part-Time Employees

Part-time workers tend to be less loyal to the operation. In addition, they have higher turnover rates and must be trained more often and supervised more closely. This last is because they do not have as much on-the-job experience as full-time workers. On the other hand, they can be laid off more easily with less risk of lawsuits or unemployment compensation claims. They also are often more eager as employees because they work fewer hours per day or week and so may be more willing to do whatever job is assigned to them.

Full-time employees need less supervision and tend to comply more with company regulations because they have more to lose and are more likely to seek advancement on the job. However, they are likely to become dissatisfied with working conditions more quickly than part-time employees, will demand wage increases more often, and are more vocal about expressing their opinions about the management of the operation.

Policies to Attract and Keep Part-Time Employees

There are several procedures to help ensure successful hiring and utilization of part-time employees. First, it is preferable to hire people who actually want to work part-time. Much of the turnover of part-time workers comes from those who want to work full-time but settle for part-time work until a full-time position becomes available.

The orientation and training program is very important. It is vital that part-time workers receive the same orientation as full-time workers. There is a tendency to invest less time in these important activities because part-time employees may work only a few hours a day. Because they may work only the few hours when business is particularly busy, it is especially important that they feel comfortable in the working environment. They do not have the luxury of slack periods to get accustomed to where everything is. For this reason it is important to schedule training during those slack periods, when they would not ordinarily be working and when there is time to train.

It is also necessary to treat part-time workers like full-time staff in order to produce motivated employees. If the employees are treated like second-class citizens, they will act accordingly.

SUMMARY

Improving employee productivity begins with hiring the right kind of employee. The hospitality employees of the future will be different from those available today. In concert with changing demographics, the industry will rely more heavily on women, Hispanics, senior citizens, the handicapped, and part-time workers.

The successful utilization of employees from any of these groups will require different techniques from those used at present. While there is an up-front investment in approaching hiring, training, and coaching in a different way, the long-term payoffs will offset the up-front costs.

NOTES

[1]Hackett, Carole, "The Women Food and Beverage Manager," *Cornell Hotel and Restaurant Administration Quarterly* 21, no. 3, November 1981, 85.

[2]Ehrlich, Paul, Loy Bilderback, and Anne H. Ehrlich, *The Golden Door,* New York, Ballantine Books, 1979, 242.

SUGGESTED READINGS

Dee, Dorothy, "Older Workers: The Industry Work Force of the Future?" *Restaurants U.S.A.,* September 1987, 10–13.

Durocher, Joseph F., "What the Hotel Manager Needs to Know," *Lodging,* October 1983, 63–66.

Ehrlich, Paul R., Loy Bilderback, and Anne H. Ehrlich, *The Golden Door,* New York, Ballantine Books, 1979.

Glyde, Gerald P., "Underemployment of Women: Policy Implications for a Full Employment," from *Women in the U.S. Labor Force,* Ann Foote Cahn (ed.), Joint Economic Committee, New York, Praeger Publishers, 1980, 130–35.

Hackett, Carole, "The Woman Food and Beverage Manager," *Cornell Hotel and Restaurant Administration Quarterly,* 21, no. 3, November 1981, 79–85.

Hall, Chester G., "Future Manpower Projections of the Hospitality Industry," Paper presented at the World Hospitality Congress, Boston, 1981.

Kohl, John P., and Paul S. Greenlaw, "National-Origin Discrimination and the Hospitality Industry," *Cornell Hotel and Restaurant Administration Quarterly,* 21, no. 2, August 1981, 26–29.

Mills, D. Quinn, "Human Resources in the 1980s," *Harvard Business Review,* July–August 1979, 154–62.

Mintzberg, Henry, "The Manager's Job: Folklore and Fact," *Harvard Business Review,* July–August 1975, 49–61.

Morrison, Malcolm H., *Foodservice and the Older Worker,* National Restaurant Association Current Issues Report no. 2, October 1984.

Peters, Jim, "Alternative Labor Pool," *Restaurant Business,* September 1, 1987, 183–87.

Reamy, Lois, "Women at Work! Life on the Cutting Edge of a Social Revolution," *Meetings and Conventions,* November 1983, 53, 72–77.

Reid, Robert D., "A Profile of the Employment of Older Workers in the Foodservice Industry," Paper presented at the Annual Conference of the Council on Hotel, Restaurant and Institutional Education, Seattle, 1985.

Riger, Stephanie, and Pat Galligan, "Women in Management: An Exploration of Competing Paradigms," *American Psychologist* 35, no. 10, October 1980, 902–10.

Russell, Cheryl, "The News About Hispanics," *American Demographics* 5, no. 3, March 1983, 15–25.

Stead, Bette Ann, *Women in Management,* Englewood Cliffs, N.J., Prentice-Hall Inc., 1978.

Stokes, Arch, "Part-Time vs. Full-Time Employees: What Are the Pros and Cons?" *Foodservice Marketing,* February 1980, 129–33.

LOCATING THE OLDER WORKERS

Aging in America, 1500 Pelham Parkway, The Bronx, N.Y. 10461; (212) 824–4004 or (800) 845–6900 outside New York State.

American Association of Retired Persons, 1909 K Street, N. W., Washington, D.C. 20049; (202) 872–4700.

Green Thumb Inc., 5111 Leesburg Pike, Falls Church, Va. 22041; (703) 820–4990.

National Association for Hispanic Elderly, 2727 W. Sixth Street, Los Angeles, Calif. 90057; (213) 487–1922.

National Caucus and Center on Black Aged, Inc., 1424 K Street, N.W., Washington, D.C. 20005; (202) 637–8400.

National Council on the Aging, Inc., P.O. Box 7227, Ben Franklin Station, Washington, D.C. 20044; (202) 479–1200.

National Council of Senior Citizens, 925 Fifteenth Street, N.W., Washington, D.C. 20005; (202) 347–8800.

National Urban League, Inc., 500 E. Sixty-second Street, New York, N.Y. 10021; (212) 310–9000.

Source: Dorothy Dee, "Older Workers: The Industry Work Force of the Future?" *Restaurants U.S.A.,* September 1987, 13.

LOCATING THE HANDICAPPED WORKERS

National Restaurant Association, 311 First Street, N.W., Washington, D.C.; (202) 638–6100. Contact Brother Philip Nelan.

Responsible Hospitality Institute, 11 Pearl Street, Springfield, Mass. 01101–4080; (413) 732–7780.

Goodwill Industries of America Inc., 9200 Wisconsin Avenue, Bethesda, Md. 20814; (301) 530–6500.

President's Committee on Employment of the Handicapped, 1111 Twentieth Street, N.W., Washington, D.C. 20036; (202) 653–5006.

Association for Retarded Citizens of the United States, 2501 Avenue J, Arlington, Texas 76006; (817) 640–0204.

Rehabilitation Services Administration, 330 C Street, S.W., Washington, D.C. 20202; (202) 732–1282. Referral to state offices of vocational rehabilitation.

Paralyzed Veterans of America, 801 Eighteenth Street, N.W., Washington, D.C. 20006; (202) 872–1300.

Architectural and Transportation Barriers Compliance Board, Room 1010, 330 C Street, S.W., Washington, D.C. 20202; (202) 472–2700.

Epilepsy Foundation of America, 4351 Garden City Drive, Landover, Md. 20785; (301) 459–3700.

National Federation for the Blind, 1800 Johnson Street, Baltimore, Md. 21230; (310) 659–9314.

United Cerebral Palsy Associations, 66 East Thirty-fourth Street, New York, N.Y. 10016; (212) 481–6300.

Source: Jim Peters, "Alternative Labor Pool," *Restaurant Business,* September 1, 1987, 187.

APPENDIX: UNDERSTANDING THE EMPLOYEE OF THE FUTURE

Two employees from each of the groups projected to be of greatest potential impact for the hospitality industry were asked the following questions:

1.   How did you get this job?
2.   What is your motivation for working here?
3.   Do you feel as if you are a minority? Does this affect you on the job?
4.   Do fellow employees treat you differently? Do managers treat you differently?
5.   Has management done anything special to accommodate your needs? What could it do?

The supervisors of these employees were then asked:

1.   Why did this person get this job?
2.   This person is a (appropriate group named). How does this affect your management style?
3.   Do other employees treat this employee differently?
4.   What are the positives and negatives about having a (appropriate group named) working for you?

The variety of responses points up some of both the benefits and difficulties—for employees and management—in hiring members of these groups.

DEBBIE

I started as a waitress, bartender, etc., and got into the management program about six years ago. As a manager, you have to go through all parts of the restaurant—bar manager, service manager, and kitchen manager—before you are promoted to general manager as Ron is. I've already been in all the positions, so kitchen manager is my last step.

I've been in the restaurant business all of my life. I started in this business when I was sixteen, and I enjoy the people side of it. It's a service I don't think is ever going to die away. People need to eat, they need to drink; they need to be pampered that way. It's not a phase that's going to go away. It was something I felt was very strong and stable for myself. I wanted to get into Bennigan's because it has an excellent training program to get into the

The author wishes to thank Meredith Cole and Mike Suter for their participation in the collection of material for these interviews.

restaurant business, so I know that if and when I decide to leave or go into business for myself, I have the background to back it up.

With Bennigan's, I feel that they treat me no differently, as they would any other manager. I don't feel that I'm discriminated against because I am a woman, but there is a very small percentage of women with Bennigan's. I've always felt that they could use more, but it takes someone who is real strong and is willing to work sixty to seventy hours a week. A lot of women can't handle this. I've seen a lot of women managers go through, and many leave for easier jobs. They're not looking for the long hours—it's not a job that's easily done.

I think that when they first meet me they don't quite know how to take me. Once they get to know me and I get to know them, they treat me just as well as any other manager.

I can hold my own just as much as they can. If anything, I think they have more respect for me for being able to do the job that they can do. I'm not discriminated against at all.

I don't feel that I have any needs that are different from the other guys. I've seen a few women go through, and it really depends on your regional manager. Some might lean on women a little harder just to make them better managers. It's just a real tough job to get into. It's hard to explain, but I just don't feel that they do anything different for me. This company fills just about every need that I have. Every year we go to seminars where they stress quality of life and try to help us understand: this is what you need to do with your day; this is how you need to structure it. They are just really good about that here. If I was with another company I would probably have a few complaints, but not with Bennigan's. Still, they have about a 30 percent turnover for management, so they try to do the best for the managers they keep.

SUPERVISOR'S COMMENTS

Deb has been with the company for five and one-half years. She was a unit employee, waitress, and hostess for about three years. She got into the job not just because she was a unit employee for so long, but because she is a strong-personality person who can direct people.

I don't think that it makes a difference in my management style. I have had women managers before whom I did have to make adjustments for. Deb does not use her being a female as a crutch, or the opposite end where she uses it to bludgeon people with. She is a women and she is a manager; it really hasn't entered into things at all. If anything, she probably gets harder shifts than the guys do, because she is, at this point, one of my most capable managers. She is not favored or babied in any way, and I have had to do that with one assistant manager I had in the past who was not very strong willed—very emotional. That doesn't affect Deb at all.

I think when a new employee just comes into the store—and especially cooks, because Deb is my kitchen manager—cooks are not used to working with women kitchen managers. It is more of a rarity to work for a woman manager in the kitchen. When people first come in and start working, they are a little leery of what to expect. They're like: "A woman manager . . . Whoa! OK—" Once somebody has worked with her, though, I think they see her as hard but fair, so I don't think that she is treated differently at all. I've never seen any repercussions from the fact that she is a woman.

There is an advantage in the fact that she has a woman's point of view. When we sit down at our weekly meetings as a management team, having a woman's point of view is probably to our advantage—although I don't feel that there is a huge difference or anything, like we're the macho guys who say we've got to do things this way and she'd say, "No, I think we'll do it this way." If anything, she's probably more the macho female. I think there are advantages just because I think there is a good mix of personalities.

Disadvantages, in Deb's case anyway, are only very short term and that is, as I said, when people don't know her. There is some stigma attached to female managers. My mentor or first restaurant manager, who taught me everything I know, was female, so I'm very open to any point of view. So I don't have any preconceived thoughts, even though I've had woman managers who could not take the business and ended up quitting.

I think that nationally I would say it's pretty true that they do not have a large measure of success in our industry—whether it's because of the pressure or the long hours, I'm not qualified to say. But there is not a great number of females out there who are very successful in this business. I hate to think that it is just because they are females.

My experience is I've worked with six female managers now in my five and one-half years with Bennigans, and they have all left the company except for Deb—and she will be a general manager. She will go all the way with the company because she has what it takes. She's been an assistant manager for two years now, and she's certainly not getting any special treatment. I don't see any advantages or disadvantages solely because she is female.

For every female manager I've had quit the company, I've had a male manager quit also because he couldn't handle it also. I would say that a greater percentage of females I've worked with have not made it for one reason or another, but maybe that's just because I've worked with fewer. For the six females I've worked with there's been thirty males. I don't see any real differences except in individual personalities.

SOLIDAD

I just applied for this job and I've had it for eleven months since yesterday. I do the laundry here. I was afraid when I first started because I don't speak English right. I couldn't understand everyone. But after that, everything was fine. Everyone was friends.

When I would talk, my boss would try to understand me and she would help me. She would say, "Talk slow and nice and everyone will understand you." That was good.

Nobody treats me differently here because I am from Mexico. Everybody is happy here so management doesn't need to do anything for me. I first started here on December 19th. In January, just two weeks later, my manager made me employee of the month. I was happy about that. We are a family here and I feel like an important person. I had to go back to Mexico for a wedding and they gave me time off with no problems. Everyone understands when you have problems here and that's nice. I'm here every day and I like it.

At first you don't feel comfortable because you work with black and white people. I was afraid they wouldn't like me because I am the only Mexican here, but everybody liked me. At first, there were four people in the lanudry, then three, then two, and now I'm the only one. My manager knows I can handle it, and I like that.

SUPERVISOR'S COMMENTS

When Solidad first came to this country, she couldn't speak any English and she was so ashamed. She didn't want to try to speak English because she was afraid people would laugh at her. Now she speaks pretty good English. It's a little broken, but you can understand every word she says. She's a beautiful person. All of the girls work together here, and that's nice. They don't resent me because I'm new. I'm nice with them and they're nice with me.

It doesn't make any difference in my management style that Solidad is Hispanic. Everyone is equal. Everyone is a person. I don't think the other employees treat her any differently either, not with her personality. I don't think you could.

She is a good worker. She's dedicated to her job, which is great. She's just a nice person to have around. I just met her and I like her so much. I think the majority of the problem with turnover of Hispanics is the language barrier. Filling out all that paperwork and communicating with people is difficult for them. I think that this holds back a lot of really good workers.

We need to let these workers know that we're here to help them and get them on the right road. Most of the bosses do this. When they hire a person, they're going to help them get ahead; I know they would. I've worked with a lot of Hispanics, and they really did get ahead, thanks to bosses and co-workers. Oh, yes, that means a lot! When you have the right people to work for it's good. This place is like a family place, but I can't say all places are like this.

AL

I was referred to Fenway Park by one of the owners who was the partner to the gentleman who owns the place. I was the executive chef down at the Holiday Inn; now I am the kitchen manager here.

The main reason I chose to work here is because I got tired of the corporate hassles. I like it here because it's independently owned and it's a lot easier to work here.

I don't really feel that anyone treats me differently because I'm Hispanic. I've never really had that problem.

Management doesn't do anything special for me. Well, except that I do have a catering business on the side, and they do work with me on my hours, but that doesn't have anything to do with the fact that I'm Hispanic.

SUPERVISOR'S COMMENTS

I hired Al as kitchen manager on the basis of his qualifications, not on the basis of anything else. So the fact that he's Hispanic is not important. Al has good qualifications. He came through some of the local chain hotels like the Holiday Inn.

The fact that Al is Hispanic does not change my management style. It changes some of the conversation in that my management (style) is a personal one. Because I have some Hispanics working for me, I know some Spanish words so that I can go back in the kitchen and talk to them on a person-to-person or family-to-family basis. I'm Italian and they are Hispanics; therefore, I kid them a lot about my ethnic food, their ethnic food, and things like that. Hispanics are strong family-oriented people. They come from the basics of life and that's how I approach them. I don't treat them like they're automatons, because I think that when you get into such an impersonal management style, that's a completely different way than the way we do things here. We try to strive on a systematic basis here to achieve our goals, but on a person-to-person basis we're closer to the situation. So if they're Spanish or hillbilly American, when they come here we always try to relate to them and where they are from, what they've been doing, and what their life is about, as far as how they perceive life and work.

We do have problems when our kitchen balance is not right. We probably have a fifty-fifty ratio of Hispanics to Anglo-Americans. Then we get out of that balance and they don't work as a team; we've had problems with them saying, "Those Mexicans don't speak English, I can't get them to do any work, etc." This is when the white guys feel threatened in their jobs. They rile up, as a group, against the Mexicans because they are frustrated with their positions and they have to strike out at someone. The best way to handle this is to set them down and say, "You've got a problem; what is it?"

You only get that kind of discrimination when you group them. When you don't group them you can't discriminate against them because they're on an individual basis. We could group 18-to-21-year-olds and 21-to-24-year-olds, because I manage these two groups differently too. This is an independent operation, so on that basis, I have to manage on a personal basis. When you have high volume, you need to group people and apply strict management principles. We don't need to be highly regulated, but that's not to say I wouldn't like to be. The management style I have here puts me under a lot of pressure. I'm hopping around here so much I don't have much time to be creative. I'm not saying that's the right way to do things, because it's not.

If you have Hispanics working for you, you have to have all their papers in line for Immigration and that can be a problem. I have twenty employees and four of them are Hispanic. They have a better work ethic than most white Americans. They are filling the positions that most white Americans won't do. A white American looks at a dishwashing job as a temporary setback to something better. A Hispanic, on the other hand, may look at it as a step up from picking potatoes in the fields. Also, Hispanics are more stable. Where it might take a Hispanic two hours to wash ten trays of dishes—and it would take a white American one and a half hours—he will do it at a lower stress level, which means less chance of burnout.

The only disadvantage I find is the paperwork. As a small business owner, I have to keep up with every new law and regulation. Sometimes I can't do this and I get fined, and I can't afford that. This is the only deterrent I can find for hiring Hispanics.

CHARLOTTE

I do the dining room, dishes, grill, and salad bar. Dishes and grill are when I don't have dining room. I work four hours a day, six days a week. Actually, I work six hours a day on Saturdays. I saw an ad in the paper for this job. I answered the paper ad and got the job.

I've worked in fast foods of all kinds for the past forty years. This job was handy and close to home.

I definitely feel like a minority here. There is a real generation gap. The younger generation has a lot of different things that concern them than an older generation does, so I just plug on and do my work.

Oh, no, management doesn't treat me any differently. I work harder, though. That's because the younger ones really don't buckle down. The older people, I guess we're grinding the wheel a little more. I don't think I have any influence over them or anything; I just do my own thing and hope they help out.

Management hasn't really done anything special for me. I work like everybody else. I'm (also) handicapped, so that makes me a little different. I can't hear so I can't do cashier, I've got cataracts in both my eyes so I can't read the meters out there, and that's the main reason why I'm in dining room.

I'd like to see the younger ones pitch in and help a little more. They just walk by. There work is there, but I do a lot more work than I should. If there is a whole bunch of dishes stacked up, they don't put them away. Or if they are dirty, they don't think to wash any of them. That is not my main job. My main job is here on the floor, and when I see there isn't anything to do out here I help out in the back.

SUPERVISOR'S COMMENTS

Basically, Charlotte came in and filled out an application and I hired her.

I don't think that the fact that Charlotte is older makes any difference as far as management goes. I manage each of my employees a little differently. They all have different personalities. Charlotte is old enough to be my grandmother, and I have to treat her with a certain amount of courtesy and respect. Sometimes, if she has a problem or needs help I treat her a little more gingerly, but basically I don't treat her any differently than any other employee. I try to find out what motivates my employees, what turns them on and what turns them off, what brings them up and what brings them down if they're too far up.

I think that some employees don't give her the courtesy and respect that she deserves. She hustles for any person. Nobody really gives her a hard time, but I think that some of them in their nonverbal communication won't give her quite as much. They don't go out of their way sometimes because they know that Charlotte will take care of things. I don't know if it's conscious, but I can see it. They don't have friendship or camaraderie because they don't have as much in common.

I try to treat everybody the same, but I try to adjust to the fact that she has different motivations; therefore, I try to work with those.

Charlotte works for about four hours and she hustles for four hours. Sometimes she gets tired and sits down for a couple of minutes, but that's very seldom. She's a very mature individual. If she calls in sick I know she is really sick. She knows the value of the job. She knows that if she calls in sick, then someone else is going to have to do her job.

ART

I just came in and applied for the job, and they hired me.

It's right down the street from where I live. I need the extra money and it keeps me busy.

It's kind of hard working with all of these kids around here. Some of them work hard, but some of them don't pull their weight. I don't mind doing my job, but I don't like doing other people's work.

The kids all get along pretty well, but I don't talk with them much because we don't have much in common. So I guess they treat me kind of different.

I take the bus to work, and I have a hard time seeing at night. John understands, so he lets me work mornings so I get home before it gets dark.

I work hard, but sometimes I wonder if anybody cares. I know I'm not going to be moving up in the company at my age, but it would be nice if someone would tell me that I'm doing a good job.

SUPERVISOR'S COMMENTS

We needed some people. Art came in and applied, and I hired him. He seemed like a pretty nice guy who wanted to work and would do a good job.

I treat Art just like everybody else. He does have some special scheduling problems, and he took longer to train because he moves a little slower, but now he's just like one of my other workers.

Art doesn't talk to the other workers much, but they seem to work together OK. He just goes about his work and does a good job.

As I said before, Art moves a little slower and his schedule isn't very flexible, but unlike some of my other workers, I think Art appreciates his job a little more. I can depend on Art to be here. He hardly ever calls in sick.

FRANK

I was a resident at the (mental health) center and I wanted to get job placement, so I went to the student union and worked over there until they changed it. So then I had a guy named John I used to work for at the student union, until they moved me to Towers. At Towers I worked for Kurt, and then they moved me over here before they closed Towers.

I like to wash the dishes, the silverware, the pots and pans, and stuff. I'm pretty good at it.

Nobody really treats me any different; I just go ahead and do my work.

Brent (the supervisor) doesn't ever go back to see what I'm doing. I put the pots and pans in with the dishes, and when I get caught up I do the silverware. I only get help in the afternoons. At breakfast I do it all by myself.

The only thing that I wish they would do better is to get someone to put away the groceries. I told him this on Monday. I said I would do the freezer in the morning and the next guy who comes in could do the walk-in storeroom. If I go do other things there would be nobody in the dish room. Sometimes all the people don't show up and I'm the only one who does so I do the work. I hold it all together here.

SUPERVISOR'S COMMENTS

Frank has been a dishwasher here for eighteen years and seems reasonably content with it, which is pretty amazing in itself.

I have no idea how Frank got his job. ARA has only been here about six years, and before that the foodservice was run by the university, and they hired him originally. I'm sure that the people who hired him are long gone by now. I believe that because of the targeted-jobs tax-credit program for hiring certain groups of people, the government will reimburse us and, depending on the cause, it can be a very large portion of their hourly wage. That helps us a lot.

Frank has got a couple of peculiar habits that I think require a little more patience than with other employees. He really enjoys rearranging things in the storeroom. We have a chemical storeroom where we keep all of our paper goods, soda tanks, those sort of things. Just about every day he will rearrange the whole thing, or he will rearrange the setup in the dish room. Fortunately, it's not the kind of thing that is going to throw the whole operation into confusion. He takes a peculiar sense of pride in doing this sort of thing, and he always wants me to come and look at what he's done and see if it's all right. I can't really put him off, because it's in my interest to just look at it right then and say, "It looks good, Frank." Otherwise he's after me the whole day. I just think he requires a little more patience, and that is no problem.

I don't think anyone really treats Frank any differently. He's got a couple of things that really work in his favor. Number one, he's been here so long. Second, he's our most regular employee. He takes the bus here, and he is always on time. He never misses one day. He does his job and he works really hard. I think he's got the respect of the people who work here, and he's treated like everybody else. I've been in a couple of situations before where I've worked with someone who is developmentally disabled and they haven't been treated as well. Generally, if you just treat them like human beings, they will perform.

I've found that as a rule, mentally handicapped people are my most reliable employees. It sounds kind of strange, but they almost don't know better to call in sick when they're not well enough to work. Frank is very reliable. He's always here, and I just can't say enough good about that—particularly in foodservice, which is upset often by attendance and problems with turnover rate. It's really nice to have someone you know is going to be there and works really hard.

I think that with people who aren't mentally handicapped, it would be difficult to find someone who would be willing to work in that position for eighteen years. He's happy to work back there, and that's great. The only disadvantages I can think of are that I need to be a little more patient with him and explain things a little more carefully and thoroughly to him. But the small amount of time that that takes is not really a problem. The payoff is a lot better in the end, so I don't really consider that to be a disadvantage.

With Frank it's kind of a unique story. I don't really have to spend a lot of time with him, and I think that if and when I do, the people who work here know and appreciate what he does so much that there really isn't any resentment there at all.

NANCY

I got hired by a manager named David. My friend Kathy is the one who suggested this place. I've been working here for six months and two years. I work in the lobby and I don't particularly like it. Nobody helps me when I need it. Mostly I'm by myself. I barely get any help when I ask. I talked to Theresa and the supervisor, Scott. They said Brandy would help me, but she hasn't helped me at all yet. I stay here because I need money and I'm afraid I won't get work anywhere else.

I just watched a tape for training and then I started working. I did not go through the McJobs program.

I feel like I'm just not part of their working team anymore. I mean, all they care about is themselves. When I ask them something, they just kind of ignore it like I'm not there. That makes me upset. My friend Laura says this place is a joke and managers don't care about anything but themselves.

The first few weeks that I started here was pretty nice. I got along. But since the corporation took over, things have been getting worse. Nobody helps me when I need it. I talk to managers about it, but they just seem to ignore it.

The days that my friend Kathy works I don't work, and the days that I work she doesn't. We're working together tomorrow and I'm glad about that. It's nice to have a friend around. When I'm by myself, things get difficult. Managers just don't care.

My mother drives me to work and I get off at two now. I have Sunday and Monday off, which I like, so at least they do that for me.

SUPERVISOR'S COMMENTS

This location used to be a franchise, but the company bought it out. Nancy was here when we took over.

It takes two people to do the job when Nancy is working because she's a little slower than some people. We have another handicapped girl working in the lobby, and when they're working together it's OK, but when they work alone there is a problem because they are a little slower. Also, Nancy has a bad temper and you have to approach her a little differently.

I don't think other employees treat Nancy any differently because she's handicapped.

I think that hiring handicapped people looks good in the eyes of the public. We're an equal opportunity employer and when other people see that we hire handicapped people, they tend to visit the restaurant more often. It is a little more costly, though. You need highly productive people to work at McDonald's. It's a fast-paced place.

The McJobs program has a specific trainer who trains them and ships them out to other stores, and then we treat them just like any other employee. They get performance reviews, raises, they get reprimanded when they're late, like everybody else. I have a handicapped sister, and that helps me understand them better. Some managers just don't understand. They think they're a burden and not worth the trouble. It's really the personality of the individual managers that makes the difference.

Nancy is limited to just the lobby. It would take a lot of time and patience to train her on anything else. Maybe if she went through the McJobs program, she could broaden her horizons a little.

MARIA

I met Bijan at the Harvest when I was working there, and he told me that he needed someone at Writer's Manor. I wasn't very happy at the Harvest so I figured I would try it out.

When I first started, I didn't like the job. I like it much better now that I feel like I know what I'm doing. I would like this job to lead into something else. This job is much better than the Harvest.

The fact that I'm part-time doesn't really affect my job. I believe that I do the best job that I can while I am there. I kind of feel inferior to people who have been there a while and work forty hours a week, but there is nothing I can do about that.

Other employees don't really treat me any differently. People who have been there a while sometimes don't know who I am and don't talk to me very much, but I know it will be a while before that happens.

Managers don't really treat me any differently either, because while I'm there I do my work. They expect me to do that.

I just asked management for one day off when I couldn't work because I am in school late. In that way they really accommodate my needs.

It really bothers me when Bijan watches me, because I just don't feel comfortable. Steven (the front-desk supervisor) just lets me be myself, but Bijan stands over my shoulder and he looks directly at me. He embarrasses me in front of the customers. I think it has to do with the fact that I'm new mostly.

SUPERVISOR'S COMMENTS

I used to work with her at the Harvest restaurant, and she said she was looking for a job that was not that hard. If she wanted to go home early she could, and if it was real slow she could do homework. She came in and applied for the job, and she got it.

What I do with my part-time people is that they come in and tell me what hours they can work. Then I go to my schedule and if those hours will work, then I hire them. If they don't, then I won't hire them. Maria, for example, can't work Thursday nights.

I don't think that people treat Maria differently because she is part-time.

The advantages of Maria being part-time are that when things are slow you can usually cut part-time workers' hours. When things pick back up you can put them back on again. You can't do this with full-time people because that job is their life. They depend on that forty hours; that is their income. Cutting hours will not hurt a part-time person as much as it will a full-time one. The disadvantage to part-time people is you can't ask them to work extra days. They usually have other things they have to do. With full-time people, you can change their schedules around a little more. They don't usually have school or a second job or something like that.

In my experience, I have never had any special problems with my part-time people. I have heard that people have problems with loyalty of part-time people, but I have never had any problems with that.

AUDREY

Well, my sister worked here, and one day I just came in and Liz asked me if I wanted a job, and I took it.

I don't feel like anyone treats me differently because I'm part-time. There's not really any difference between part-time and full-time work, because when you're there you just do what you have to do.

Sometimes Liz has to fit in my schedule around school, but that's the only thing she really does.

Management doesn't really need to do anything else, because everything is pretty easy here.

SUPERVISOR'S COMMENTS

Audrey's sister worked here, and she came in with her mother, and I needed some dinner assistants. I thought it would be a good idea for Audrey to work a couple of hours a night, a few days a week, to make some extra money. It's hard to find part-time employees.

Originally, management had to make some changes for part-time employees. We work on a supervisory program here. I'm not required to be here all the time, but I would never leave Audrey here all by herself. There's really no point in teaching her how to open (the place) because she will never have to do that. She's come a lot further than I expected.

I think that part-time workers get jobs that others don't want to do. They get to do the bad jobs.

Audrey is restricted in her scheduling. I can work her weekends and nights. She has other pressures that restrict when she can work. It's very easy to get burned out here, but since she only works a couple of hours a day, that's not likely to happen. Also, since she is young, if she decides she wants to work more in the future, or in the summers, she already knows about the restaurant.

3 | IMPROVING PRODUCTIVITY: DESIGNING THE WORKPLACE

The interaction of employees and the environment in which they work affects productivity; designers must develop facilities with productivity in mind.

OBJECTIVES OF FACILITY PLANNING

There are several objectives involved in planning a new facility or revamping an existing one.

First, the planner aims to ease the production process. Spaces are arranged and laid out to ensure a smooth flow of people and things.

A second objective is to minimize the cost and time required to handle goods within the operation. This means moving many items mechanically rather than by hand; routing things over straight paths while minimizing backtracking; and carrying a minimum amount of inventory while ensuring proper storage to protect materials from damage.

The planner must also try to minimize the investment in equipment. Case-by-case cost-benefit analysis will determine to what extent machines should replace people.

Because of the increasing costs of building, the planner must make full use of both horizontal and vertical space for workplaces, aisles, and storage, so that work can be completed in a minimum amount of wasted space without the feeling of being cramped.

Equipment must be maintained. The wise planner will select surfaces that can be easily cleaned. Maintenance comes into play in the design of equipment. Placing kitchen equipment on wheels, for example, allows for ease of movement during cleaning.

The hospitality industry is greatly concerned with cost control. This is another objective when planning facilities. Portion control, for example, can be made

Adapted from *Foodservice Facilities Planning, Third Edition*, by Edward A. Kazarian, New York, Van Nostrand Reinhold, 1989.

easier by selecting serving utensils of an appropriate size. Similarly, employee costs can be controlled through the efficient layout of individual work stations, designed in accordance with the tasks to be performed there.

Facilities also should be designed with flexibility in mind. The operation may need to expand; the menu may be changed if the original choices do not appeal.

PLANNING THE TYPE OF FACILITY

There are several sequential steps in the development of a property that will determine how productive the end product is. A market analysis is conducted to determine the potential customers or guests. From this information, a menu—to use the example of a restaurant—is developed that will appeal to the market segments being sought. The type of service and operating characteristics are set, equipment characteristics determined, and the resulting space requirements and arrangements finalized.

Market Analysis

Various factors can be identified to give a picture of the type of menu desired. Occupation is the first. Students interested in bulk food at low prices, health-conscious secretaries, and expense account executives will seek different menu offerings. The income level of the target segments is crucial. The more discretionary income is available, the more can be spent on dining out. The educational level of the market is related to both income and occupation. Generally speaking, the higher the educational level, the greater the incidence of eating out.

Age and sex are also important factors. Certain foods appeal more to a younger crowd. Some foods also are more popular with women, or with men; chicken à la king, for example, is a traditional light luncheon favorite of women's groups.

The reasons people eat out will influence what is put on the menu. If a particular restaurant caters to the so-called special occasion crowd, for example, there will be a number of flambéed items and flamboyant drinks. The marketplace can be broken down into three broad segments: the captive market, the mass market, and the status market. Those in the captive market eat out because they have little or no choice. This includes people in prisons, institutions, hospitals, and colleges. Their primary motivation is physical—eating simply to refuel. The mass market is concerned with other things. It may be a change in routine, convenience because both spouses are working outside the home, or a means to get away from the kids. The status market is concerned with ego needs. To see and be seen is important. It may be a way to impress a date or a business client, or it may be a special occasion such as a birthday or anniversary. Each group will look for different items on the menu.

The final point to be considered here is the pattern of arrival. The planner needs to know the likely travel flow in terms of numbers per hour as well as the likely composition of the customers: singles, couples, families, or groups.

Menu Development

Menu offerings will be developed in accordance with the market segments being pursued. In turn, the menu will serve as a basis for future layout and design options.

The frequency of changes must be considered. A menu may be completely fixed, such as a fast-food operation. Another option is to have a generally fixed menu with seasonal changes—two to four a year—or changing specials, to give repeat business some variety while offering the chef the opportunity to take advantage of special prices in the marketplace. This is also a convenient method of recycling leftovers.

Certain operations change their menus every day. This may be appropriate where the menu is limited and the business consists of heavy repeaters, such as at a camp or resort. Consideration should be given in the planning stages to balancing the types of foods each day in order that one work station—the grill, for example—is not overburdened. Cafeteria-type operations tend to use a menu that repeats on a two- to six-week basis. Other operations incorporate daily or cyclical changes but keep certain popular items standard on the menu.

The size and extent of the menu must also be considered. The more limited the menu, the less equipment will be needed. The more extensive the menu, the slower the service, as well as more storage space and equipment that will be needed. A more extensive menu does appeal, however, to a larger number of potential customers. A decision also must be made on the type of service available: à la carte or complete meals.

At this point the particular items can be chosen. This should be done in accordance with certain guidelines:

The items should appeal to the customers being sought.

They should be profitable. Profitability can be measured in terms of *food cost percentage*—the ratio of food cost to selling price—and in *dollar contribution margin*—the difference in dollars and cents between the selling price of one item and its food cost.

They should be easy to produce. The easier and faster the items can be produced, the less time, labor, and equipment will be needed.

They should be readily available at all times.

They should be easy for the employees to prepare. It is pointless to put items on the menu that the staff cannot prepare with a high level of consistency.

Menu balance must be considered. It is important that no one piece of equipment or work station be overwhelmed because of the mix of offerings.

The items should be compatible with each other and offer a balanced selection.

Price is also important. A range of prices will give customers the option of choosing a lower-priced item they may feel offers better value. Excessive price spread—the difference between the most and least expensive entree—encourages sales of the lower-priced dishes. The highest-priced entree should be no more than twice that of the lowest-priced one.

Food Preparation

Various methods are available to prepare the same item. The extent to which a restaurant will use prepared items is important in determining the type of equipment and relative space required. For example, a meal can be prepared from scratch using only fresh raw ingredients, from a combination of fresh and preprepared items, or from precooked frozen portions. The choice will determine how much area is required for storage, prepreparation, and cooking.

Type of Service

There are several different methods available to serve food to the customer. In table service operations, servers bring the food to the customers' tables. These types of service units require more square feet of space per seat than other types.

Counter service is where the customers sit at a counter. Popular at breakfast and lunch, this operation typically features a limited menu and high turnover and requires a minimum of space.

Booth service allows a certain amount of privacy. Combinations of the above three methods of service are common.

Tray service is used in airlines, hospitals, and similar types of facilities. Room service in hotels requires areas for loading the carts. Cafeteria service specializes in low- to medium-priced meals.

Restaurants may also be self-service. This can be accomplished with a buffet, with an entirely take-out operation, or with vending machines.

The type of service chosen will have implications for the absolute space required as well as the relative distribution of that space among the various functions.

At this stage, the type of equipment necessary to serve the desired menu can be determined. Dividing the estimated number of items to be prepared per hour by the hourly capacity of each piece of equipment will determine the amount of equipment required.

PLANNING SPACE ARRANGEMENTS

The productive use of space and of the people who operate that space is achieved by applying certain principles of flow to the functions inherent in the operation.

Identifying Functions

The first step is to identify on paper all of the functions that take place in an operation. In a restaurant, for example, goods are received and sent to either dry or refrigerated storage. From there they might go to preparation, then to the cook, server, dining room, and dishwasher.

Productive use of space occurs when two functional areas—receiving and storage, for example—are placed near each other. Evaluation of flow can be undertaken for materials, employees, guests, or paperwork in order to minimize the flow for what is considered important. The same type of analysis can be accomplished for a guest entering a hotel or restaurant in order to ensure a minimum of guest inconvenience—in getting to the room, for example.

Flow Principles

Whichever criteria are considered important, the principles to minimize movement are the same. Wherever possible, flow should be along straight paths. In addition, the amount of cross traffic, backtracking, and bypassing should be kept to a minimum.

Keeping flow in a straight line—over the shortest distance—is crucial. Cross traffic causes bottlenecks and congestion; consequently, it should be avoided. Backtracking occurs when a person moves from one place or piece of equipment to another, then returns along the same path. This probably cannot be eliminated but should be cut down as much as possible, perhaps with wide aisles or circular routes of flow. Bypassing occurs when someone has to move past one or more pieces of equipment to perform the next stage in a process. Different arrangements of equipment, fixtures, and areas may be necessary to find the best arrangement.

Flow diagrams or string charts—in which pieces of string are used to simulate movement—can be useful in finding the best arrangement.

LAYOUT CONFIGURATIONS

Five layouts are common in the design of equipment and workplaces. A single straight-line arrangement—in which pieces are placed along a wall or in an island—is simple but limited in the number of pieces that can be accommodated.

An L-shaped arrangement can accommodate more pieces of equipment and can be used where space is limited to keep pieces of equipment or workplaces separated better.

A U-shaped arrangement is also suitable where space is limited, but the lack of space limits it to where only one or two employees are working. An additional restriction is that pass-through movement through the area is not possible.

A parallel, back-to-back arrangement allows for centralizing the utilities required for the two banks of equipment, which are set up parallel to each other, their backs adjacent to each other.

FIGURE 3–1 EXAMPLES OF EQUIPMENT ARRANGEMENTS.

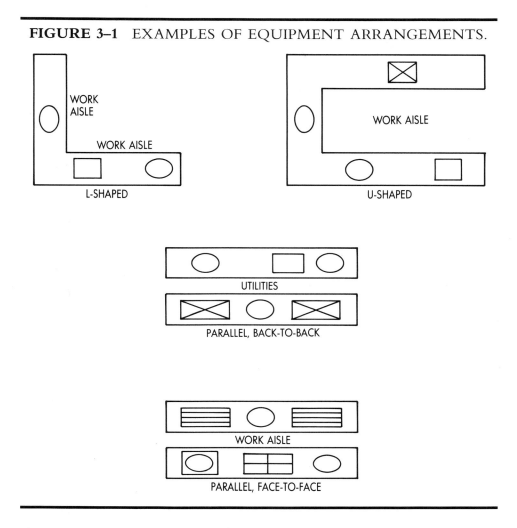

A parallel, face-to-face arrangement consists of two rows of equipment facing each other, with a work aisle in between. In this arrangement, two utility lines are required.

The four more complex arrangements are shown in figure 3–1.

SUMMARY

The design of the operation affects employee productivity. Productivity can be increased by taking into account employee, material, guest, and paperwork flow in the development stages of a new facility. The layout of existing operations can be changed, though at greater expense than for a new facility. By taking the principles identified in this chapter into account, owners can achieve more output from the same amount of employee effort. The result is increased productivity.

SUGGESTED READINGS

Kazarian, Edward A., *Foodservice Facilities Planning, Third Edition*, New York, Van Nostrand Reinhold, 1989.

APPENDIX: IMPLEMENTING DESIGN AND LAYOUT—THE BANK OF ENGLAND

During the past decade, the Bank of England has embarked on modernization and refurbishment plans for its London premises. In the midst of this, there was a need to review the foodservice facilities at all levels. The catering facilities were outdated and highly labor-intensive. The equipment installed was obsolete and energy-intensive. There was also a need to replace main boilers and elevators in the central catering block, which is separate from the main bank buildings.

The particular building that will be examined had been developed over the years to provide a variety of services:

> First floor: quick lunch bar, waitress service based on a typical mid-1950s highway service station
>
> Second floor: conventional meat-and-vegetable cafeteria
>
> Third floor: management dining room and salar bar
>
> Fourth floor: carvery
>
> Fifth floor: coffee shop and table tennis room
>
> Sixth floor: coffee shop

One of the system's obvious flaws was that there was a washing machine on every floor but only a single kitchen, in the basement.

Foodservice in industry is therapeutic: employees perform better if they know that their lunch is going to be well served and nicely presented in pleasant surroundings, and after such a meal there is a tendency for morale to be higher in the afternoon.

In this building, however, it was evident from customers' comments that there was general dissatisfaction with the services provided, and the participation rate—the percentage of bank employees who used the catering facilities—had dropped to approximately 45 percent. Among the employees' complaints was that the menu was divided illogically between floors, so that someone who wanted roast beef could not dine with a person who wanted a salad.

The catering staff, which is generally forgotten, was also asked to express a view. The employees pointed out that their working conditions were less than satisfactory and indeed, in some cases, hazardous.

Following consultation, it was decided to appoint a designer specializing in catering, who, together with the company's own management team, set about reviewing the service requirements and making recommendations as to future service styles.

Source: Brian T. Watts, managing director, B. E. Services Limited.

PROJECT DESIGN BRIEF

The brief was given to the catering designer after wide consultation. It was divided into two parts, covering foodservice and general requirements.

Foodservice

The project design shall be based on the concepts produced by the consultants in conjunction with the bank and its catering company.

The cost of the foodservice equipment element of the budget shall be totally recoverable over a five-year period through reduced operating costs, brought about by increased efficiency as a result of the overall concept.

The aim shall be to provide catering facilities of a very high standard.

A wider choice of foods shall be made available.

Food shall be made available in bar areas.

Entertaining facilities for guests shall be provided.

The working conditions for catering staff shall generally be improved.

General

On completion of the contract, the building will be capable of a further twenty years of life under normal maintenance conditions.

Energy conservation will have utmost priority.

Environmental standards shall conform to the latest codes of practice.

The building shall comply with all current legislation.

Standby electrical facilities shall be maintained.

All finishes and installations shall be easily maintained.

To enable the design brief to be carried out the consultants were given several instructions:

Survey each floor and determine principal service risers and drops for possible structural alterations and effects on proposed layouts. Relate all services to building drawings for reference.

Survey each floor for possible structural alterations, particularly with regard to centralization of the dishwashing activities.

Propose a style of service for each floor.

Propose conceptual sketch layouts for each floor.

Prepare schedules of new equipment with budget costs.

Prepare schedule of building projects, together with budget costs.

Prepare schedule of services, together with budget costs.

Produce a report embodying all proposals, sketch layouts, budget costs, and schedules.

COMPARISON OF OLD AND NEW

Serving Areas and Dining Rooms

The old-style cafeterias (fig. 3–2) were traditionally formed with a single line and all items served to the customer. Some move toward self-service had been made, but due to the poor design this was largely ineffective. The result was that long lines developed and there was more customer dissatisfaction.

It was decided early that the carvery, salad bars, and conventional cafeteria would be combined onto two floors, enabling the customers to circulate through a free-flow area, helping themselves to all items on the menu.

It was also decided to reject the idea of long counters open on one side, as these proved to be energy-, capital-, and labor-intensive. New counters were designed that enabled customers to move around all four sides, helping themselves (fig. 3–3).

Needless to say, the caterers became concerned about the effect on portion control, so it was decided to price band all items where possible, seeking to control the portions of only high-cost items such as meat. Vegetables and salads could be freely taken by the customer in any quantity, the theory being that the likely increase in food usage would be more than offset by the saving in staff. Employees widely accepted this concept.

Another decision was to introduce a fast-food bar to the unit. During all service times, members of the kitchen staff took part in serving the food, to enable them to see the customers and vice versa. This used the staff to greater

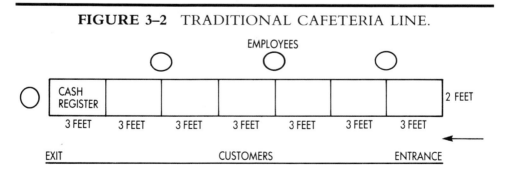

FIGURE 3–2 TRADITIONAL CAFETERIA LINE.

IN THE TRADITIONAL CAFETERIA LINE BOTTLENECKS OCCUR WHEN THE FIRST CUSTOMER IN LINE ORDERS SOMETHING THAT REQUIRES A WAIT. OF AN AREA OF FORTY-TWO SQUARE FEET, ONLY EIGHTEEN SQUARE FEET ARE USED FOR SELLING. THREE SERVERS AND A CASHIER ARE REQUIRED.

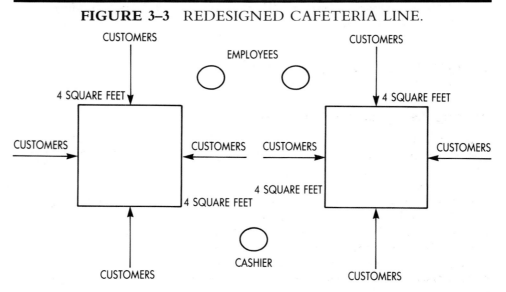

FIGURE 3–3 REDESIGNED CAFETERIA LINE.

IN THE REDESIGNED CAFETERIA LINE, THERE ARE NO BOTTLENECKS. OF AN AREA OF THIRTY-TWO SQUARE FEET, ALL IS USED FOR SELLING. THE SERVING AREA CAN BE STAFFED BY TWO SERVERS AND A CASHIER.

effect and, incidentally, improved the food quality, as the cooks were forced to face the customers and give them the food that they had helped produce.

Other fundamental changes were made:

Removal of all double boilers in favor of hot plates and attractive warming dishes

Removal of vinyl or polished floors in favor of carpeting in all areas, including along the walls up to about three feet off the floor

Use of postformed laminated materials and ceramic tiling

Increased emphasis on refrigeration and food display

Alteration of serving areas to reflect and become part of the dining areas rather than the kitchens

Introduction of air-conditioning

Reliance on customers to clear tables themselves, allowing a single centralized washing area to be developed for china, crockery, and glassware. All washing up of tableware then was centralized on a single floor in the building, using conveyor belts to move used trays to a central point, and mobile carts to move glassware from the bars; this permitted the closing of five separate washing areas and enabled five staff members to take care of all the washing–up and clearing operations

With this last step, the company moved away from employing separate cleaners, except for the rest rooms. Otherwise, all of the catering staff were expected to help clean the building.

The main features of the washing areas included:

- Daylight for washing-up staff
- Ceramic tiles of various colors
- Open storage of machinery and detergents, in place of storage cupboards
- Air-conditioning
- Full heat recovery on automatic dishwashing machines
- Removal of waste bins in favor of waste-disposal units
- Introduction of labor-saving devices such as automatic removal of cutlery from trays

These changes enabled the company to recruit and hold a number of key staff in an area that traditionally has a high turnover.

Bar Areas

An early decision was made to include licensed facilities in the building and firmly link them to the service of food, with emphasis on soft furnishings and tables. This lessened their image as London bars; instead they were seen as an extension of the lunch service. Customer and staff alike welcomed the move.

The bar designs themselves were radically changed from those of the traditional London pub, all optics, beer pumps, and cash registers placed on the front of the bar to enable the bar staff to serve customers face-to-face. It was observed that the staff in the traditionally designed bar spent approximately 25 percent of the time walking backward and forward. The design changes reduced this wasted movement by 25 percent.

In addition, the storage cellar was moved to the same floor as the bar, with immediate access by bar staff. An automatic beer dispenser was installed.

Kitchen Design

As in all other areas, the designers and management consulted the workers who would be using the kitchen. As a result, a number of design features were built into the kitchens that enabled them to be operated hygienically, safely, and economically:

> Where possible, cantilevered or mobile tables with no drawers or shelves underneath were used. (Kitchen drawers typically contain items that are not used but that the staff cannot bear to throw away.)
>
> Refrigeration featured stainless steel, glass-fronted doors, standardized roll-in trolleys, and plastic containers.

Ovens all were set at a high level to avoid any bending, and on wheels with flexible power connections.

Stoves had solid doors and open frames, with no ovens underneath, and all were cantilevered.

Wet steaming equipment was fixed to a waterproof base in order to permit easy cleaning.

Ventilation could be washed automatically without grease filters, and had built-in fire protection over sensitive equipment.

Full heat recovery from refrigeration and main ventilation was provided.

Kitchen stores were abolished.

NET RESULTS

As a result of the expenditure, the staff required to operate the building has been reduced from 230 to 86. These employees undertake additional duties, such as the cleaning of the building, but are still able to provide new services such as guest suites, foodservice in the bar, and operation of a wine bar with foodservice.

Despite fears that portion sizes would increase, the reverse was evident. The average vegetable and salad portions taken have, in fact, decreased. Meanwhile, the customer participation rate has risen to 83 percent.

It is now five years since the redesigned building opened. In that time, the unit has been viewed by twenty-five hundred visitors and has served an average of fifteen hundred people per day. No further major redecoration or replacement program has been necessary, and there is general pride in the unit among catering staff and customers alike. The employer and the employees now view their catering as something to be proud of; the latter are better motivated and view their own jobs as being an important part of the bank's operations.

4 | IMPROVING PRODUCTIVITY: EMPLOYEE SCHEDULING AND TASK PLANNING

One of the restaurant industry's major costs is for payroll and benefits; the industry average is more than 30 percent of sales. The control of this cost should be of obvious concern to management.

Improved scheduling of employees and planning of their tasks can help significantly. Industry consultants have indicated that potential savings of 10 to 20 percent of labor costs can be expected through employee scheduling. This could represent savings of 3 to 6 percent of sales.

ESTABLISH PRODUCTIVITY STANDARDS

The first step in establishing employee schedules is to determine a *productivity standard* for measuring future performance. Lothar A. Kreck defines a standard as "a definite level or degree of performance established by management that is proper and adequate for a particular purpose."[1] There are several ways to establish standards.

Industry Norms

Various attempts have been made to come up with industry-wide standards for use in the hospitality industry. Pannell, Kerr, Forster, a well-respected consulting firm, developed broad measures of restaurant standards over several years. These measures are outlined in table 4–1.

It is not wise, however, to apply industry standards to a hotel or restaurant without consideration of the specific characteristics of the operation. Industry standards are averages for the industry and must be used for general guidance only. They do not take into account the age of equipment, the complexity of a menu, or the ability of the staff.

TABLE 4-1: RESTAURANT PRODUCTIVITY STANDARDS

Covers served per service staff member per meal period:

Formal dining room	12–15
Coffee shop with open kitchen	35–50
Coffee shop with separate kitchen	25–35
Regular dining room	18–22
Captain or hostess coverage per service	1 per 4–8
Bus staff coverage per service staff member	1 per 4–5

Source: "How to Precontrol Your Payroll Costs," Theodore Mandigo, *Foodservice Marketing*, April 1982, 30 (Edgell Communications, Cleveland).

Time Studies

Time studies are useful for measuring repetitive activities involving the same product or service. This makes their use more difficult in the hospitality industry, in which the work often consists of many different activities and the handling of many different products. In work sampling, well-defined events are observed and recorded. An event might be the registration of a guest or the unloading of dishes from a dishwasher. As a result, data can be developed on times devoted to the different tasks carried out.

A technique known as Methods Time Management (MTM) is useful in this regard. Manual work is split up into basic movements, each of which is timed. Times are expressed in Time Movement Units; one TMU equals one-millionth of an hour. The Swedish Institute for Food Service has conducted research using this technique. When calculating time needed to make a dish, the degree of convenience is important, because there is generally an inverse relationship between the degree of convenience and the amount of labor involved.

The MTM system can analyze only manual operations and does not measure time spent in processing operations such as boiling or frying. To compensate for this, a contingency factor must be worked in, depending on the proportion of manual time to processing time. Assuming a ratio of 40 percent manual time to 60 percent processing time, the contingency factor would be 1.5 (60 divided by 40). The manual time to prepare the dish would be multiplied by this factor.

Standard times can be established for each item on the menu. When combined with sales forecasts, a standard is produced for scheduling purposes.

When timing tasks, certain considerations are important:

Try to select employees whose work speed is in the middle range.

People will work faster when being observed and timed.

Take unscheduled events—such as equipment breakdown—into account.

Past Production Records

The most practical method of developing productivity standards is to keep operating statistics over a period of time, noting those periods when service and quality were at a level that produced guest satisfaction with the fewest number of employees.

Standards would be set for each department, in a restaurant, for each meal period. In a hotel housekeeping department, the standard might be the number of rooms cleaned per employee hour, which equals the number of rooms cleaned divided by the number of hours worked by room attendants. By analyzing a test period of at least a week when there are no unusual operating conditions, standard figures can be produced.

Characteristics of Good Standards

To be useful, standards must be easy to use and implement. Managers must be able to rely on them repeatedly. They must be accurate enough to compensate for different employees and changing circumstances. They also must be a true representation of the task.

DEVELOP A FORECAST

Forecasting is part science, part art. It is also a key to the successful control of labor costs. Employees are scheduled by applying standards to a forecast of customers, guests, or covers.

Prepare Forecast

A forecast then can be developed for each market segment. The existing number of occupied rooms is taken as a base. To this is added or subtracted a forecast of rooms based on the growth, stability, or decline of each segment, the competitors' edge or lack thereof in the marketplace, and the availability of resources to exploit any advantage.

Similar techniques would be appropriate for forecasting restaurant demand.

A ten-day forecast, starting on a Friday, also has advantages. It allows the forecaster to estimate customer counts for employee scheduling during a full pay period. It also allows a preliminary full weekend forecast. This is particularly important as so many hospitality businesses have weekend business that is totally different from what is experienced during the week. It is desirable to update the forecast halfway through, taking into account any new information such as the cancellation of a convention or a prediction of snow.

DEVELOP STAFFING GUIDES

Once a standard has been set using one of the methods outlined above, we have a figure for determining how many staff hours are required for varying levels of forecasted business. A staffing guide shows how these hours should be scheduled to provide the required level of service with a minimum of unproductive labor.

A staffing guide is usually prepared for the average level of business expected. Forecasted sales can be plotted for each half hour of operation, and then the appropriate number of staff hours per half hour can be scheduled. The most productive arrangement is probably a staggered schedule. In such a schedule, people come in to work at different times depending on the flow of business. While two servers may operate a station during peak meal times, one may come in early to open the station while the other may stay late to close up.

REPORTING AND EVALUATION

Too often a system is set up but insufficient concern is given to maintaining it. Over a period of time, small deviations from standards grow into major cost problems.

The key in evaluating the system is to compare actual performance with the standards, to report any significant deviation in a timely manner, and to take steps to correct any discrepancies.

The manpower required for scheduled housekeeping employees is contained in table 4–2. In this particular example, productive scheduling is a product of the efforts of two people: the front–office manager who produces the forecast and the executive housekeeper who schedules accordingly. If the front–office manager projects 80 occupied rooms and is correct, the score is 100 percent. If only 70 rooms are occupied, however, that error will result in excess staff hours being scheduled. At a level of 80 occupied rooms, 43 hours of work by day housekeepers would be required, while 37 hours would be needed for 70 occupied rooms. The wasted 6 hours must be "charged" to the front–office manager, bringing the rating to 86 percent (of the hoped-for 43-hour staffing need—37 divided by 43). It is as bad, though, to be understaffed with a score of 114 percent as overstaffed with 86 percent.

TABLE 4–2: MANPOWER REQUIRED FOR HOUSEKEEPING SCHEDULED EMPLOYEES

Occupied rooms	Hours of work by day housekeepers	Hours of work by laundry
100	53	20
90	48	19
80	43	17
70	37	16

The other side of control is to determine how well the executive housekeeper schedules. If 90 rooms were forecast and actually sold, the standard for day housekeepers would be 48 hours. If they actually spent 50 hours performing the work, the executive housekeeper's productivity in scheduling would be 48 divided by 50, or 96 percent. A score above 100 percent might indicate that rooms were not being cleaned well enough to meet the quality standard.

At the room attendant's level, a score can be given after room checks. A measure of the employee's performance can be given by dividing the number of items checked as satisfactory by the number checked as unsatisfactory.

PRINCIPLES OF EMPLOYEE SCHEDULING

Several principles can be identified that, when put into practice, will result in more productive employee scheduling.

Schedule Split Shifts

A split shift means scheduling employees for two time periods during the day with time off in between. For example, employees may work lunch service, be off for a few hours, then return to provide service at dinner. This concept is feasible where employees live close to the operation. It does, however, make for a very long day for the employee. It would also encounter strong opposition if the employees were unionized.

Schedule Irregularly

The idea of irregular scheduling is that an employee should be called in to work at the time that business warrants, rather than starting at the same time each day. For example, if guests check out later on weekends than during the week, it makes sense to bring in housekeepers later on these days.

Use Part-Time Personnel

It is unproductive to staff for peak periods using full-time employees. Full-time personnel can provide a steady, well-trained core of employees to meet average business conditions, while part-time workers can be used to supplement that core during peak periods.

Use a Staffing Guide

As noted above, a staffing guide links forecasted business and productivity standards to determine the number of employees needed at each hour of the day. Its use is critical to establishing control of labor cost.

STORING EMPLOYEE LABOR

The flow of business in the hospitality industry is erratic. At times during the day there are few customers or guests; at other times there are lines of people waiting to be served or to check in. At times, then, employees have nothing productive to do, yet they are being paid for their time. The idea of storing employee labor is to utilize the employee's time when demand is low in ways that will contribute to the organization when business is brisk.

Find Slack Time

The first step in this process is to determine whose time is slack at what periods. This can be accomplished through observation. Which employees are standing around; when is that occurring?

Planning in Advance

Advance planning is necessary to utilize properly the slack time that has been identified. Advance planning of menus, for example, might reveal that a particular entrée to be served in a few days requires a great deal of prepreparation. Slack time could be used, say, to steam cabbage leaves in preparation for stuffed cabbage rolls. Or servers could fold napkins for a major banquet the following day. The key is knowing what is ahead and using slack time to carry out tasks in order to save time later.

Preparation and Storage Constraints

Employee labor can be stored only within quality and safety constraints in the preparation and storage of certain items. Food items cannot be prepared too far in advance, for fear of spoilage. Flower centerpieces for a function will wilt if put together too far ahead of the occasion.

Within the constraints of quality and safety, though, management can identify who has any slack time and, with knowledge of short-term future events, can put that slack time to productive use. The products of the employees' efforts are then stored until the demand for them occurs. The employees' labor, thus, is effectively stored.

IMPROVING EMPLOYEE SCHEDULING

Management seeks to give maximum service at minimum cost. Better scheduling can result in significant cost savings while still maintaining the level of service. What is needed is a method for approaching scheduling problems. What is known as *decision trees* can help, by setting down the range of possible scheduling decisions and their potential consequences in an organized fashion.[2]

Define the Problem

The first step is to determine the nature of the problem. If we are concerned with weekend staffing, it would be necessary to concentrate on examining the sales and customer counts for past weekends. Business for a hotel or restaurant is often different during days of the week or months of the year. A hotel may enjoy nearly full occupancy in midweek but be empty on weekends. The rule of thumb is that if guest or customer counts vary by more than 10 percent for a particular time period, a separate analysis should be conducted. If Monday through Friday occupancy is 80 percent and weekend occupancy is 65 percent, these require two distinct staffing decisions.

Determine the Staffing Alternatives

Management's challenge is to schedule employees under conditions of demand uncertainty. To reduce that uncertainty, management uses past data as a foundation for future demand projections. Let us assume that the problem is staffing for Sunday brunch. The customer count for the previous year's Sundays would be plotted on a line, omitting any unusual days such as Mother's Day or Easter Sunday. These occasions would require separate consideration. Having plotted the previous business, management can divide the data into three levels of demand: low, medium, and high. A staffing pattern can be determined for each level of demand by applying productivity standards to the customer counts. For the low demand of 90 to 120 customers, four servers and three cooks might be needed; for 120 to 150 customers, it might be six servers and four cooks; for the high demand of 150 to 200 customers, eight servers and five cooks might be appropriate. It might be found, for example, that out of fifty previous Sundays, customer demand was low on ten, medium on twenty-nine, and high on eleven days. The median number of customers—the midpoint when arranging the data in ascending order—is 100, 135, and 170 for the low, medium, and high levels, respectively. This information, as described in figure 4–1, helps determine staffing needs.

Because of the uncertainty of demand, the restaurant could end up with employees standing around idle if business is less than forecast, or with unhappy customers waiting excessive amounts of time if demand is more than forecast. To reduce the uncertainty, management next should determine the probability of each level of demand. This is the number of days with a level of demand, divided by the total number of days. The results in our example are .2 (ten divided by fifty) for low demand, .58 (twenty-nine divided by fifty) for medium demand, and .22 (eleven divided by fifty) for high demand.

Costing Out the Alternatives

If we assume that the cost per employee for brunch is $14 for servers and $30 for cooks, we can determine the staffing cost per shift at various levels of business. For low demand, the employee cost would be $146 (four servers at

---

FIGURE 4–1 CUSTOMER COUNTS FOR SUNDAY BRUNCH.

LOW	MEDIUM	HIGH
MEDIAN 100	MEDIAN 135	MEDIAN 170
	XXXXXX	XXXXX
XXXXX	XXXXXXX	
---	---	---
XXXXX	XXXXXX	XXXXX
	XXXXXX	

90	120	150	200

EACH *X* REPRESENTS A SUNDAY. OVER THE PAST YEAR, ON TEN SUNDAYS THE RESTAURANT HAD BETWEEN 90 AND 120 CUSTOMERS, ON TWENTY-NINE DAYS BETWEEN 120 AND 150 CUSTOMERS, AND ON ELEVEN DAYS BETWEEN 150 AND 200 CUSTOMERS. THE MEDIAN NUMBERS FOR THE PERIODS OF LOW, MEDIUM, AND HIGH DEMAND WERE 100, 135, AND 170, RESPECTIVELY. STAFFING LEVELS ARE SET TO SERVE THE THREE LEVELS OF DEMAND. IF THE RESTAURANT EXPECTS LOW DEMAND AND STAFFS ACCORDINGLY, THE MAXIMUM NUMBER OF CUSTOMERS THE EMPLOYEES COULD HANDLE WOULD BE 120. STAFFING FOR MEDIUM DEMAND, EMPLOYEES COULD HANDLE 150 CUSTOMERS. STAFFING FOR HIGH DEMAND, EMPLOYEES COULD HANDLE 200 CUSTOMERS.

$14 each plus three cooks at $30 each); for medium demand, the cost increases to $204 (with two additional servers and another cook); for high demand, the cost jumps to $262 (with two more servers and one more cook needed).

Determine the Revenue

To determine the expected revenue, it is necessary to know the average customer check. This is obtained by dividing total sales revenue by the number of customers. Let us assume that the average check is $12. Projected revenue is obtained by multiplying the median number of customers at a given level of demand by the average check.

If we scheduled eight servers and five cooks, demand could be handled at all levels. At a high level of demand, revenue would be $2,040 (170 customers at an average of $12 each); with medium demand, revenue would be $1,620 (135 times $12); with low demand, revenue would be $1,200 (100 times $12).

If we scheduled six servers and four cooks, demand at low and medium levels could be handled. The appropriate revenue figures would still be $1,200 and $1,620, respectively. At a medium level of staffing, however, the maximum number of customers who could be handled without loss of service would be 150 (fig. 4–1). Customers beyond this number would be unwilling to wait for the time necessary to be seated and served. Thus, maximum revenue even during high demand would be $1,800 (150 times $12).

If we scheduled only four servers and three cooks, they could handle a maximum of only 120 customers. Staffing would be sufficient to handle low demand; the revenue generated would be $1,200. At medium or high demand, however, maximum revenue would be limited to the 120 customers who could be handled successfully with a low-demand staff (fig. 4–1). Maximum revenue for both medium and high demand would be limited to $1,440 (120 times $12).

Prepare the Decision Tree

A decision tree identifies the decisions to be made and their consequences. By incorporating measures of uncertainty, expected payoffs for each decision can be estimated in order to arrive at the best choice. A decision tree for this problem (which need not be vertical to be called a tree) is depicted in figure 4–2. Management must make a decision to staff at a high, medium, or low

FIGURE 4–2 DECISION TREE FOR RESTAURANT STAFFING.

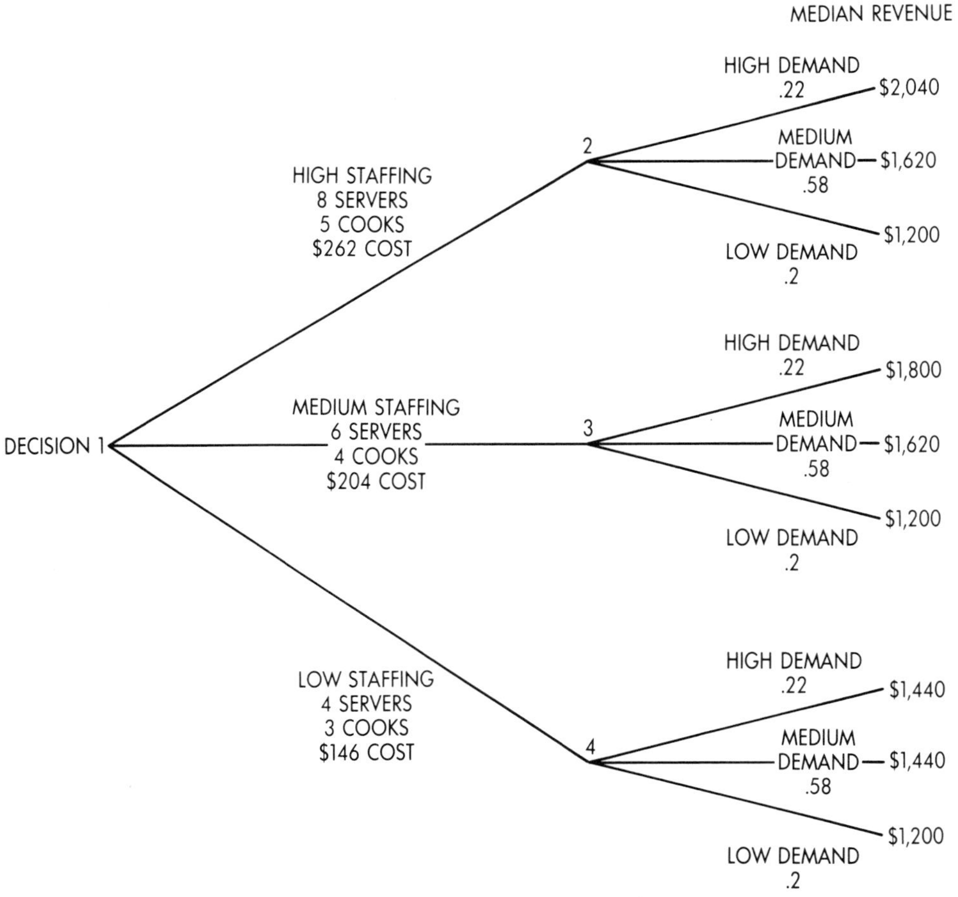

level. The employee cost of that decision is $262, $204, or $146, respectively. The tree branches off into a line for each level of staffing.

Customer demand may be high, medium, or low, so each staffing branch is divided further. The probabilities associated with those levels are listed, as is the expected revenue at each level of demand.

Evaluating the Consequences

The next step is to determine the yield or net revenue from each alternative, to arrive at the best choice.

The expected average revenue is found by multiplying the probability of each alternative by its yield and adding the totals. This is known as the *expected value (EV) method*. Referring to figure 4–2, the expected value, EV, at high staffing is $1,628.40. (EV = [.22 times 2,040] plus [.58 times 1,620] plus [.2 times 1,200].) Subtracting the cost of staffing, 262, the net yield is $1,366.40. At medium staffing, the EV is $1,611.60. (EV = [.22 times 1,800] plus [.58 times 1,620] plus [.2 times 1,200].) Subtracting the cost of staffing, 204, the net yield is $1,371.60. At low staffing, the EV is $1,392. (EV = [.22 times 1,440] plus [.58 times 1,440] plus [.2 times 1,200].) Subtracting the cost of staffing (146), the net yield is $1,246.

Choosing the Best Alternative

The net yields for high, medium, and low staffing are $1,366.40, $1,371.60, and $1,246, respectively. Given the assumptions that have been made, staffing at a medium level is preferred. When demand is not as expected, employee labor could be stored in ways identified previously.

Management may decide to staff at a lesser level, however, to generate occasional lines of waiting customers. This strategy may be important from a marketing perspective; a line of customers may generate a reputation for the restaurant as an action place. It should be noted, however, that if our assumptions hold true, over the long run high staffing will generate higher net yield.

The above discussion does indicate that the decision tree can only establish the net yields of the alternatives. The decision rests with management. That decision may be influenced by marketing or service considerations outside of net revenue.

Sensitivity Analysis

Sensitivity analysis refers to the process of recalculating the yields based on different assumptions. If wages increase or the probability of demand is reduced, the decision tree must be recalculated to arrive at updated net yields.

SCHEDULING WITH COMPUTERS[3]

Several computer systems presently exist that can effectively perform employee scheduling, using a personal computer and printer to interface with the company's software. Typically, three functions are performed: planning, control, and analysis.

Planning

The planning function can be performed at the personal computer directly or from work sheets prepared by the system. Planning includes forecasting and scheduling and is the first step in time management. Planning begins by forecasting the measures of performance for the business—sales, customers, or rooms occupied, for example. These measures are chosen because management wants to control labor in relation to them.

Next, managers must decide who works, what job they will perform, and when they will be scheduled. A software package can show managers the previous week's schedule and ask only for changes to be made. As managers schedule employees for various jobs, they are shown the results of their scheduling and the impact on the forecasted performance measures so they can achieve their targeted labor costs. Each employee can be scheduled individually to begin and end work at any time during the day and at any valid job. Employees can be scheduled for any number of different jobs and time periods during the day. This last feature accommodates split shifts, for example.

A report is then generated showing all the employees who have been scheduled inadvertently for overtime. A wide variety of overtime rules such as hourly limits, weekends, and holiday nights can be entered. The program checks the schedule against the rules to determine whether any of them apply. If so, management can modify the schedule to permit any desired amount of overtime—or none. When management is satisfied with the weekly schedules, they are printed for posting and saved for transmission to a unit where employees will "clock in."

Control

The old employee time clock—now called in some systems the employee terminal unit—controls the schedules, never allowing employees to deviate from them unless management approves the change. Because schedules may change without much warning, however, management has full control of any changes by making a simple input at the unit at any time. A single unit typically can handle up to five hundred employees.

Employees may arrive for work and check in at any time. If an employee checks in prior to his or her scheduled start time, the unit issues a receipt showing when that employee is scheduled to begin work. If the employee is asked to work earlier than scheduled, however, a supervisor can start the employee at that time by making a simple manual input at the unit.

If an employee checks in later than the scheduled start time, the unit starts the employee at the next quarter hour. Employees who are not scheduled to work but are called in at the last minute can also be scheduled on the spot by a supervisor at the unit.

At the time employees check in, they are requested to enter a job code, which designates their department and pay code. The unit then checks to see if they are reporting for the job scheduled by management and prevents them from checking in for an unscheduled job. Thus, the system can ensure that each employee is being paid at the correct rate and that the hours and costs are allocated to the proper areas.

When employees leave work they are automatically given a receipt by the unit, which shows them which job or jobs they performed, when they came in and went out, and how many hours they have accumulated so far, for each day during the present pay period.

The receipt also shows any changes the supervisor made on the time card. Thus, employees can audit their paycheck for each day of the pay period. When the pay period ends, the receipt on that day will agree with the payroll information.

If an employee attempts to check out later than scheduled by management, the system will inform the worker that supervisor approval is necessary. This control feature ensures that supervisors are alerted in real time that their scheduled labor costs are going to be higher than planned. At that time or later, the supervisor can take whatever action is appropriate for checking out the employee.

For businesses that require employees to keep track of tips or sales, the unit can be set to require employees to enter that information before receiving the departure receipt. This prevents the problem of having to track down employees who do not make the required reports. Reported tips or sales are automatically incorporated into the payroll preparation.

A buffer can be set into the system to allow employees to check out at any time up to twenty-four hours past their scheduled ending time without supervisor intervention. This allows management wide latitude in determining how long they can let employees go beyond their scheduled time before supervisors must be informed.

At any time during the day, supervisors can receive reports showing who is scheduled to be working, by department, and the labor costs accumulated by that department so far that day.

The old-time card system is eliminated; employee interaction with the system is through a telephone-like keyboard. Employees can access only their own daily schedule information through their employee number. Supervisors have access to all data and functions through a security code, which they can change at any time.

At the end of each day, the unit transmits the employee activity data it has collected back to the personal computer and receives in return the schedules in effect for the next two days.

Analysis

The analysis function begins when the personal computer has received the day's employee data. Reports are prepared showing how the actual labor hours and dollars for that day compare with those that were scheduled, and compares the labor costs with actual measures of the business entered in the personal computer. These analyses are prepared for every department and, if desired, for every employee. Thus, management can see every day how labor costs compare with the targets and measures chosen.

Managers can also be alerted to potential overtime situations before they occur. These reports show which employees are in danger of going into overtime if their schedules are not modified. Management can then take actions to prevent overtime.

TASK PLANNING

Task planning involves the analysis of specific actions involved in carrying out a job, in order to establish a more productive procedure for completing that job.

Select the Task

The first step in this process is to select the task to be analyzed. For the novice task planner, it is wise to select a simple task such as buttering bread or assembling salads. A complex task such as cleaning a room might be broken down initially into components such as making the bed and dusting the room. As the task planner develops more skill and confidence, more complex and time-consuming tasks can be identified and analyzed. It is preferable to select tasks that can cause bottlenecks in production or are frustrating for employees.

Determine the Factors Affecting the Task

A variety of factors affect each task to be analyzed. All factors must be identified and made part of the analysis.

Raw Materials

Tasks are affected by the accessibility and storage of raw materials used in performing the job. It is important that all materials be easily accessible to the work area. In one hotel studied, it was found that 20 percent of a room cleaner's time was spent in getting linen from the linen room. A major reason for this was that a linen shortage made adequate stocking impossible. The answer was to establish a system of stocking linen and other supplies in a closet on each floor. Because cleaners had adequate, accessible supplies, they were able to clean sixteen rooms instead of thirteen in a regular day. This resulted in a savings of 10 percent on the housekeeping payroll. A key principle is that the handling of materials does not add to their value. Such handling, therefore, should be kept to a minimum.

Process Used

The process used refers to the steps taken in completing the task. The proposed process should be identified early in the task analysis. For food preparation, this would involve identifying each item on the menu and its proposed preparation method. The process of cleaning a room might be: make the bed; clean up loose trash; empty ashtrays into a wastebasket; clean the bathroom, doing the floor last; clean the venetian blinds; dust surfaces and furniture; vacuum the floor; and rearrange the furniture.

Desired Finished Product

The standard of performance desired affects which tasks must be performed. A fine restaurant emphasizing its use of fresh ingredients will require different preparation methods for its menu items than a fast-food operation that relies heavily on convenience products. Each aims at producing a quality product—within the boundaries of the price-value relationship. That is, there must be a customer perception that the value received is more than or equal to the price paid.

Quantity to Be Produced

The method of preparation and even the process can be affected by the quantity to be produced. For large-quantity jobs, the capital investment for a piece of equipment may be less in the long run than the labor cost of several employees.

Hamburger patties may be prepared in different ways, depending upon the quantity to be produced. Large numbers can be prepared by portioning the ground meat on a baking tray on top and pushing gently to flatten the patties. The second tray is then ready for filling. Another large-quantity method is to spread the meat evenly in a rectangular baking pan, cover with waxed paper, flatten with a rolling pin, and cut into squares before cooking. Small quantities can be shaped by hand.

Work Area

Work stations should be sufficiently large to allow for the tools and utensils necessary to complete the required tasks. Tasks that require the use of the same tools or utensils should be performed at the same place, whenever possible.

Available Equipment

It is necesary to take into account the equipment necessary and available for completing a task. Financial constraints may limit the purchase of more productive or energy-efficient equipment. In other cases, little cost is involved; the use of two French knives, for example, will double the cutting action in dicing onions. In the kitchen, difficulty in performing certain tasks often can be traced to blunt knives.

Employees

The number and type of employees used greatly affects the cost of performing a task. Maximum efficiency results from having the least number of employees necessary. It may not, however, result in minimum cost. In one operation management was extremely cost conscious, keeping staff to a minimum. But an examination of the kitchen payroll showed excessive overtime. An analysis of the operation revealed that existing employees could not complete the required work in normal working hours. The pressure was reduced by hiring two additional employees. The result was that most of the overtime payments were eliminated and overall payroll costs were reduced.

Another factor that must be considered is the quality of the service provided. Sufficient employees must be scheduled to ensure customer satisfaction. The saving of an employee's hourly wage must be weighed against any loss of business through guest dissatisfaction.

The skill level of the employee must also be considered. The key is to delegate tasks as far down the line as possible commensurate with the employee's ability to perform the delegated task. In other words, have a five-dollar-an-hour task performed by a five-dollar-an-hour employee.

Location

Proper location of each work center within the facility helps increase the productivity of each task. Easy flow of materials is important. One tool to aid this process is a flow diagram, which shows the flow of materials between the various functions for a particular operation. A typical flow diagram for a food-service facility is illustrated in figure 4–3. A study of this kind helps determine the most effective placement of one work station relative to the others. Within each department, similar flows can be identified to aid equipment placement.

Timing

Timing refers to both how long it takes to perform a task and when it has to be done relative to the completion of other tasks. With certain menu items, for example, several tasks may have to be completed at the same time. This probably means more than one employee would have to be involved. Alternatively, some tasks might be completed ahead of service and the products combined by one employee at the last minute.

ESTABLISH PROCEDURES

The answer to several questions will help determine the proper procedures to use in performing each task.

Can It Be Eliminated?

If this task or step in the process is eliminated, will the end product or service suffer? Can the purchase of a potato-peeling machine eliminate peeling by

FIGURE 4–3 FLOW DIAGRAM FOR A FOODSERVICE
FACILITY.

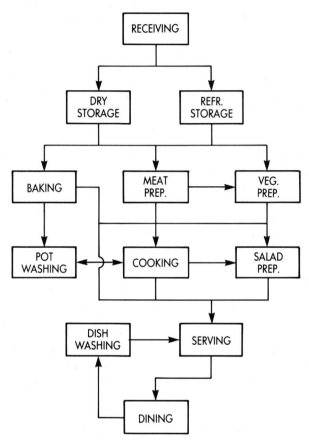

(*Source:* Edward A. Kazarian, *Food Service Facilities Planning,* New York, Van Nostrand Reinhold, 1975, 74.)

hand? If beds are not turned down at night, will guest satisfaction be diminished? Can carpets be cleaned once every nine months instead of twice a year?

The pantry in one restaurant was staffed on the basis of service for three meals a day. When the morning meal was eliminated, staffing remained the same. An analysis of service requirements resulted in fewer employee hours scheduled.

Can It Be Combined?

Can one employee perform several different jobs? Perhaps general maintenance could be performed by bellhops during slack times of the day. Can employees work with both hands at the same time to improve results?

Are There Unnecessary Delays?

Are insufficient supplies causing service slowdowns? Holiday Inns found that wheeling a small cart into the guest room saved money when cleaning the room. The materials needed were easily accessible, limiting much walking. In addition, the room attendant felt more comfortable with the door closed. Energy costs were reduced because heat or air-conditioning did not escape from the room as before, when carts were left outside the open door.

Is There Misdirected Effort?

Can a conveyor belt be used to move food and dishes? Can wheels be put on equipment to roll rather than carry it?

Are Skills Used Properly?

Do we have the right match of employee skill level and task difficulty? Does the employee know the best way to perform the job?

In one hotel, a new regulation requiring that a fire watch be maintained at all public functions caught a supervisor off-guard while a function was taking place. To fill the need, the hotel used a plumber who had not yet gone home. The plumber, working at time and a half, cost much more than was necessary for the job involved.

Are Employees Doing Too Many Unrelated Tasks?

Is the trainee manager being used as a fill-in employee? By asking employees to do too many things, do they end up doing nothing really well?

Is Work Spread Evenly?

At one hotel, five hundred room service breakfasts were served between 7:00 and 11:00 A.M. In the dining room, service was busiest between 8:30 and 9:00 A.M. The entire dishwashing crew was on duty at 7:00 A.M., although most of the soiled dishes from room service did not reach the dishwashing station until 10:00 A.M. After a study of the situation, it was decided to bring employees in at 9:00 A.M. instead of 7:00 A.M.

In figure 4–4, the stages involved in preparing macaroni are laid out. The cook begins at the worktable where the work sheet and recipes are kept. From there the process is:

- Ten steps to the pot and pan rack to get the pan
- Thirty steps to the sink to add the water
- Fifteen steps to the range carrying the pan and the water
- Fifty steps to the storeroom while the water is heating, to get the macaroni
- Fifty steps back to the range
- Ten steps to the drawer in the salad table for a spoon

FIGURE 4–4 STAGES INVOLVED IN PREPARING MACARONI.

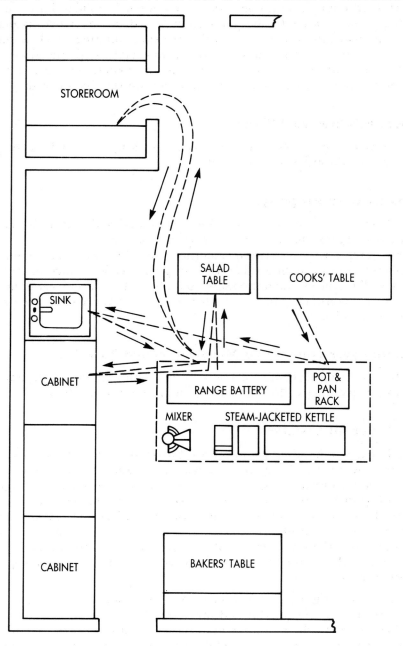

STOREROOM

SALAD TABLE

COOKS' TABLE

SINK

CABINET

RANGE BATTERY

POT & PAN RACK

MIXER   STEAM-JACKETED KETTLE

CABINET

BAKERS' TABLE

(*Source:* Lynne Nannen Ross, *Work Simplification in Food Service,* Ames, Iowa, The Iowa State University Press, 1986, 7.)

- Ten steps back to the range
- Fifteen steps to the cabinet for salt
- Fifteen steps back to the range
- Fifteen steps to the sink for a little more water
- Fifteen steps back to the range

This process required the cook to walk a total of 235 steps. In figure 4–5, a simplified process is suggested for this task. Beginning at the worktable, the cook walks 10 steps to the steam-jacketed kettle, turns on the hot-water faucet located above it, fills the kettle, and turns on the heat; walks 20 steps to the cabinet to get the macaroni and salt; walks back to the kettle; and adds the macaroni and salt, stirring them with a spoon that is stored on a rack over the kettle. The entire process requires that the cook walk only 50 steps.

PRINCIPLES OF MOTION ECONOMY

Various time and motion studies have resulted in the development of principles to minimize unproductive body movements.[4]

Make Rhythmic, Smooth Motions

An overlapping figure-eight stroke or a circular motion requires less energy than short back-and-forth strokes. This principle can be applied to such tasks as spreading sandwiches, stirring various items, or cutting with a knife.

Make Both Hands Productive

Both hands should be performing similar tasks at exactly the same time. When the hands move symmetrically, there is less body strain. The steps involved in using both hands to make grilled cheese sandwiches are outlined in figure 4–6. The tray is buttered by ladling melted butter down the center of a pan. Picking up four slices of bread in each hand, the employee simultaneously places the bottom slices in the middle of the tray, then draws them to the sides. This allows the first two slices to be covered with butter while leaving enough butter for the next two slices (each numbered 2 in the figure). The remaining slices are placed in the pan in the order shown, the employee working with both hands at the same time, moving aside already buttered slices to make room for the next slices.

The next step involves placing slices of cheese on the bread. Two slices of cheese are picked up in each hand and both are placed on the number 12 slices of bread. Then, again with each hand, the top slice of cheese is lifted from each number 12 and placed on number 11. This procedure is repeated for slices 10 and 9, 8 and 7, 6 and 5, 4 and 3, and 2 and 1.

A top slice of buttered bread is now placed on the cheese. Melted butter is

FIGURE 4–5 STAGES INVOLVED IN PREPARING MACARONI—SIMPLIFIED.

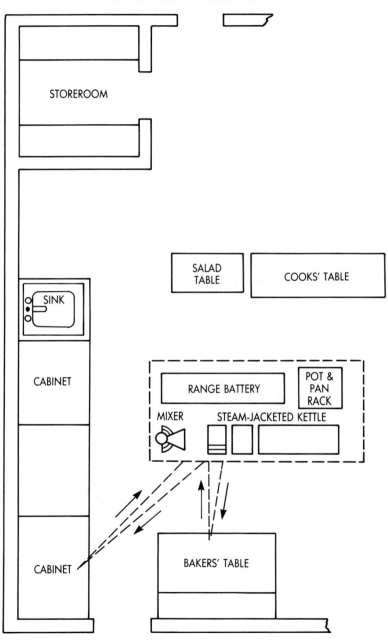

(*Source:* Lynne Nannen Ross, *Work Simplification in Food Service,* Ames, Iowa, The Iowa State University Press, 1986, 10.)

ladled into another pan. One piece of bread is picked up in each hand, patted in the butter, and placed on the cheese in the first pan. The procedure is repeated until all slices are covered. The pan of sandwiches can then be covered with waxed paper and refrigerated until it is time for toasting.

Keep Motions Short, Simple

Each motion should use the least possible time and energy. If a task can be done with a hand motion, it is a waste of energy to move the entire arm. In the cutting of biscuits, for example, they are worked on a floured breadboard, rolled out with a rolling pin, cut with a biscuit cutter, and transferred to a baking sheet. The leftover dough is then rerolled and recut.

It is more efficient, however, to roll the dough directly onto a bun pan. The dough is rolled into a rectangular shape, leaving a one-inch margin around the edges of the pan. Biscuits are then shaped into squares or diamonds using a knife or spatula, separating the biscuits as they are cut to ensure even browning. Less time and fewer motions are required. There is no need to reroll the dough and transfer it to the baking sheet.

FIGURE 4–6   STEPS INVOLVED IN MAKING GRILLED CHEESE SANDWICHES.

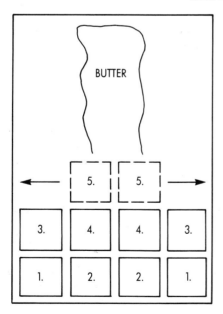 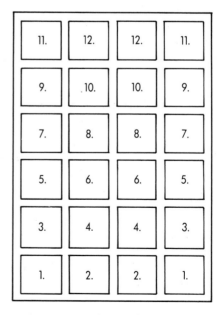

(*Source:* Lynne Nannen Ross, *Work Simplification in Food Service,* Ames, Iowa, The Iowa State University Press, 1986, 30.)

Maintain Comfortable Positions, Conditions

The proper height for mixing or beating can be found by standing erect in front of a table with the arms straight and pressing the hands flat on the table. A task such as stirring is very tiring if the forearm is higher than the elbow.

The height of the work surface should let an employee either sit or stand when working. This helps ease monotony as well as physical tiredness.

Similar consideration should be given to providing correct lighting, ventilation, temperature, and humidity while minimizing noise.

Locate Materials for Efficient Motions

There should be a definite and fixed place for all tools and materials, as close as possible to the point of use. Wherever possible, the force of gravity should be utilized to deliver both incoming and outgoing materials. Equipment that is designed for easy grasp will help employees work longer.

Use the Best Available Equipment

Purchasing equipment on wheels will offer dramatic savings in the time and effort to get things done. A simple cart can be used to make one trip from the storeroom with the entire day's supplies rather than requiring many trips during the day.

Yet another example, and one that is overlooked, involves the selection of spoons. The purchase of spoons with insulated handles reduces the chances of being burned by a hot handle during cooking.

Rely on Normal Work Areas

The normal horizontal work area is the space within which work can be done with the least energy. It can be found by making an arc over the work surface by holding the elbow close to the side and swinging the arm out from the elbow. The total normal work area includes the space covered by the combined arcs of both forearms.

The maximum horizontal work area is the space within which an average amount of energy is expended. This area can be found by making arcs over the work surface by extending the full arm outward and swinging it from the shoulder.

The normal vertical work space can be found by making an arc by swinging the lower arm in a circle from the elbow. The maximum vertical work area can be determined by extending the arm and drawing an arc in a relaxed manner. Work is less tiring if the elbow is not raised above shoulder level. The more work that can be done in the normal work areas, the less tiring it will be on the employee.

SET UP THE WORK AREA

Applying the principles of motion economy, management can set up the work area. Preferably, this will be done with employees' assistance. By involving the employees who actually perform the tasks, management will reduce resistance to any proposed changes. Furthermore, it is vital that tasks are designed with the right employee in mind. The work area for a six-foot-three employee would be different from that of a five-foot-six employee.

Evaluate the Procedure

After a shakedown period, it is necessary to evaluate the new procedure. At this stage it is important to ensure that employees are performing the job in the new fashion. Now the employee can be involved in helping decide whether any part of the process can be eliminated, combined, or simplified.

Establish Performance Standards

Once the revised procedure has been agreed to, it is important to determine new performance standards for the task. Employees must be told what is expected of them. If standards are not met, both the job and the employee should be examined to determine what is wrong. It may be that the standard is too high or the employee is not performing up to par.

SUPERVISE AND COACH

When either a new employee is hired to perform a task or an existing employee is trained to carry out a job a new way, it is necessary to supervise closely until the procedure becomes a habit. Supervision then can be replaced by periodic coaching, stressing the positive as well as negative aspects of performance.

While the steps outlined above have concentrated on increased productivity through standardized movements, there is a danger involved. For some employees, standardized movements may be equated with boredom. An employee may change the routine of doing a job to prevent boredom. The increase in productivity resulting from minimized movements may be offset by a loss in productivity resulting from less motivated employees. The key is to ensure that there is an excellent job match between the skills and abilities required for the task and those present in the employee.

SUMMARY

Significant cost savings can occur through improved employee scheduling and task planning. Employee schedules are established by developing productivity standards, forecasting sales, and applying a staffing guide in order to maximize employee productivity.

Employees can be scheduled for split shifts or irregular hours, and part-time people can be used to cut costs. Another option is to store employee labor— or, at least, the output of that labor. A cost-benefit analysis also can be performed in order to determine the best staffing level for the operation.

Analyzing a particular task identifies the factors affecting it and can lead to new procedures that will simplify the work. Procedures also can be identified that will minimize the movements necessary to perform the job.

Once new procedures have been established, the work area can be set up anew, the operation evaluated, and new performance standards determined, with the procedures supervised until doing them becomes a habit.

NOTES

[1]Kreck, Lothar A., *Operational Problem Solving for the Hotel and Restaurant Industry*, Boston, C.B.I. Publishing Company, 1978, 28.

[2]Grinnell, Douglas, and William Remus, "Using Decision Trees to Solve Restaurant Staffing Problems," *The Journal of Hospitality Education* 7, no. 2, Winter 1983, 51–62.

[3]This section describes the TimeManager system of the TimeManagement Corporation, Minneapolis. This system is representative of the way computers can be utilized in the scheduling of employees.

[4]Ross, Lynne Nannen, *Work Simplification in Food Service*, Ames, Iowa, Iowa State University Press, 1986.

SUGGESTED READINGS

Bill, Brian, and Mark Heymann, "Productivity: A Case for Quality-Based Profit Improvement," *Lodging Hospitality*, September 1983, 48–52.

Burley, Kenneth R., "Set Labor Performance Targets as Effective Management Tools," *Foodservice Marketing*, October 1981, 24, 25.

Collins, Patrick J., "Staffing the Housekeeping Department," *Executive Housekeeper*, July 1978, 24, 28, 29.

———, "Staffing the Housekeeping Department: Phase II," *Executive Housekeeper*, August 1978, 23, 24.

Emerzian, A. D. Joseph, and John R. Coleman, "Systemizing Project Work: The Future Is Now, Part 1," *Executive Housekeeper*, January 1977, 24, 26, 56–58.

———, "Systemizing Project Work, Part II," *Executive Housekeeper*, February 1977, 30, 32, 38, 40, 42.

Grinnell, Douglas, and William Remus, "Using Decision Trees to Solve Restaurant Staffing Problems," *The Journal of Hospitality Education* 7, no. 2, Winter 1983, 51–62.

King, Carol A., "Controlling Dining Room Labor Cost," *Consultant* 15, no. 1, January 1982, 35–42.

Kreck, Lothar A., *Operational Problem Solving for the Hotel and Restaurant Industry*, Boston, C.B.I. Publishing Company, 1978, 27–34.

Lundberg, Donald E., and James P. Armatas, *The Management of People in Hotels, Restaurants and Clubs*, Dubuque, Iowa, Wm. C. Brown Publishers, 1980, 262–95.

Mandigo, Theodore, "How to Precontrol Your Payroll Costs," *Foodservice Marketing*, April 1982, 29–32.

Miller, John C., "Scheduling Staff Profitably," *Hospitality*, September 1983, 29–31.

Osenton, James R., "The Stored Labor Concept," *Increasing Productivity in Foodservice*, Jule Wilkinson (ed.), Chicago, *Institutions/Volume Feeding Magazine*, 1973. 135–46.

Ross, Lynne Nannen, *Work Simplification in Food Service*, Ames, Iowa, Iowa State University Press, 1986.

Skroder, Pen, "Optimization of Labor Productivity Through Labor Cost Analysis," *Journal of Foodservice Systems* 1, 1981, 127–204.

APPENDIX: IMPLEMENTING EMPLOYEE SCHEDULING—A RESTAURANT EXAMPLE

The subject of this study is a moderately priced 175-seat restaurant in a downtown area. It is open from 6:30 A.M. to 1 A.M., Monday through Saturday. The normal staffing is as follows:

- Early shift, 6:00 A.M. to 2:00 P.M.: twelve servers
- Middle shift, 2:00 P.M. to 10:00 P.M.: six servers
- Late shift, 5:00 P.M. to 1:00 A.M.: four servers

Everyone gets a one-hour meal break and works a seven-hour day. The schedule requires a total of 154 server-hours a day.

During a typical six-day week, the restaurant serves 10,040 covers, with an overall server productivity of 10.9 per server-hour. When Saturday activity is excluded, productivity is slightly higher: on average, 1,705 weekday covers are served, or 11.1 covers per server-hour (table 4–3). These figures indicate that Saturday productivity is lower than average and is pulling down overall server productivity. The largest volume of business is done during the week, however, and affords a greater potential for savings. In table 4–3 the Monday through Friday activity is broken down by meal period. Afternoon productivity is higher than the overall average, but on a very low volume of business.

SETTING PEAK STANDARDS

The manager plotted the flow of business by hour. This showed where the business peaked. Staffing was also charted (fig. 4–7) and hour-by-hour productivity calculated (table 4–4). This showed what was being achieved at peak hours and where the slack in the schedule was. The higher the covers per server-hour, the better the productivity.

Next, staffing standards were developed by determining the coverage needed to service the peak periods. There were at most eleven stations in the 175-seat dining room. The manager estimated that at lunchtime people sat down, ate, and left in thirty minutes or less during the noon to 1:00 P.M. period. Because parties of three are seated at tables for four and single guests are seated at tables for two, it is unlikely that all servers would have all seats occupied at one time. It was assumed, therefore, that only 75 percent of the chairs are occupied even when the restaurant is at full capacity. Thus, the most a server could

From "Controlling Dining Room Labor Cost," Carol A. King, *Consultant* 15, no. 1, January 1982, 35–42.

		Average covers	Server hours scheduled	Covers per hour
TABLE 4–3:	SERVER PRODUCTIVITY BY MEAL PERIOD (WEEKDAYS ONLY)			
Breakfast	6–11 A.M.	520	48	10.8
Lunch	11–2 P.M.	450	36	12.5
Afternoon	2–5 P.M.	175	12	14.6
Dinner	5–10 P.M.	435	46	9.5
Late supper	10–1 A.M.	125	12	10.4
Total/average		1,705	154	11.1

attain at a 16-seat station during the hour would be two seatings of 12 people, or 24 covers. This figure assumes that there is a waiting line and that whenever a table is vacated, another party is waiting to sit down. It also assumes that people are able to be served as quickly as they wish, with no slowdowns or delays in service.

With 24 covers per station or server per hour, the manager estimated that a maximum of 262 people could be served at the twelve stations in the peak lunch hour. In other words, for every 24 covers served in that hour, one more server would be required. But the analysis of the week studied shows that only 8 servers were needed instead of 12 because an average of 200 people, not 288, were served from noon to 1 P.M. (table 4–4).

ADJUSTING THE PEAK STANDARDS

But there is a catch. With only 8 servers either four stations would have to be closed down, 22-seat stations would be assigned to servers (175 seats divided by 8 servers), or a combination of the two. What happens if the 200 customers do not arrive at even intervals and the dining room does not turn over according to plan? What would happen if three-quarters of them arrive at the beginning of the hour? If the restaurant is operating with reduced seating, 50 people would be forced to stand in line for a half hour, upsetting many guests on short lunch breaks. An alternative would be to fill those big 22-seat stations, taking the risk that some of the servers will get stuck and give slow service. In fact, between 8 and 12 servers are needed for this situation. The manager decided to try 10.

The manager then examined the breakfast service. Here a 60 percent utilization of seats was assumed (the number of actual customers divided by the number of seats available), because there are more single people and parties of two at breakfast than at lunch. A maximum of 2.5 sittings per hour was estimated. This resulted in a 175-seat maximum of approximately 260 people during the

FIGURE 4-7 STAFFING CHART—ORIGINAL AND REVISED.

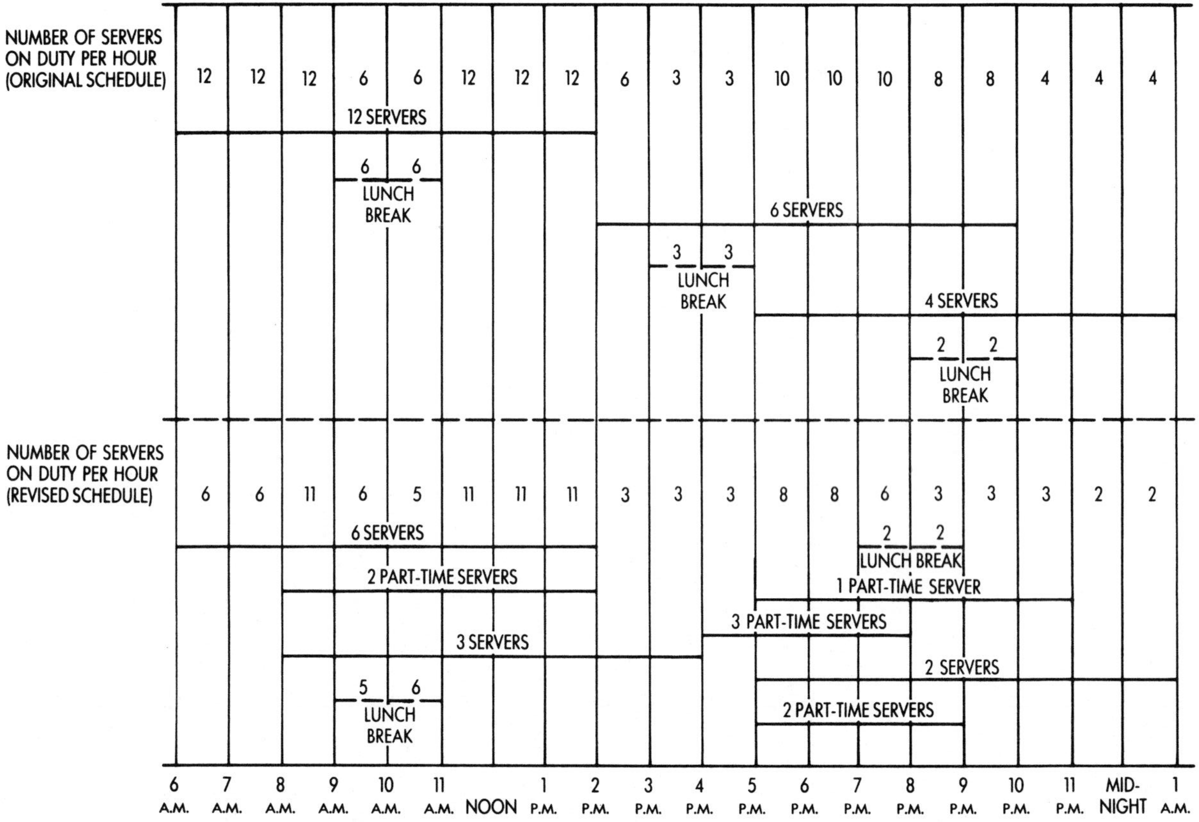

	6 A.M.	7 A.M.	8 A.M.	9 A.M.	10 A.M.	11 A.M.	NOON	1 P.M.	2 P.M.	3 P.M.	4 P.M.	5 P.M.	6 P.M.	7 P.M.	8 P.M.	9 P.M.	10 P.M.	11 P.M.	MID-NIGHT	1 A.M.
NUMBER OF SERVERS ON DUTY PER HOUR (ORIGINAL SCHEDULE)	12	12	12	12	6	6	12	12	12	6	3	3	10	10	10	8	8	4	4	4

Original schedule: 12 SERVERS (6 / LUNCH BREAK / 6); 6 SERVERS (3 / LUNCH BREAK / 3); 4 SERVERS (2 / LUNCH BREAK / 2)

	6 A.M.	7 A.M.	8 A.M.	9 A.M.	10 A.M.	11 A.M.	NOON	1 P.M.	2 P.M.	3 P.M.	4 P.M.	5 P.M.	6 P.M.	7 P.M.	8 P.M.	9 P.M.	10 P.M.	11 P.M.	MID-NIGHT	1 A.M.
NUMBER OF SERVERS ON DUTY PER HOUR (REVISED SCHEDULE)	6	6	6	11	6	5	11	11	11	3	3	3	8	8	8	6	3	3	2	2

Revised schedule: 6 SERVERS (5 / LUNCH BREAK / 6); 2 PART-TIME SERVERS; 3 SERVERS; 3 PART-TIME SERVERS; 2 PART-TIME SERVERS; 1 PART-TIME SERVER (2 / LUNCH BREAK / 2); 2 SERVERS

(*Source:* Carol A. King, "Controlling Dining Room Labor Cost," *Consultant* 15, no. 1, January 1982, 37.)

peak hour—very close to the actual average of 250 from 8:00 to 9:00 A.M. during the week (table 4–4). With lower seat utilization, however, the manager felt the servers could handle larger stations than they could at lunch. It was decided to try working breakfast with 11 servers instead of 12. This would give each server up to about 24 customers (the 260 maximum divided by 11 servers). Using the same method, it was determined that dinner service required only 8 servers.

Finally, there are periods when a minimum staff is required regardless of the volume of business. For late supper, the manager wanted a minimum of 2 servers on duty until closing. Since this business was somewhat unpredictable, 3 servers were assigned until 11:00 P.M. By 11:00 P.M. they could usually tell what the rest of the evening's business would be like. If it looked like a rush, the third person could stay on another hour.

Now the manager had peak-hour requirements for breakfast, lunch, and dinner. Unfortunately, we cannot schedule workers only for the hours we

TABLE 4–4: PRODUCTIVITY BY HOUR (WEEKDAYS)

Time period	Covers	Staffing (original)	Productivity (covers per server-hour)
6–7 A.M.	40	12	6.6*
7–8	90	12	7.5
9–9	250	12	20.8
8–10	80	6	13.3
10–11	60	6	10.0
11–12	100	12	8.3
12–1 P.M.	200	12	16.7
1–2	150	12	12.5
2–3	75	6	12.5
3–4	40	3	13.3
4–5	60	3	20.0
5–6	175	10	17.5
6–7	100	10	10.0
7–8	80	10	8.0
8–9	60	8	7.5
9–10	20	8	2.5
10–11	60	4	15.0
11–12	40	4	10.0
12–1 A.M.	25	4	6.25
Total/average	1,705	154	11.1

* For first half hour of service (after set-up time)

need them; we must give them enough work to make it worth their while to come in. In fact, most union contracts require that a worker be paid for a minimum number of hours (usually four, if the employee reports to work as scheduled). Therefore, the staffing required at peak periods at least partially determines the staffing of off-peak periods. We can utilize off-peak times for meal breaks and side work and can employ part-time employees to work only breakfast, because tips are lower than at other meals. Most servers want to work lunch as well, to make their tips. Therefore, the manager had to revise the figures for lunch and schedule 11 servers in order to have 11 for breakfast coverage. The revised schedule was charted and the productivity for each hour was recalculated. In the periods when productivity was low, shifts were staggered and part-time help substituted until each time slot was brought to an acceptable level. The revised figures are shown in tables 4–5 and 4–6 and the lower part of figure 4–7. The manager also was able to cut the opening crew from 12 to 6 by putting things on wheels to reduce set-up time.

THE RESULTS

The revised schedule required only 111 server-hours, compared to 154 required by the original schedule, about a 28 percent reduction, resulting in an increase in productivity from 11.1 covers per server-hour to 15.4. The largest increase was in late supper productivity, which rose from 10.4 to 17.8. This figure is a bit misleading, however, because contingency coverage was available if needed. The old schedule had been planned to cover higher levels of business even though they may not materialize. The new schedule provides greater flexibility. The gains in other periods were more concrete. Dinner productivity increased from 9.5 to 15.5, a gain of 6 covers per server-hour. Breakfast showed a gain of 4.5. These productivity rates represent reasonable attainable standards for the restaurant.

TABLE 4–5: SERVER PRODUCTIVITY WITH REVISED SCHEDULE (WEEKDAYS ONLY)

		Average covers	Server hours scheduled	Covers per hour
Breakfast	6–11 A.M.	520	34	15.3
Lunch	11–2 P.M.	450	33	13.6
Afternoon	2–5 P.M.	175	9	19.4
Dinner	5–10 P.M.	435	28	15.5
Late supper	10–1 A.M.	125	7	17.8
Total/average		1,705	111	15.4

TABLE 4–6: PRODUCTIVITY BY HOUR, REVISED SCHEDULE

Time period	Covers	Staffing (original)	Productivity (covers per server-hour)	Staffing (revised)	Productivity (revised)
6–7 A.M.	40	12	6.6*	6	13.3*
7–8	90	12	7.5	6	15.0
8–9	250	12	20.8	11	22.7
9–10	80	6	13.3	6	13.3
10–11	60	6	10.0	5	12.0
11–12	100	12	8.3	11	9.1
12–1 P.M.	200	12	16.7	11	18.2
1–2	150	12	12.5	11	13.6
2–3	75	6	12.5	3	25.0
3–4	40	3	13.3	3	13.3
4–5	60	3	20.0	3	20.0
5–6	175	10	17.5	8	21.9
6–7	100	10	10.0	8	12.5
7–8	80	10	8.0	6	13.3
8–9	60	8	7.5	3	20.0
9–10	20	8	2.5	3	6.7
10–11	60	4	15.0	3	20.0
11–12	40	4	10.0	2	20.0
12–1 A.M.	25	4	6.25	2	12.5
Total/ average	1,705	154	11.1	111	15.4

* For first half hour of service (after set-up time)

TABLE 4–7: COVER COUNTS BY DAY OF WEEK

		Mon.	Tue.	Wed.	Thu.	Fri.	Sat.
Breakfast	6:30–11 A.M.	545	532	545	528	450	226
Lunch	11–2 P.M.	436	427	445	463	479	483
Afternoon	2–5 P.M.	140	164	186	194	191	243
Dinner	5–10 P.M.	417	429	445	437	447	324
Late supper	10–1 A.M.	80	100	125	150	170	221
Total		1,618	1,652	1,746	1,772	1,737	1,515

We can take this analysis one step further. These productivity rates were established on the basis of averages. Averages are combinations of low values and high values. The covers served by day of the week are shown in table 4–7. Generally the figures are quite consistent. However, several are out of line. Friday breakfast is quite a bit lower than the rest of the weekdays. If this is a regular occurrence, our standard reflects lower productivity for that meal period. On Monday, business also seems to slacken after lunch. For late supper there is a wide range between the lowest day and the highest. Saturday, which we have not considered so far, shows a very different pattern of business. Separate standards could be set up for Saturday, using the same methodology the manager applied in developing weekday schedules and standards.

5 | DEVELOPING A PRODUCTIVE COMPANY CULTURE

When a company is small, the owner can impose his or her beliefs and standards about how things should be run, by being involved in all phases of the operation for all or most of the hours the hotel or restaurant is open. When the organization grows to the point where personal supervision by the owner over all phases at all times is impossible, employees need something to guide their actions—something beyond policies and procedures. That something is a company culture.

DEFINING COMPANY CULTURE

Culture can be defined in different ways. Some view it in terms of things that are directly observable about the members of a company—their patterns of speech and behavior, for example. Others see it as something an organization has—a system of shared ideas, knowledge, and beliefs. To some culture is a system of shared meanings, something an organization is.

Howard Schwartz and Stanley M. Davis define culture as "a pattern of beliefs and expectations shared by the organization's members. These beliefs and expectations produce norms that powerfully shape the behavior of individuals and groups in the organization."[1] These common beliefs are something an organization has, represent what the organization is, and are directly observable as they manifest themselves in the way people act and talk. In short, culture is "the way we do things around here."[2]

Culture is a definition of what the company is all about. Climate, the subject of the next chapter, is a measure of the employees' perceptions about what the company is all about. Measuring climate tells us how well employees are receiving the message of what the culture is. It measures the fit between the prevailing culture and the employees' values. If employees accept the culture of the organization, the climate will be good. If they do not, the climate will be bad. Culture is a long-term matter and more difficult to change than climate.

Development of Culture

A study of how a company culture develops illustrates why it is so difficult to change. It is explained by Schwartz and Davis in this way:

85

Culture is rooted in deeply held beliefs and values in which individuals hold a substantial investment as a result of some processing or analysis of data about organizational life. These beliefs and values create situational norms that are evidenced in observable behavior. This behavior becomes the basis for the formation of beliefs and values out of which norms flow.[3]

This process is illustrated in figure 5–1.

Characteristics

Successful companies place a great deal of emphasis on values. They have a clear idea of how their business should be run; they give time and attention to shaping these values, in light of the economic and business environment faced by the organization, and communicating these values to the employees; these values are known and shared by all who work for that company—from general manager to dishwasher.

An effective value system has certain characteristics:

Values should be both loose and tight. That is to say, management must set a clear direction while allowing opportunity for individual initiative in moving toward that direction.

It must emerge rather than be imposed. It should be the end product of long-term processes, not an ultimatum.

It cannot be changed at will. Consistency should be stressed and any changes dealt with very carefully. Because change requires so much commitment and energy, management should view change as a process that will occur infrequently.

It has a reasonably predictable life cycle. It can never be defined as tightly as a quantifiable goal. It does, however, emerge from being rather flexible, progressively becoming more rigid over time.

FIGURE 5–1 A MODEL OF CORPORATE CULTURE.

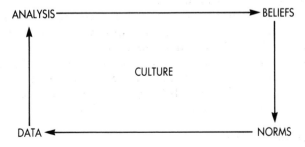

(*Source:* Howard Schwartz and Stanley M. Davis, "Matching Corporate Culture and Business Strategy," *Organizational Dynamics,* Summer 1981, 34.)

It imposes choices. An emphasis on control will limit creativity.

It can range from general management principles to reasonably specific business decisions.

It suggests movement from where one is to where one wishes to go.

TRADITIONAL SHARED BELIEFS

According to Thomas J. Peters and Robert H. Waterman Jr., the traditional culture has included several beliefs they consider inappropriate to success in today's business environment.[4]

First has been emphasis on the idea that bigger is better. As a company grows, economies of scale result. The key is to grow, carefully coordinating growth along the way.

The second aspect is an emphasis on cost control. To oversimplify, profits come from sales minus costs. Profits can be increased by increasing sales or cutting costs. This orientation stresses cost cutting as a means of being successful.

The traditional culture stresses lengthy analysis before any action. Whether in marketing or budgeting, planning and numbers are given top priority.

Entrepreneurs are not encouraged. After all, the company has spent a great deal of time and effort to develop the "perfect" system. Company officials do not want people to suggest changes to the system. All they want is someone to follow the methods that have been developed.

Another aspect is the belief that a manager's job is to make decisions. Making the right decisions is regarded as more important than and separate from their implementation.

It is also important for the traditional manager to exert control over everything. An emphasis is placed on lengthy job descriptions, detailed organizational structure, and complicated procedure manuals. People are treated solely as a factor of production.

The key to improving productivity, the traditionalists say, is to provide the correct monetary incentives. Top performers are rewarded and poor ones fired.

Quality can be controlled through inspection. Simply increasing the size of the quality control department can eliminate problems.

Traditionalists believe that all businesses are essentially the same and can be run using the same methodologies. As long as a manager can read the financial statement, he or she can control the business and make a success of it.

Traditionalists also believe they know more than the market. As long as quarterly earnings keep growing, the income statement and balance sheet can be massaged to make the manager look good, irrespective of what the marketplace tells us.

Last is the emphasis on growth. If domestic growth slows, expand into international markets or other industries—even if we do not understand the business being expanded into. (After all, the traditionalists say, all businesses are the same.)

PROBLEMS

Several problems exist in this traditional culture that make it inappropriate in today's environment. A cost-reduction philosophy, for example, leads to obsessions with cost over quality and value. Cutting costs may lead to short-term profitability, but the reduction in value to the customer will result in lost business.

In terms of motivating employees, more of them can relate to the need to increase value and quality than to cutting costs. This is because as customers themselves, they know what they demand in quality. As employees, there is little incentive to cut costs unless they are partial recipients in the resulting gains. This is not usually the case.

An emphasis on costs tends to produce conservative solutions to problems. In history it usually has been the risk taker, the person with a creative solution to a problem, who has produced a profit while satisfying the customers.

The rational approach to management can result too often in a style that is overly critical. It is easier to find economic reasons not to do something than to find such reasons as customer satisfaction to proceed. The resulting paralysis through analysis leads to a lack of new ideas. The company relies on formal systems rather than on internal values to move it forward. The result is often stagnation rather than movement.

SHARED BELIEFS FOR THE FUTURE

In researching companies that have consistently performed well from a bottom-line perspective, Peters and Waterman identified several themes they consider crucial to developing a culture that will move a company forward. The service companies they felt exemplified success are Delta Airlines, Marriott, McDonald's, American Airlines, and Disney Productions.

Bias for Action

Successful companies, it was found, are characterized first by organizational fluidity. Communications are informal. This goes beyond an open-door policy to mean that management is visible by walking or wandering around. Hotel managers of quality, according to the American Hotel and Motel Association, walk around their properties at least once a day.

This is carried over to design. Some companies have installed escalators rather than elevators in order to encourage more face-to-face contact.

Peer review is found to be a very powerful motivator. Employees have been found to respond to an informal peer review over the more formal paper-laden procedure laid down by management. The key is to provide positive reinforcement for any action that benefits the company.

An important factor is the amount of experimentation. McDonald's is constantly trying different menu items, restaurant formats, and pricing options. Holiday

Inns has numerous test sites where new operational wrinkles are tried out. It seems the key is to start out small, focusing on tangible results, and build on success. If room occupancy is down, identify one time period that is important and develop a campaign to improve the situation.

The analogy of learning to play golf can be used. We traditionally teach people to play golf by lining them up on the tee, pointing to the hole somewhere in the distance, and letting people swing. The first lesson is concentrating on how to drive. After the inevitable slice, it may take many minutes to reach the green and longer still to hole the ball, presumably the object of the exercise.

Compare that to a teaching method that lines the ball up several inches from the hole. The novice putts into the hole; then the ball is moved back slightly. It is a little more difficult but, perhaps after a miss or two, the golfer sinks the ball. In this second method we are building on success. The golfer knows right away what it feels like to get the ball into the hole. That feeling will sustain the golfer through many hooks from the tee.

The same is true in any endeavor. Select a small problem and move toward achieving some tangible measure of success in solving it. Use that as a springboard to action for another.

Emphasis on the Customer

Companies that perform well focus on the creation of revenue rather than the cutting of costs. This is particularly important in the hospitality industry, where so many of the costs are fixed. Beyond a certain point, costs cannot be cut without closing down the operation. Once that break-even point is reached, fixed costs have been covered and the difference between revenue and variable costs flows right to the bottom line. This does not mean that management should not be concerned with controlling costs; it does mean that the focus should be on the revenue side of the equation.

Increased revenue comes in part from listening to the customer to determine unmet needs and wants. This requires active involvement on the part of top management, an orientation that stresses people (both customers and employees), and a high degree of measurement and feedback. The philosophy set at the top is toward service and quality. A service orientation will lead to profitability; an accent on profits alone may not lead to service to the customer. A profit objective is also less likely to get employees involved. More employees can relate to the externally focused objective of service or quality rather than to the internally focused goal of profits, unless they are directly involved through profit sharing—and most are not.

This aspect of corporate culture is practiced in a variety of ways. Disney has an annual week-long program in which executives leave their desks, put on a costume, and literally get close to the customer. In addition, employees are called cast members; personnel is referred to as casting. Eight hours of training are required before ticket takers are allowed to go "on stage." Marriott is obsessed with its Guest Satisfaction Index. It is said that up until his death, Bill Marriott personally read every complaint letter than came to the head office. (Whether or not this is true is not as important as the perception by Marriott employees that it was true.) McDonald's personifies this as Quality, Service, Cleanliness, and Value. To that company, QSCV leads to profits. Few companies include a customer impact section in employee job descriptions, yet this inclusion would stress to all employees—especially back-of-the-house ones—the importance of the guest.

Entrepreneurship

Entrepreneurship—or *intra*preneurship—is the ability to be big and act small at the same time. As people climb their career ladder or as companies embark into the marketplace, they take certain risks along the way. They try new things. Much of their success may be due to this tendency. There are few constraints to acting this way because the individual or the company has little to lose. It is easy to take chances. As the individual and the company grow and become more successful, they gain the material benefits of their success: new car, house, sales, profits. Now they become more conservative in their decision making. The reason? Now they have more to lose. A wrong decision here could mean a loss of position, either in the corporate hierarchy or in the marketplace. This can induce the tendency to make few if any decisions, to take few if any chances. The behavior that developed their success is changed in order to maintain that success. The result is often a decline in personal and business fortune.

The key is to encourage new ideas. Being willing to encourage ideas also means being willing to tolerate mistakes and failure. Mistakes should not be accepted or condoned; however, they must be tolerated. This may seem contradictory, but the point is that if the culture is such that employees are unwilling to try or suggest new ideas for fear they will fail and be ridiculed, the company will stagnate.

The food and beverage manager of a pier in the south of England introduced a snack menu of hot dogs and soda during the intermission of a wrestling match held weekly on the facility. Never in the years of the attraction had such a thing been tried. The first night the idea was so successful the team ran out of everything. The next morning the young manager reported to his superior that everything had sold out. Instead of giving compliments, the superior berated the food and beverage manager for lousy forecasting!

People Orientation

The realization that results are achieved through and by people is critical. This involves showing—and meaning—respect for the individual. It means the company has to be willing to spend time and money in selecting the right kind of people, training them in how best to perform, setting clear and reasonable expectations, and giving them sufficient autonomy that they can contribute to the job.

People orientation functions in several ways. First is the language that is used. Crew members work at McDonald's, cast members at Disney. Second, people-oriented companies view themselves as an extended family, which includes the employees' families. We have previously mentioned a Chicago restaurateur who, recognizing the importance of the family to his Hispanic employees, encouraged them to bring their families to visit the workplace. Marriott approaches the problem of employee theft not only through a control system, but also by encouraging a feeling of family such that employees would not steal from each other. A third point concerns the chain of command. While the formal chain of command is used for major decisions, informality marks day-to-day communication.

Training is intensive at people-oriented companies. A well-constructed training program tells the employee that the job being performed is important enough to require extensive employee preparation, and in turn that the employee chosen to perform it also must be important. The reverse, of course, is also true. When a new employee is merely told to "observe Fred" for two hours as the extent of the training program, we are giving signals about the unimportance of the job and the person performing it.

Training begins with the selection and socialization of new employees. The intensity of the recruitment process indicates to new employees how important they and the job they perform are to the company.

People orientation also manifests itself in the amount of information shared by management. Typically, employees are excluded from receiving information on the company's financial condition. In part this is due to the competitive nature of our society. If financial information is given to employees, the figures may end up in the hands of the competition. Another reason is that if we tell the employees how well we are doing and how much they contribute to that, they will want to share in the rewards! (Of course, if they really do contribute all that much to the success of the property, perhaps they should share in its success.) The companies that have tried sharing information feel that any loss of information to the competition is more than compensated for by the increased employee loyalty that comes from feeling trusted.

Information is not given to employees to berate them for doing a poor job. Control comes from peer pressure. It is fairly easy to shield poor performance from the boss—but not from one's peers. Internal competition for results is encouraged. A danger lies in that too much internal competition can result in a situation in which an individual schemes to look good at the expense of the operation. The key is to identify very carefully what is to be used to measure success.

Values to Live By

Top companies figure out what they stand for, communicate that to their public, and live it. All policies and actions are based on this set of beliefs or values. Companies that performed better financially had values that were qualitative and less precise, rather than quantitative and exact.

The Peters and Waterman research identified common characteristics of these company values. First, profit comes from doing certain things well, rather than being an end in itself.

The values chosen also are successfully aimed at inspiring employees in the lower ranks of the organization.

It is further noted that businesses are a combination of contradictions. At any one time, there are pressures to provide service while cutting costs, to be operations oriented but also innovative, to be formal while encouraging informality, and to exhibit control while stressing the importance of people. The values that seem to work best are those where management comes down strongly on one side of these contradictions. Narrow in scope, these values include a belief:

- In being the best
- In the importance of the details of execution
- In the importance of people as individuals
- In superior quality and service
- That most members of the organization should be innovators and the organization should be willing to tolerate failure
- In the importance of informality to enhance communication
- In the importance of economic growth and profits[5]

Restaurant Services Inc., a Seattle-based restaurant company, took out a two-page newspaper ad, signed by its employees, managers, and purveyors, to let the public know what its values were. They were expressed as Our Tenets of Excellence:

1. We wish to contribute significantly to the quality of life of our guests by providing the best food, spirits, service, and ambiance at a fair price.
2. We unconditionally guarantee all that we do, 100 percent.
3. We seek to manage honestly and with thorough explanation.
4. Our employees' goals are: doing *whatever* is reasonable to satisfy our guests; professional appearance and demeanor; honesty.
5. We strive for the cleanest, freshest restaurants in Seattle.
6. We, in sum, want to be the best.[6]

This is significant in that the company is going on record as stating its values to employees and customers alike. Such a public display not only helps convince the public that the company is serious, but also puts pressure on management to live up to them.

Values tend to be laid down by and through the personality and actions of a leader.

Stick to What You Know

The more successful operations expand into areas related to their basic expertise. "A business is a business is a business" is not true. Many conglomerates have found, to their distress, that moving into an area they know little about can court disaster. This was the case when Heublein acquired Kentucky Fried Chicken. They found that the liquor business, in which product quality can be controlled at the factory, is very different from the restaurant business, in which quality control is important at each of the "mini-factories" where the food is produced and consumed.

Simple Form on Three Pillars

A successful culture depends in part on a relatively simple organization with a small corporate staff. Authority is pushed down to the operating level, where the action is. IBM has a policy of a three-year staff rotation. Those in staff positions know that very soon they will be out in the field working under the policies they helped develop. This has turned out to be a marvelous system of checks and balances.

To meet the needs for efficiency around the basics, regular innovation, and response to major threats, Peters and Waterman suggest a three-pillar approach to organizational design. The pillar of stability seeks to establish a simple form and develop broad, underlying values for the company.

The second pillar, entrepreneurship, focuses on developing new activities into new, self-contained divisions.

The so-called habit-breaking pillar seeks to encourage a willingness to reorganize regularly on a temporary basis to take advantage of trends in the marketplace or particular management strengths.

Loose and Tight

The future-oriented company culture exhibits at one and the same time a tight central direction while maximizing individual autonomy. Certain things are controlled very rigidly. These include the values the company lives by, an action focus, regular communication with rapid feedback, peer pressure, concise paperwork, and a focus on the outside—on the customer.

Holding firm to these ideas allows the organization to encourage, if not demand, looseness in other areas. Experimentation is encouraged, as is informal communication. Positive reinforcement is given and maximum individual autonomy sought.

Being both loose and tight means knowing what to control and what to let go of. This framework, which provides employees with security, also gives them the confidence to become innovative and help move the company forward.

IMPLEMENTING A COMPANY CULTURE

In order to implement the culture appropriate for a company at a particular point in time, a series of questions must be asked. These questions are fundamental to the success of a business and reach right to its core.

What business are we in today and do we see ourselves as being in five to ten years from now? This is the difference between being in the telephone or the communications business, or between being in the hotel or the tourism business.

What are the most important characteristics of these businesses? Here it is important to identify how fast these businesses are growing, what the present market share is, and what the competition is like.

What are our goals and strategies for these businesses? Certain basic decisions must be made. Do we intend to lead the industry, to develop a strategy for short- or long-term profitability?

What shared values will help implement these strategies? A short-term profit strategy will require a certain type of value system; an emphasis on employee development as the key to long-term profitability will suggest a different set of values.

Implementation of a culture takes place at three levels within the organization: the *mission and strategy,* the *organizational structure,* and *human resource management.*

At the first level, the concern is with developing a culture that is consistent with the overall mission and strategy of the business. At this stage it is also necessary to understand that the mission of the business may very well be influenced by the personal values of the people at the top. There have been instances in which the founders of certain hotel and restaurant companies have held strong beliefs against drinking alcohol. These personal beliefs have translated into policies prohibiting the serving of alcohol in their company-owned properties. In a situation like this, no amount of feasibility analysis will result in a change. The issue is one of values, not economics.

As for organizational structure, there are three concerns. First, there is the need to develop a managerial style consistent with the technical and political structure of the organization. As an example, we can contrast the cultures necessary for a functional or a matrix organization. In the functional organization, the traditional straight-line organizational chart holds true. An example is given in figure 5–2. In a matrix organization, power is balanced by both product and function (fig. 5–3). A manager is appointed for each specialized project and given sufficient staff to complete the job. The project manager is given authority over the staff within that project. The manager in charge of marketing the budget division is responsible to the vice president for the budget division, while indirectly reporting also to the vice president of marketing. While a more traditional chain-of-command management style is appropriate for the functional organization, the matrix format requires more emphasis on negotiation.

A second concern with organizational structure is in the development of subcultures appropriate to the particular function of a department. Sales and accounting are two obvious extremes. The accounting function concentrates on cost reduction and efficiency. The sales function focuses on filling rooms or seats and making deals. The culture for each will be different. We would not want a conservative sales department or an adventurous accountant.

The third concern is how to blend the various subcultures so that they can coexist for the good of the whole. The key is to develop a company culture

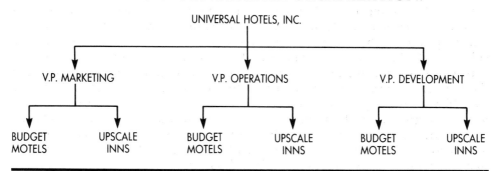

FIGURE 5–2 FUNCTIONAL ORGANIZATION.

UNIVERSAL HOTELS, INC.

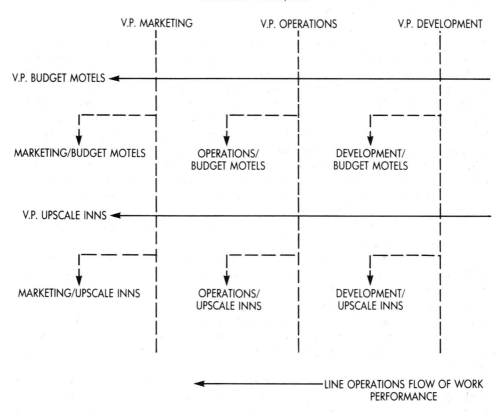

FIGURE 5–3 MATRIX ORGANIZATION.

UNIVERSAL HOTELS, INC.

strong enough to transcend any departmental subcultures—one culture that everyone can identify with over and above the system within each department.

In the third level, human resource management, an impact on culture can be made in selection, development, and rewards. In selecting employees, attention can be placed on how a particular person would fit into and reinforce the culture of the business. Candidates should be turned down if it is felt that their personality was inconsistent with that of the organization. Companies that use the human resource system to reinforce the culture spend a great deal of time and effort on training and development. The orientation and socialization process involves a great deal of emphasis on the values of the company. The Disney organization is particularly adept at this. Every employee takes a course entitled *Traditions 1,* which traces the development of Disney and stresses the qualities that the company emphasizes in itself and its employees.

Finally, companies reinforce the preferred values system by rewarding and promoting those employees who exemplify what the company wants to stand for.

CULTURE TYPES

In their book on corporate cultures, Terrence E. Deal and Allan A. Kennedy identify four generic cultures that derive from the degree of risk associated with the company's activities and the speed with which the companies and their employees receive feedback on whether strategies have been successful.

They termed the high risk, quick feedback type the *tough guy/macho culture.* Police departments, surgeons, advertising, management consulting, and entertainment are examples of where this type of culture prevails. The emphasis on quick feedback diverts attention and resources from long-term investments. The accent is on producing today, at the expense of tomorrow. Because competition is stressed, cooperation is essentially forgotten. It tends to be difficult to build a strong cohesive culture, because of the high turnover caused by people who fail in the short run.

The *work hard/play hard culture* tends to be found in organizations where risks are low and feedback is quick. The fast-food or quick-service companies fall into this category. Success comes from persistence. This value system is to find a need and fill it. The accent is on the team rather than on the individual. In this culture a great deal of work gets done. It is ideal for active people. The major danger is that quality can be sacrificed for quantity. As such, the better companies constantly stress the need for quality in meeting customer needs. A second difficulty is that this type of culture requires a great deal of energy from its employees. As employees age, they may lose the necessary stamina and burn out.

The *bet-your-company culture* is typically found in a high-risk environment with slow feedback. Capital goods industries, oil companies, and investment banks are all examples of this type of culture. Decisions come from the top down. The business meeting is very important. To survive it is necessary to be able to feel comfortable in making decisions without knowing for a long time whether they will pay off. Such organizations move extremely slowly and are subject to short-term fluctuations in the economy and cash flow problems as they wait for the long-term payoff.

Last, there is the *process culture,* characteristic of low-risk environments with slow feedback. Typical of banks, insurance companies, and heavily regulated firms, this culture leads to an emphasis on how something is done rather than on what is done. Great attention is paid to being on time, being orderly, and attending to detail.

Each culture described above is usually found in certain industries. A hotel company, however, may take on some or all of the characteristics of, for example, a process culture. Similarly, within a hotel or restaurant there may be several subcultures with the patterns given above. The key is to ensure that the culture implemented is appropriate for the mission of the company and that subcultures are not allowed to override the culture chosen as appropriate for the organization as a whole.

CHANGING COMPANY CULTURE

To change the culture within an organization, it is first necessary to identify it.

Identifying a Culture

The best way to identify the prevailing culture within a company is through a series of interviews with individuals and small groups, asking employees to describe the rules for survival within the company. In other words, what are the rules of the game? The result is a number of statements about the behavior necessary to succeed in a particular environment. These statements then can be fed back to small groups of managers in order to reach agreement on the cultural norms of the company.

A useful matrix to describe the culture is the way tasks are handled in the context of various relationships. Management tasks can be described as follows:

- Innovation
- Decision making
- Communication
- Organization
- Monitoring
- Appraisals and rewards

For each of these tasks, employees are asked the survival rules in terms of the following relationships:

- Company-wide
- Boss-subordinate

- Peer
- Interdepartmental

Let us take decision making as an example. Employees would be asked how decision making is typically handled company-wide, between boss and subordinate, between peers, and among departments. They may answer that the key is to gain the consensus of the group, that the right people must be involved, that any action requires many sign-offs, or that department managers are encouraged to show individual initiative and decisions are made unilaterally from the boss down.

Culture and Strategy

Having identified the prevailing culture, it is necessary to compare it with what is required to further the company's future strategy. Earlier we looked at the future shared beliefs deemed important for corporate survival. By looking at where the company is compared to where it wants to go, we can set out priorities. First, management determines in which direction the company should go. Next, it identifies the culture that will take the company there. The components of the culture are given one of three levels of importance: high, medium, or low. Third, the existing culture is overlaid with the desired culture to determine the degree of compatibility: high, medium, or low. The resulting matrix determines the degree of risk in changing the existing culture to one that will help the company reach its new strategy. This process is shown in figure 5–4.

For example, there is a tremendous change in the culture when a single operation decides to franchise. An individual has built a tight concept with a formula that works in terms of menu items, methods of preparation, level of service, and control of costs. To develop a strategy of expansion will require a different culture. Typically, a concept has been built on personal supervision. Decision making will tend to be autocratic. To expand as a franchise, tight standards are necessary. These standards must be rigidly adhered to by managers and employees not under the direct supervision of the entrepreneur. The key element of strategy, then, is a tightly controlled product, delivered in a decentralized way. Both elements would be rated of high importance in figure 5–4.

To what extent would these elements be present in an entrepreneurial organization? Certainly the tightly controlled product would be, because the restaurant, for example, would be under the direct supervision of the owner. It is unlikely that any decentralized decision making goes on, however. Decisions would be made by the owner rather quickly, with little or no consultation with others. A scoring system is used to aid in evaluation: 1 indicates that the risk is negligible, 2 that it is manageable, and 3 that it is unmanageable. The first element of culture—a tightly controlled product—would rate a score of 2 while the other element—delivered in a decentralized way—rates a 3. A

FIGURE 5–4 ORGANIZATIONAL CULTURE AND CORPORATE STRATEGY.

HOW IMPORTANT IS THIS TO FUTURE STRATEGY?	TIGHTLY CONTROLLED PRODUCT		DELIVERED IN A DECENTRALIZED WAY
OF HIGH IMPORTANCE	2	3	3
OF MEDIUM IMPORTANCE	1	2	3
OF LOW IMPORTANCE	1	1	2
	PRESENTLY EXISTS	EXISTS SOMEWHAT	DOES NOT EXIST

TO WHAT EXTENT IS THE DESIRED CULTURE PRESENT?

(*Source:* Adapted from Howard Schwartz and Stanley M. Davis, "Matching Corporate Culture and Business Strategy," *Organizational Dynamics,* Summer 1981, 41.)

principal difficulty in franchising, in fact, is the willingness to have the concept managed by others not under the original owner's personal supervision.

This type of analysis allows management to determine the major problems to be faced in moving the existing culture to one that will help the operation achieve its new strategy. Attention should be directed at specific parts of the company's culture that are important to the future success of the operation and are presently nonexistent in the corporate culture.

MANAGING COMPANY CULTURE

Once it is deemed important that a change in company culture occur, the next stage is to ask, "How can that change be implemented and managed?" In implementing change, managers must be concerned about two things: how fast they can implement change and how much control they will have over the end result.[7]

Low Control, Low Speed

Traditional methods of implementing change have been ineffective. A typical example of the low-control, low-speed method is human resource development. Building teams from the bottom up is a strategy that takes a great deal of time to implement (low speed). In addition, experience has shown that the final result tends to be something other than what was originally envisioned (low control).

High Control, Low Speed

Instituting a formal planning process was originally a high-control, low-speed method of implementing change. The effect of planning on the organization had an impact after the employees had developed the experience and skills necessary to utilize the concept fully. In the beginning, managers had a great deal of control over the results of the planned process. But it is now argued that in many organizations strategic planning has become a routine, politicized part of the structure and does not help the organization adapt to changes in the environment. Thus, planning has moved from a strategy of high control and low speed to one of low control and low speed.

High Control, High Speed

The same is true, it is argued, for structural solutions as a means of implementing change. Structural solutions include such things as decentralization and the splitting of the company into divisions. Originally a high-control, high-speed change method, it, too, has moved to low control and low speed. In the area of control, management has overestimated the durability of such change in the face of changes in the external environment. Consequently, structures tend to remain in place after the environment supporting such structures has changed. Thus, management loses control over the end result of the change. Similarly, management underestimates the time difference between changed structure and changed behavior. The result is a move from high speed to low speed.

To implement and manage a different culture requires the use of strategies over which the manager has high control, and which can be put into place relatively quickly. Three things can be controlled very quickly: symbols, the patterns of activity that are generated, and the settings chosen for any interactions.

Symbols

Symbols within a company have three functions. First, they are descriptive of what the company is all about. Second, they can be used to control the energy within an organization by inspiring or motivating those within the company. Third, they maintain the system by reinforcing the way things are done and by guiding the way the company changes.

Symbols may be verbal or consist of specific actions or certain materials. Verbal symbols are such things as myths, legends, stories, slogans, jokes, rumors, or names. Consider the strength of Caterpillar's 24-Hour Parts Service Anywhere in the World, IBM's IBM Means Service, and McDonald's' Quality, Service, Cleanliness, and Value, compared to the weaker Delta gets you there. (Gosh, I would hope so!) To the surprise of researchers, successful companies have qualitative rather than quantitative slogans on a two-to-one ratio.

Stories help preserve the culture of the company by conveying organizational values to newcomers. Thomas Watson, Jr., son of the founder of IBM would tell of the nature lover who enjoyed seeing the wild ducks fly south each October. He began feeding the ducks. Soon several of them spent the winter in the pond on what was fed them instead of continuing the flight south. As time went on, they flew less and less. After several years they were so fat and lazy they could barely fly at all. The point he made was that it is possible to tame wild ducks but never to make tame ducks wild again. At IBM it was the wild duck that would succeed, because the tame duck would never go anywhere.

While the story was used to express IBM's tolerance for the maverick innovator, one employee remarked upon hearing the story that "even wild ducks fly in formation." This immediately became part of the wild ducks story, because it made the equally valid point that we must all go in the same direction.

Hotels and restaurants have their own stories of employees who struggled to work in a blinding snowstorm or managers who worked twenty hours straight after a tornado hit a nearby community.

Various actions are also symbolic of the way a company operates. Examples are rituals, parties, rites of passage, meals, and the way the day is started. Rituals give the culture a tangible, meaningful form. Rituals may include the honoring of retirees to demonstrate the importance of loyalty to the company. It may, as in the case of Disney, mean the times that management takes on a customer service job to show the importance of the guest. The manager who is willing to pitch in and get involved in the back of the house as well as in the more glamorous front jobs sends a powerful message to employees.

Certain college graduates bemoan the fact that as part of the company training program, they must peel carrots for two weeks. Surely, they argue, it does not take two weeks to learn the difficulties involved in this task. Yet this may be a rite of passage—like basic training—to show the importance of every detail in satisfying the customer.

In the hospitality industry, many operations are very class-conscious in the way meals are given to employees. Certain people are allowed to dine in the hotel's restaurants while others are relegated to the employee dining room. Managers can demonstrate their particular culture by setting democratic rules for employee meals and requiring that managers eat with employees, unless they are conducting business with a client.

Material symbols include status symbols, awards, badges, and pins. In a company with a strong culture, there are many opportunities for material symbols. It may be the pins, flags, and plaques at weekly Tupperware meetings or membership in IBM's Hundred Percent Club, for those who have consistently met their sales quota. The key is that the standards are set so that 80 percent of the sales force will meet the goal and be able to join the club. Why is the quota so low? The key in any incentive is not to motivate the superstar; he or she will get there in any case. The trick is to offer an incentive to get above-average performance from the average performer. Setting the standard so that 80 percent can attain it will do this.

Patterns

How these symbols are used will determine their ultimate success or failure. The key to success is to apply these symbols of change as positive reinforcement in a consistent and frequent manner. It is far easier to get desired behavior by rewarding the positive than by trying to stamp out the negative. If customer service is important, have supervisors reward an Employee of the Moment whenever especially good service is seen.

Settings

Managers can further influence culture through the settings in which they interact. They imply the importance of a meeting by making a decision to attend. One hotel manager hired this author to develop and deliver an orientation program for new employees. For the first few sessions, the general manager attended for a few minutes to deliver his personal philosophy to the new employees. Thereafter it seemed that something more important always came up. The employees were told how important they were to management. But the actions of the manager belied the message.

The location of meetings are also important. Being summoned to the manager's office implies a more formal tone than when the manager drops in to the kitchen to discuss a problem. Selecting a formal setting for a meeting or party can imply greater status to it.

Management can use the meeting agenda to send signals. How much time is spent discussing costs against customer satisfaction? The order of items can be crucial. Some managers will put items unimportant to them at the top of an agenda so that by the time they reach the items they want approved, all dissension will be over.

Messages also can be sent based on who makes presentations at meetings. Does the general manager control the show, or are department managers urged to make presentations and proposals? The answer can tell a great deal about management style.

Last, those who control the minutes control the history of the meeting. Editing the proceedings of what has gone on can be done—not to distort the truth, but to emphasize what the manager wishes to stress.

SUMMARY

The development of a corporate culture—the way we do things around here—is useful to let employees know clearly what the company stands for. It means that knowing the values considered important, they will be more likely to act according to what the company wants, even when supervision is not direct.

Management must decide what is important and how to implement it. Implementation can occur when managers spend time and effort in persistently stressing, through words and action, what is important.

NOTES

[1]Schwartz, Howard, and Stanley M. Davis, "Matching Corporate Culture and Business Strategy," *Organizational Dynamics,* Summer 1981, 33.

[2]Attributed to Marvin Bower, quoted in *Corporate Cultures: The Rites and Rituals of Corporate Life,* Terrence E. Deal and Allan A. Kennedy, Reading, Mass., Addison-Wesley Publishing Company, 1982, 4.

[3]Schwartz and Davis, 33–34.

[4]Peters, Thomas J., and Robert H. Waterman, Jr., *In Search of Excellence: Lessons from America's Best-Run Companies,* New York, Harper & Row, 1982, 42–44.

[5]Ibid., 285.

[6]*The Seattle Times,* January 16, 1984, A6–A7.

[7]Peters, Thomas J., "Symbols, Patterns and Settings: An Optimistic Case for Getting Things Done," *Organizational Dynamics,* Autumn 1978, 19–20.

SUGGESTED READINGS

Baker, Edwin L., "Managing Corporate Culture," *Management Review,* July 1980, 8–13.

Boje, David M., Donald B. Fedor, and Kendrith M. Rowland, "Myth Making: A Qualitative Step in OD Interventions," *The Journal of Applied Behavioral Science* 18, no. 1, 17–28.

Dandridge, Thomas C., Ian Mitroff, and William F. Joyce, "Organizational Symbolism: A Topic to Expand Organizational Analysis," *Academy of Management Review* 5, no. 1, 1980, 77–82.

Deal, Terrence E., and Allan A. Kennedy, *Corporate Cultures: The Rites and Rituals of Corporate Life,* Reading, Mass., Addison-Wesley Publishing Company, 1982.

Peters, Thomas J., "Symbols, Patterns and Settings: An Optimistic Case for Getting Things Done," *Organizational Dynamics,* Autumn 1978, 3–22.

———, "Excellence at the Top: A Leadership Style That Works," *Cornell Hotel and Restaurant Administration Quarterly,* 20, no. 3, November 1980, 13–23.

Pettigrew, Andrew M., "On Studying Organizational Cultures," *Administrative Science Quarterly* 24, December 1979, 570–81.

Sathe, Vijay, "Organizational Culture: Some Conceptual Distinctions and Their Managerial Implications," working paper, Division of Research, Harvard Business School, 1984.

Schwartz, Howard, and Stanley M. Davis, "Matching Corporate Culture and Business Strategy," *Organizational Dynamics,* Summer 1981, 30–48.

Tichy, Noel M., "Managing Change Strategically: The Technical, Political, and Cultural Keys," *Organizational Dynamics* 10, Autumn 1982, 59–80.

APPENDIX: IMPLEMENTING COMPANY CULTURE—A HOTEL EXAMPLE

Because of the rapid growth of the company being studied, as well as increasingly competitive markets and external economic and social factors that affected the hotel industry, it was felt that stronger, more centralized management policies were needed in order to provide for greater consistency of performance.

OBJECTIVES

There were several major objectives in this project:

Through the participation of all general managers and members of the operating team, determine the framework for future policy decisions and performance standards.

Provide a significant body of information about areas of strength and concern, as perceived by all general managers and operating team members.

Establish a clearly defined statement of norms, or principles, that would guide future actions and provide for greater consistency of performance.

Clearly define a framework to help ensure long-term rather than short-term decision making.

Build a team concept and strengthen the ties between the general managers and the operating team.

APPROACH

With the services of an outside consultant, a four-step process was proposed.

First, the general managers in each of the four regional divisions must participate in a full-day seminar to cover several matters:

- A common understanding of the process being undertaken to define the norms or principles of the company
- A common vocabulary for talking about areas of strength and concern
- The collection of information regarding those areas of strength and concern

The second step was the compilation and categorization of all data collected, followed by the feedback of that data to the operating team (comprising regional

105

supervisors). The operating team then would assess the information and organize it in order of importance to the accomplishment of the company's objectives.

In step three, the discussion would be summarized, and norms or principles for the operating division of the company would be negotiated among the vice presidents.

Finally, the norms of the company would be announced in the form of some type of celebration.

It was recommended that the four-step process take place over a six-week period.

Location

Two options were considered for the location of the four full-day meetings of general managers: at company headquarters or in the four regions.

Having the meetings at company headquarters would mean all the general managers would be coming to the home base. For a number of them, it had been a long time since they had visited the head offices of the company. Bringing them in would reacquaint them with the company, and would set the tone for the meetings. The unspoken message would be that the process was important. Additionally, the corporate office would be able to exert more influence over the process.

The disadvantages of this option were that it would involve travel time and cost for the participants.

Travel time and cost would be reduced by having the meetings in the field. Also, the corporate office would be coming to the managers.

After much consideration, however, it was decided to hold the meetings at the head offices.

LEADERSHIP SEMINAR

It is vitally important that a project of this nature have the overt support of top management. To accomplish this, a leadership seminar was held. The participants—the operating team—were corporate officers of the company. This summation of the topics covered and the discussion that ensued will give the reader a picture of the thinking of top managers at the beginning of the project.

Autonomy

Important elements of autonomy included the ideas that you don't dictate when it isn't required and that there was a need to address priorities across the board. There was considerable disagreement as to how general managers would respond to more centralized policy decisions.

Individual comments addressed the need for understanding where responsibility lies, what the company expected overall from the general managers, and difficulties in communication.

The company system was described as a group of satellites that float in space and only occasionally come back in and dock.

There was considerable discussion of the concepts of "can versus must," with some people believing in the need to sell policy changes to general managers and others believing that a direct statement of intent should be adequate to ensure compliance.

It was noted that most members of the operating team were former general managers who historically had operated with a high level of autonomy, so current managers should not be more resistant to change than the team members would have been. It was suggested that once a budget was prepared, any deviation should require approval.

Regarding the growth of the company, it was indicated that in the past strong general managers had done what they had to do and flourished. Now management had become more complicated, and there was a void to be filled through corporate direction. Today's demands and pressures were different. The old system worked and was easier because the company was smaller.

It was agreed that autonomy could be preserved if corporate officials chose correctly what policy decisions it would make and how they would be preserved.

Hospitality

There was considerable discussion of both the necessity and difficulty of defining hospitality. It was also stated that performance standards should be established based on the provision of hospitality.

Words used to describe hospitality included welcome, warm, important, family, fun, empathy, concern, friendly, caring, home, comfortable, secure, happiness, recognition of the guest, gentleness, smile, sincerity, and enthusiasm.

Performance Standards

It was stated that performance standards should be more specific across the board, and that there should be specific requirements with regard to service for guests.

Policies

There was considerable discussion of the concept of uniform policies and their impact on autonomy. Some people said uniform policies already were in place but were not being uniformly administered.

Supportiveness, Sharing of Ideas

There was a mixed response to how new ideas were believed to be received. Several people said there was a tendency to shoot down a new idea; others disagreed.

The word *cautiousness* was used to describe how ideas were brought to the table.

There was considerable discussion, too, about the notion of the company as a family and the need for everyone to "come home" on occasion. Several items were thought to reinforce the family concept:

- Relationships that go beyond 8:00 A.M. to 5:00 P.M.
- Genuine concern for the well-being of people
- The existence of a family room, library, and provision of liquor
- The pride of belonging
- Sibling rivalry (but not competing at the expense of someone else)

Participants noted that communication and relations with the development group could be improved. The operations group perceived itself to be stronger than the development group. Physical separation tended to increase the finger pointing.

It was indicated that the group needed to spend time on strategies. A case-study approach was suggested, in which up-front preparation would be required. There was general agreement that the time spent in meetings could be more effectively utilized. There was some disagreement about whether or not meetings were merely reporting sessions.

Participants stated that people should feel comfortable to say, "Hey guys, here's a mess, help me out."

The group noted it should meet more often, with the meetings serving as a vehicle for deciding on specific issues.

Definition of Norms

The leadership seminar led to its own clearly defined statement of general norms, or principles, divided into three categories: existing positive factors, existing negative ones, and desired goals (table 5–1). This was intended to help the general managers as they met in the four-step process to set new company standards.

STEP 1: THE GENERAL MANAGERS MEET

The agenda for each regional meeting of the general managers sought input on both current and desired performance standards, the identification of support systems currently in place, and recommendations for additional systems support.

8:30 to 8:45 A.M.: Introduction

8:45 to 10:30: Summation of the leadership seminar presented to the operating team

10:30 to 10:45: Break

10:45 to noon: General discussion of current performance standards

TABLE 5-1:	DEFINITION OF NORMS	
Existing/Positive	*Existing/Negative*	*Desired*
Integrity is foremost in all dealings	Development and operations need better communication, common goals.	An atmosphere where employees develop skills, and feel a sense of accomplishment, and provide a quality guest experience
Decentralized management structure	Financial management strains working capital	Get away from *we* versus *they* problem with development
Results oriented within liberal framework	Few operating policies or required procedures.	Programs and systems to increase the guest experience
Allows its people great flexibility	Only specific situations evaluated	Adequate funds to enable the general manager to provide quality hotel service
Reinvestment keeps properties up to date	Too much input delays decisions, causes confusion	What is good for the whole, not a region
Openness and ability to go to the top with an idea or problem	Expectations sometimes not communicated effectively or consistently	Performance standards for each position
Workers given responsibility	Company has short-term outlook	Annual evaluations based on these standards
Company is people oriented and progressive	Communication is a problem at the corporate level	Communicating expectations and priorities consistently
Broad parameters to operate properties	People are defensive	Communicating positive and negative consequences clearly
Individuals can be like owners	People don't use each other for resources	Resources available, and their use encouraged, to attain objectives
Group has a good sense of humor under stress	Bottom-line awareness, not a strong commitment to overall quality	Fast-moving, well-thought-out long-range plan
Strong sense of ethics	Poor communication downward on change from decentralization.	Rewards for more than just the bottom line
Support for each other and concern for our people	Acceptability of quick-fix financial solutions over long-term position and business levels	Long-term strategies, with commitment from development and operations
	Overemphasis on cutting expenses	Honest evaluation of ideas and how to build on them
	Underemphasis on generating sales	

TABLE 5–1: DEFINITION OF NORMS (*continued*)		
Existing/Positive	*Existing/Negative*	*Desired*
		A high degree of guest satisfaction
		Define hospitality and commit to it
		Equate hospitality, quality of guest experience, and the bottom line
		Time to develop benefits of hospitality, guest experience
		Compromise *today* between profitability and guest satisfaction, to compete effectively in the future

Noon to 1:00 P.M.: Lunch.

1:00 to 3:00: Individuals' identification of existing performance standards

3:00 to 3:15: Break

3:15 to 5:00: Individuals' perceptions of current and desired systems that support performance standards; individuals' preliminary ranking of standards in order of priority

Results

After all the input of the general managers, nearly twenty categories of performance standards were proposed. They were in the areas of accountability; autonomy; basics; cash flow, ROI, and working capital; cleanliness; communication and feedback; community involvement; creativity and innovation; energy conservation; fire and safety; food and beverage; guest experience and hospitality; orientation; people development and training; planning and the marketplace; profitability and the bottom line; remodeling and physical conditions; and sales.

STEP 2: ORGANIZING COLLECTED INFORMATION

The company then proceeded to the second of the four steps, with the operating team meeting to assess the data that the general managers had collected. The agenda included both review of the information and efforts to organize it in order of priority.

8:30 to 8:45 A.M.: Introduction

8:45 to 10:00: Review and explanation of collected information from general managers, including perceptions of current and desired performance standards

10:15 to noon: Review of desired performance standards and preliminary priority planning.

Noon to 1:00 P.M.: Lunch

1:00 to 2:00: Review of current and proposed systems recommendations

2:00 to 3:00: Breakup of operating team into smaller units of three people to set priorities for desired performance standards, as well as systems support necessary for reinforcement

3:00 to 3:15: Break

3:15 to 5:00: Small units' reports on prioritization, reason for selection, and specific systems recommendations for support

STEP 3: NEGOTIATING STANDARDS

The third step in the process involved two separate meetings to negotiate the new standards, with an agenda prepared as well for a third session if required.

Agenda, Session 1

1:00 to 1:45 P.M.: Review of compiled information on performance standards and systems

1:45 to 3:00: Setting of individual priorities for the standards

3:00 to 3:15: Break

3:15 to 3:30: Agreement on the first standard to be defined

3:00 to 5:00: Definition of the first standard; identification of current systems support; recommendations for additional systems support

Agenda, Session 2

8:00 to 8:15 A.M.: Review of previous standard

8:15 to 8:30: Determination of second standard to be defined

8:30 to 10:00: Definition of second standard; identification of current systems support; recommendations for additional systems support

10:00 to 10:15: Break

10:15 to 10:30: Determination of third standard to be defined

10:30 to 11:30: Definition of third standard; identification of current systems support; recommendations for additional systems support

11:30 to 1:00 P.M.: Lunch

1:00 to the end: Definition of remaining standards; identification of current systems support; recommendations for additional systems support

Agenda, Session 3 (If Required)

The agenda for a third session was prepared, if needed, to complete the definition of standards, identification of current systems support, and recommendations for additional systems support.

RESULTS

From the sessions in step three, several performance standards were agreed upon and announced, completing the four-step process:

Mission: To provide quality management services for the benefit of our clients and for the increased long-term profitability of the company.

Premise: We will be held accountable for achieving our mission with honesty and integrity through established performance standards. The degree of achievement of performance standards will be recognized by a change in the level of responsibility, compensation, and continued employment.

Communication and feedback: The timely, accurate, and appropriate exchange of information.

Planning: The development and execution of short-term and long-term strategies based on anticipated economic climate, market position, and physical condition of the property.

People development: The training, education, and coaching of individuals to enable them to realize their full potential to accomplish the operations mission.

Hospitality: The behavior on our part that results in our guests feeling welcome, being comfortable, and having their needs satisfied.

Quality environment: The creation of physical surroundings that are pleasant, clean, and secure.

House profit: The accomplishment of profit objectives through adherence to the budget.

Basics: The adherence to the required operational controls, procedures, and policies as established in the basics manual.

Sales: The achievement of budgeted sales through aggressive, innovative, and persistent selling and marketing techniques.

Food and Beverage: The timely preparation and attractive presentation of quality food and beverages appropriate to the market.

6 | DEVELOPING A PRODUCTIVE ORGANIZATIONAL CLIMATE

In the previous chapter, we discussed the importance that management identify a corporate culture—the way we do things around here—that through its implementation would create conditions to produce motivated employees. While managers may feel that they have correctly identified the necessary elements and have introduced strategies to implement them, it is the employees' perceptions that are important. A sender may believe that a message has been sent, but communication does not take place unless and until the message has been received. What employees receive—their perceptions of the culture set by management—is termed organizational climate.

CLIMATE WITHIN ORGANIZATIONS

What do we mean by the climate within an organization? When employees say they never know what is going on or they belong to a tightly knit group or the only time they hear from the boss is when they have done something wrong, they are talking about the climate of the organization. Unlike the weather, organizational climate is not something that can be seen or felt directly, though we can probably sense the climate in a restaurant or hotel by observing the employees' behavior as they interact with guests, fellow employees, and management.

Although the weather is something that cannot be changed and must be accepted, management can take definite action to modify organizational climate.

Two of the first writers on organizational climate were George Litwin and Robert Stringer. In their book[1], they identified climate as consisting of a set of properties of the work environment. These properties were based on the perceptions of the people who worked there. Further, how the employees perceived the climate was found to influence both their motivation and behavior. Litwin and Stringer were also able to measure the perceived climate of the work place.

The above definition encompasses several things. First, climate is perceptual. It is the employees' perception of what exists, not necessarily what actually does exist; these two may or may not be the same thing. Management may

114

feel that high standards are set; the employee may feel differently. It is the employee's perception that will influence employee motivation and actions. If the perception is that high standards do not exist, the employee may decide: "If management doesn't care about the standard of service given to the guest, why should I?"

Second, climate can be measured. A variety of dimensions have been suggested. This chapter will explore what can be called a six-dimensional model in some depth.

Research has also shown that although the climate within an organization is stable over time, it can be changed by management action.

A MODEL OF ORGANIZATIONAL CLIMATE

A model of how the climate within an organization develops and influences job behavior is suggested in figure 6–1. The influences on climate—the external environment, differences in the structure of the organization, and personal differences in the style and behavior of management—are moderated by the norms of the group of which the employee is a member, as well as the individual's tasks and personality, to produce, in effect, three types of climate. The individual has a perception of the climate that exists within the company. To the extent that this is shared by the other employees in his or her department, a group climate is formed. Where there exists a collective perception within the property, an organizational climate can be described—one that is generally agreed on to be descriptive of the operation as a whole.

The individual then develops in his or her mind a map of the perceived climate, which acts as a screening device to reinforce that perception. Research has shown, for example, that the longer an individual has been working within a certain climate, the more difficult it is to change that person's perception of it. On the basis of the individual, group, and organizational climates, employees develop expectations that, moderated by the employees' ability and personality, affect motivation, satisfaction, and job performance.

External Influences

The external environment surrounding the company influences the type of climate that is appropriate. We can speculate, for example, that the availability of labor will help shape the extent to which the company values employees. When the competition for employees is stiff, management will adopt a stronger employee orientation than when labor is plentiful.

Organizational Influences

There is an assumption that close physical proximity between workers and management will produce greater employee identification with management goals and objectives. Additionally, some feel that a smaller property will produce

FIGURE 6–1 A MODEL OF ORGANIZATIONAL CLIMATE.

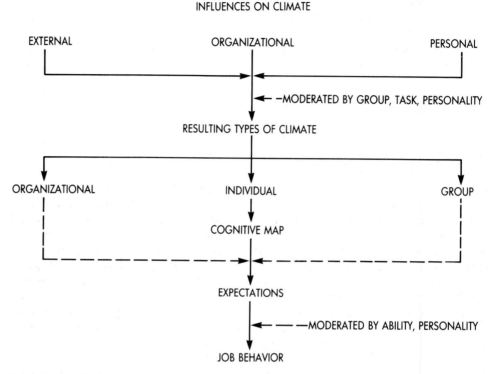

(*Source:* Adapted from R. H. George Field and Michael A. Abelson, "Climate: A Reconceptualization and Proposed Model," *Human Relations* 35, no. 3, 1982, 195.)

a greater feeling of teamwork than a larger operation. The results of research on the effect of size on organizational climate are mixed. While some studies have shown that increasing size reduces job satisfaction of employees, all agree that size alone is not a decisive determinant of organizational climate.

Although insufficient studies have been completed to produce generalizations, one study found a significant relationship between climate and the type of technology. Employees in companies that used small batch and process technologies perceived more favorable climates than those in operations using mass production techniques.

Studies have also looked at the orientation of the organization in terms of its effect on employee perception of climate. It has been found that highly bureaucratic structures are more likely to be perceived as closed systems, with a less satisfactory climate. In another study, employees felt they had more individual autonomy and were rewarded more when they perceived that the company had an orientation toward customers rather than stockholders.

Personal Influences

Individuals bring with them biases toward seeing what is around them. Individuals who grew up inherently suspicious of management will tend to see negatives in everything management does. They may view things differently from another employee who was raised to believe that management is not out to get the workers.

Moderating Influences

The external influences on climate are moderated by several factors. It has been shown, for example, that perceptions of climate vary among employees at different levels in the management hierarchy. Perceptions are also influenced by the type of job that employees perform and the type of person they are. One study found that when an experimental group was given more discretion to make decisions, those in the group showed more motivation toward responsibility and achievement, felt a closer relationship to management, and felt that rewards were tied more closely to performance than a control group did. They were also more successful in sales and profitability than the control group.

Employees can conduct a simple exercise to determine what motivates them to do a good job. People are motivated by many different factors. Some are internal factors, such as a need for power or achievement; others are connected to the job itself, such as the desire for challenging work; while still others are influenced by a supervisor or manager, such as the need for feedback or praise. The employee should take a few minutes to list, in no particular order of importance, the factors that motivate him or her to do a good job. Then review the list. Which items are directly influenced by the supervisor? There are certain things that an individual manager can do little about; for example, perhaps, pay and benefits. But the supervisor can directly influence other things, such as recognizing employee achievements and giving some decision-making authority. The list is likely to contain more manager-influenced items than the employee expected. Many people—including managers themselves—are surprised to realize the number of items important to creating motivation that can be influenced by the boss.

For employees who place great importance on the work situation, certain dimensions of climate are more important. Such employees prefer task-oriented management actions that seek to get the organizations moving. They also enjoy friendly social relationships while not wishing to be burdened with what they consider merely busy work. For those who see the work situation as being less important, the emphasis sought is on maintaining pleasant relationships while reducing dissension and disruption.

Dimensions of Climate

At least ten questionnaires have been developed to measure the climate within an operation. This research has resulted in descriptions of climate in anywhere from four to seven dimensions, or key aspects. A well-respected model is that of the Forum Corporation.[3]

The Forum model describes the climate of an organization in six dimensions: three dealing with performance, three with development. The performance dimensions are *clarity, commitment,* and *standards.* The development dimensions are *responsibility, recognition,* and *teamwork.*

Clarity refers to how well the employees understand the goals and policies of the company, in addition to how clear they are about their own job. It is the feeling that things are organized and run smoothly, not confused. Too often, employees are not given a written job description when they join a new hotel or restaurant. They must pick up the elements of their job from existing employees. If they feel unclear about what they should be doing relative to others in the operation, they would have a low score on this dimension. In general, companies do not tell employees enough about their overall goals and objectives. Perhaps the feeling is, "They're just not interested." But the result is that employees do not know what is important to the company. If they are not clear about that, they will be unclear about how to act in work situations. "If a customer complains, what should I do?" or "If my boss makes a pass at me, what can I do?"

Commitment is the extent to which employees feel continually committed to achieving the goals of the company; the extent to which they accept company goals as being realistic; the extent to which they are involved in the setting of such goals; and the extent to which their performance is continually evaluated against the goals of the operation. Companies have certain goals, such as profitability, return on investment, customer satisfaction, and cleanliness. These goals are achieved (or not achieved) by the efforts of the employees. Company goals can be met only if employees are in some way committed to achieving them. The greater the commitment, the more likely it is that the objective will be achieved.

Standards measure the degree to which employees feel that management emphasizes the setting of high standards of performance, and the extent to which they feel pressure to improve their performance continually. Strange as it may seem, employees often have higher standards than the company does. This can occur in an operation that is very bottom-line oriented. In an effort to achieve that all-important profit, concessions are made in the areas of customer service, equipment maintenance, and employee training and development. Employees, in particular those who have been with the operation for an extended time, may feel that standards toward the customer have been slipping. This will influence how they feel toward the company and may well affect their performance. *In Search of Excellence,* in comparing companies that emphasized financial objectives with others emphasizing nonfinancial objectives (such as customer satisfaction or cleanliness), found that the latter actually produced better bottom-line results than the companies that stressed financial objectives. One explanation is that few layers of employees can relate to the financial objectives of the operation; many more layers can relate to something such as customer satisfaction. They may not share in the profits of the company, but they have all been customers.

Among the development dimensions of climate, responsibility is the feeling employees have that they are personally responsible for the work that they do, that supervisors encourage them to take the initiative, and that they have a real sense of autonomy. The employee who has to check with the boss before he or she can do anything does not have this. Some supervisors, while complaining that their subordinates will not leave them in peace and will not make decisions for themselves, do not encourage employee initiative. They criticize employee decisions without being constructive; they will not tolerate employee opinions that differ from theirs. One explanation for this behavior is that the supervisor, while critical of the employees' lack of initiative, wishes to keep a close check on them. This paternalistic feeling comes from the belief that if employees can make decisions and initiate actions without them, the supervisors will not be needed. The way this type of supervisor feels needed is to force employees to check with him or her about even the most minute details of a job.

The second development dimension is recognition: the feeling that employees are noted and rewarded for doing good work, rather than receiving criticism and punishment as the predominant form of feedback. In a climate such as this, rewards and recognition outweigh threats and criticism, there is in place a promotion system that helps the best person rise to the top, and the hotel or restaurant has a reward structure related to excellence of performance. It sometimes seems, however, that the only feedback employees get is when something is amiss. When we hear, "The boss wants to see you," most of us will immediately think, "What did I do wrong?" A major reason is the idea of management by exception. Under this accounting term, targets are set and, if met, the property is on target and no remedial action need be taken. If sales or cost projections are out of line, however, a red flag goes up to initiate corrective management action. Thus, if things are going well, the manager, who has many demands on his or her time, will pass over that department to concentrate on the problem areas. The result is that the only time employees hear from the manager is when things go wrong. Under this type of climate, in fact, employees may perform negatively in order to receive some feedback— even if it is criticism. The fact is that an absence of feedback—extinction is the psychological term—is more punishing than punishment. This idea is as prevalent for children at home and students in the classroom as it is for employees in the workplace.

Teamwork is the third development dimension. This is the perception of belonging to an organization that is cohesive, one where people trust one another, and where employees feel personal loyalty and the sense that they belong to the organization. It is the feeling of *us* working together, rather than *us versus them,* whether that be management versus workers or kitchen versus dining room. We all like to feel that we are part of a winning team. Consider how this can work for or against a hotel. We know that the most effective form of advertising is word of mouth. A negative comment from a friend can outweigh the effect of an advertisement costing thousands of dollars. If we assume that a hotel has two hundred employees and that each one talks to one hundred people each week, both in and out of work, each and every week there are twenty thousand messages going out about that hotel that could be positive or negative. "Oh, you work at the XYZ Hotel; how is it?" "You wouldn't believe the way they treat us; I wouldn't trust that new manager as far as I could throw him!" Result? One lost customer.

Job Behavior

Numerous studies have found a correlation between organizational climate and job performance. Climates seen as supportive have produced higher performance than those perceived as less supportive. Employee-centered climates have not always led to higher performance levels. One major factor seems to be the consistency with which climates are perceived. Employees who perceived that a climate was always rules oriented or always employee oriented performed better than in situations in which the climate perception changed.

That link is not as clear or as persuasive, however, as the relationship between climate and job satisfaction. Supportive climates lead to job satisfaction.

But is there a link between job satisfaction and job performance? Most of the studies conducted prior to 1950 assumed that there was a positive relationship between job satisfaction—the extent to which an individual perceives getting satisfaction from the job—and productivity. Literature reviews in the fifties indicated that there was little evidence of a significant relationship between satisfaction and performance. It has been demonstrated, however, that there is a consistently negative relationship between job satisfaction and turnover. That is, the greater the job satisfaction, the less the turnover. Links, while less strong, have also been found between satisfaction and absenteeism, and between satisfaction and on-the-job accidents. Greater satisfaction is related to less absenteeism and fewer on-the-job accidents.

The link between satisfaction and performance seems to be related to the type of job. The relationship is greater for jobs that call on higher levels of skills and knowledge.

The traditional viewpoint that high morale leads to good performance has given way in some quarters to the reverse notion, that good performance leads to high morale. When an employee achieves a measure of job success (performance), that leads them in turn to being satisfied with their job. Academic rigor aside, in the hospitality industry, which relies on guest-employee contact so much, it is hard to believe that a dissatisfied employee can give complete and hospitable service to a guest.

Moderating Influences

At this level there are also external individual factors that moderate the link between climate and job behavior. One is the ability of the individual employee. In an innovative climate, employees who have the skills to produce in an unstructured setting will be more productive than those of lesser ability. Another factor is the employee's personality. Those with a high need for order perform better in a highly structured climate, while those with a high need for autonomy perform better in an environment in which decision making is decentralized.

MANAGEMENT'S ROLE IN CHANGING CLIMATE

While organizational climates tend to be stable over time, they can be changed. The key, first of all, is to determine what problems, if any, exist within the organization and then to apply appropriate plans of action to correct them.

Determining the Problem

A picture of the hotel or restaurant's climate can be gained through either formal or informal means. A variety of instruments are available to measure climate in a variety of dimensions. The number of items in a questionnaire can vary from a low of 1 to a high of 254. Most questionnaires consist of between 20 and 80 items. A case study at the end of this chapter uses 36 items.

These questionnaires generally can be used in any type of business or organization, with the questions personalized to make them more relevant to the employees filling them out.

The number of categories used in surveys can also vary. Previously used surveys have been characterized by a common core of dimensions: autonomy, structure, reward, consideration, warmth, and support. Beyond this core, considerable diversity can take place. This chapter suggests the six dimensions of clarity, commitment, standards, responsibility, recognition, and teamwork. Larry E. Greiner and Robert O. Metzger suggest the following categories are appropriate:

Immediate supervision: effectiveness of the relationship between employees and their immediate supervisors

Innovation: flexibility and creativity in the organization

Personal growth and advancement: opportunities to develop within the organization

Recognition: extent to which employees feel they are rewarded for good work

Teamwork: cohesiveness and intradepartmental loyalty and cooperation

Organizational clarity: understanding of the organization's goals and employees' expectations

Responsibility: extent to which employees feel they are delegated appropriate amounts of responsibility and authority

Decision making: employees' active voice in organizational or departmental decisions

Performance standards: employee and organizational concern for high performance standards

Organizational vitality: extent to which the organization is dynamic, venturesome, innovative, and responsive

Communication: effectiveness of dissemination of information about operations and activities within the organization.[2]

When Holiday Inns developed its own survey internally, the following categories within dimensions were used:

Employee and the job: skill utilization, job satisfaction, and working conditions

Supervision: support, two-way communication, and performance planning

Rewarding performance: compensation, benefits, and employee development

Management and the employee: senior management, middle management, and organizational commitment

Mutual support: work group, between groups, and communication in general

An organization consists of tasks, structure, people, and technology. In general, climate questionnaires show a strong emphasis on people, moderate emphasis on structure, moderate to slight emphasis on tasks, and slight or no emphasis on technology. This emphasis on people-oriented questions may be due to a combination of two reasons. First, climate is related strongly to job satisfaction. Second, most of these questionnaires have been developed by professionals with a strong background in psychology, and naturally they are more interested in the human side of the organization.

While the survey method is an exact and relatively inexpensive way of measuring climate, other informal methods of gauging employee feelings are available. During regular employee meetings, the same themes may keep coming up, indicating problems in one or more areas. On regular tours of the property, managers may be able to identify employee concern over some topics. It should be pointed out that employees may be fearful or otherwise unwilling to share their feelings in open meetings or even face-to-face sessions with the manager if a feeling of trust is not felt. One of the strong features of a survey program is that individual anonymity is assured. The result should be a true representation of the organization's climate.

Patterns of Climate

Four patterns of climate frequently emerge. These are *structural, motivational, reinforcement,* and *clarity-teamwork.*[3]

A structural climate is one that has very high scores on clarity and standards while exhibiting relatively low scores on the other four dimensions described above. Clear and specific procedures have been established for each job. The manager has developed a strong system of management information and control. However, this person also may tend to spend an undue amount of time in the office, and individual responsibility and commitment to goal achievement may be lacking. Nevertheless, this type of climate has been found in high-performing companies. As long as none of the scores is particularly low, this would be considered a good climate.

In the motivational climate, scores on responsibility and commitment are very high while scores on the other four dimensions—clarity, standards, recognition, and teamwork—are moderate. Management has hired and encouraged employees with strong feelings of personal responsibility for individual performance. A difficulty arises if this is not matched by an emphasis on performance control and teamwork.

Teamwork and recognition are the strongest dimensions in the reinforcement climate. Typically, this profile would not be found in a high-performing organization unless there was also a high score in at least one other dimension. For example, it may be that reinforcement is given for any type of performance and that teamwork is emphasized at the expense of getting the job done properly.

In the clarity-teamwork climate, the organization functions because employees know clearly what they are supposed to do and feel a shared sense of identity in performing the job. While some stability exists, such organizations do not tend to perform at a high level. Morale is usually low and the company can experience a great deal of turnover.

Is There a Best Climate?

The best climate is the one that works. Just as management practices influence the type of climate within a company, so the climate affects employee motivation. The best climate, then, is the one that stimulates the appropriate motivation desired. David McClelland of Harvard developed a three-pronged theory of motivation; he called the social motives the *need for achievement,* the *need for affiliation,* and the *need for power.* He saw individual motivation coming from the pursuit of one of these three social motives.

The need for achievement is the need to excel in a particular task. Individuals high in this need stress outperforming others, meeting or surpassing a self-imposed standard of excellence, having unique accomplishments, taking a long-term, advanced view toward advancing the business, and having plans to overcome personal and environmental obstacles. As depicted in figure 6–2, commitment and responsibility are strong stimulants of achievement motivation.

The need for affiliation exists when a person shows concern about establishing, maintaining, or restoring positive relationships with other people. Such people want to be liked and accepted, are concerned about people both in and out of work, and desire to maintain positive interpersonal relationships on the job. Recognition and teamwork are strong stimulants of affiliation motivation.

The need for power is manifested by a desire to influence others. This person is characterized by powerful actions that arouse strong positive or negative feelings in others and a concern for reputation or position. Standards and clarity are strong stimulants of power motivation.

In a hotel or restaurant setting, in which departments must work closely together to ensure guest satisfaction, a climate that encourages affiliation or group motivation would tend to encourage high performance rather than one that encourages individual motivation.

FIGURE 6–2 HOW CLIMATE AFFECTS MOTIVATION.

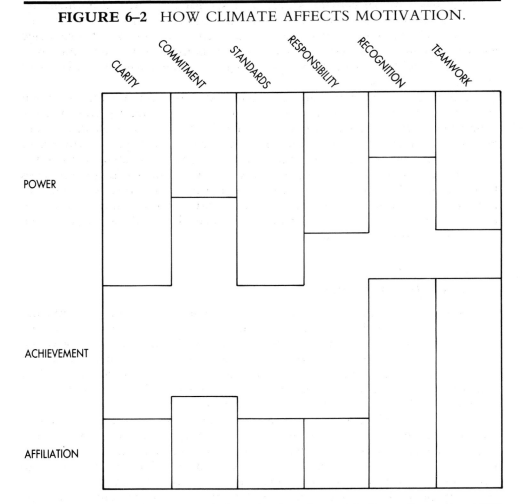

(*Source: The Language of Organizational Climate,* handout, Boston, The Forum Corporation, 1979.)

Plans of Action

Try this test: An elevator door opens at the fifth floor. The elevator is empty. Four people get in and the elevator descends to the fourth floor, where two people get out and three get in. At the third floor, four get out and one gets in. At the second floor, no one gets out and three get in. At the first floor, the door opens. Now quick: what's the answer?

Most people say the answer is five. But a few ask, "What's the question?" The point is that it is necessary to identify the problem before recommending a solution. In the case of organizational climate, we assume that a company

FIGURE 6–3 ORGANIZATIONAL CLIMATE AND MANAGEMENT ACTION.

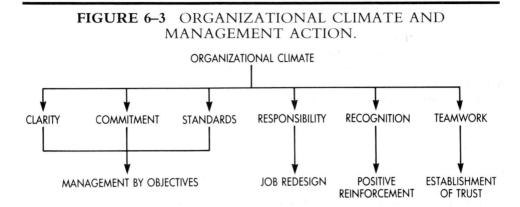

wishes to have a reasonably high level in all of the six dimensions described above. Improving different dimensions of climate requires different techniques (fig. 6–3).

Where standards, clarity, or commitment is low, a program of management by objectives is suggested. Management by objectives is concerned with developing goal commitment among employees by involving them in the setting of the standards.

Where responsibility is low, a program of job redesign is called for. Job enlargement consists of giving the employee different tasks to do as part of the job. Job enrichment involves passing on some of the traditional functions of management to the employee.

When recognition is lacking, management should implement a program of positive reinforcement. Positive reinforcement means giving employees rewards and encouragement when they do something right.

When teamwork is lacking, management must take responsibility for establishing trust between management and employees and among groups of employees.

The following chapters will expand upon the implementation of these techniques.

SUMMARY

Managers cannot directly motivate employees, because motivation must come from within the individual. However, managers can establish a climate within the organization that in turn can produce the conditions to encourage the development of motivated and productive employees.

Climate can be described in terms of six dimensions: clarity, commitment, standards, responsibility, recognition, and teamwork. By measuring the level of these six dimensions, managers can determine what problems, if any, exist within the company and can take appropriate action.

Problems in the areas of clarity, commitment, or standards suggest the need for a program of management by objectives. Low scores on responsibility point the way for job redesign. When recognition is perceived as being low, positive reinforcement may be necessary. When teamwork is lacking, management must establish an atmosphere of trust.

NOTES

[1]Litwin, George H., and Robert A. Stringer, Jr., *Motivation and Organizational Climate,* Cambridge, Mass., Harvard University Press, 1968.
[2]Greiner, Larry E., and Robert O. Metzger, *Consulting to Management,* Englewood Cliffs, N.J., Prentice-Hall, 1982, 213.
[3]*The Language of Organizational Climate,* handout, Boston, The Forum Corporation, 1979.

SUGGESTED READINGS

Field, R. H. George, and Michael A. Abelson, "Climate: A Reconceptualization and Proposed Model," *Human Relations* 35, no. 3, 1982, 181–201.
The Forum Corporation, *The Manager and Motivation,* unpublished monograph, 1977.
————, *The Language of Organizational Climate,* unpublished monograph, 1979.
Friedlander, Frank, and Newton Margulies, "Multiple Impacts of Organizational Climate and Individual Value Systems upon Job Satisfaction," *Personnel Psychology* 22, 1969, 171–83.
Garin, Robert H., and John F. Cooper, "The Morale-Productivity Relationship: How Close?" *Personnel,* January–February, 1981, 57–62.
Hellriegel, Don, and John W. Slocum, Jr., "Organizational Climate: Measures, Research and Contingencies," *Academy of Management Journal* 17, no. 2, 1974, 255–80.
Holiday Inns Inc., Organizational Climate Survey, Memphis, Tennessee, 1984.
Joyce, William F., and John W. Slocum, Jr., "Climates in Organizations," in *Organizational Behavior,* S. Kerr (ed.), Columbus, Ohio, Grid Publishing, 1979, 317–33.
Payne, R. L., and D. C. Pheysey, "G. G. Stearn's Organizational Climate Index: A Reconceptualization and Application to Business Organizations," *Organizational Behavior and Human Performance* 6, 1971, 77–98.

APPENDIX: IMPLEMENTING ORGANIZATIONAL CLIMATE— A CASE STUDY

The organizational climate study is a management tool that can increase employees' involvement in their jobs while fostering open, two-way communications. Both results can lead to increased customer satisfaction, repeat business, and bottom-line profits.

Using this tool, you can influence your work group's climate and ultimately that of the entire property. By acting on the results, you will boost the productivity of your work group while increasing its confidence in you and in its ability to get the job done.

There are no easy or instant answers. However, you will have a method for identifying both the strength of your work group and those areas that interfere with its performance. The success of this program depends on your commitment to follow through with action as a result of the survey.

Organizational climate is how your employees perceive the people and things that influence their work. It consists of how they view:

Clarity: To what extent do employees understand what is expected of them?

Commitment: To what extent do employees accept the goals of the company and department?

Standards: To what extent do employees believe that tough, challenging goals are set by management?

Responsibility: To what extent are employees allowed to use their own initiative?

Recognition: To what extent do rewards and recognition outweigh threats and punishment?

Teamwork: To what extent do people trust and respect each other?

The way employees view these items will affect their behavior on the job. If you know what employees think and feel about what it is like to work in your property, you can begin to reinforce the things that help them work better and remove the things that get in the way of providing good customer service.

The climate will vary from department to department, because each group is affected by the different jobs those employees do, the conditions under which

The author is indebted to the Holiday Corporation for the use of the guidebooks from its organization climate survey. This case draws heavily from the process identified therein.

they work, and the style of their department managers. There is an overall property climate, however, that represents the combined views of the employees.

THE SURVEY PROCESS

The five steps in the organizational climate survey are:

1. Employees fill out surveys.
2. Managers fill out surveys.
3. An independent data-processing firm analyzes the responses.
4. Department heads review problems identified by the surveys and meet with their employees to review and discuss feedback, analyze problems, identify issues, and develop action plans that will resolve them.
5. Department heads meet with their supervisors to report progress toward dealing with the issues identified.

PRE-SURVEY COMMUNICATION

The department heads whose staffs are to be surveyed need to understand the reasons the property has been chosen for the survey and an overview of the process. The reasons for surveying, along with expectations and goals of the process, are best explained by the general manager. This should be accomplished as part of a regular staff meeting.

Once department heads understand the survey process and its benefits, they will need to communicate that information to their employees in a staff meeting. In communicating the process, several key points should be stressed:

Completed surveys will be kept confidential. Employees will not sign the surveys and will not be identified by their individual responses.

General managers and department heads will receive the employees' surveys in feedback packages. Survey results will be discussed with employees for objective setting and action planning.

General managers and department heads will receive a feedback package only if they have five or more direct reports. To protect the employees' anonymity, survey results from any group of less than five people will be combined with results from another appropriate group or groups reporting to the same manager.

General managers and department heads will be the first ones to receive a feedback package including their own employees' results.

An independent data-processing firm will tabulate survey results and prepare feedback packages. Completed survey forms will be destroyed after results have been tabulated. The data-processing firm will also use computer programs that protect employees' anonymity.

Setting the Date

When planning the climate survey, consider the following before selecting survey dates:

- Schedule around heavy business periods
- Avoid scheduling during the budgeting process
- Avoid scheduling during staffing changes
- Allow at least fourteen days' lead time

One week is usually an adequate amount of time to allow for administering the survey at your property. Remember that you are checking the climate of your property at a particular moment in time. To be effective, the survey should not be extended over a period of more than two weeks.

Once you have established the days on which the survey will be administered, schedule a meeting with the supervisors to plan for the survey of each of their employees.

THE SURVEY: EMPLOYEES

This survey is designed to get your ideas on what it is like to work at this property. It is not a test; there are no right or wrong answers. The best answer is *always* just what you think. The purpose of the survey is to measure employee attitudes and opinions, and the work climate of this property. You should respond to each statement as honestly as you can so your answers, along with those of other employees, will provide a measure of what it is like to work at your property.

Your answers are completely confidential. No one at this property will see your filled-in survey. To be sure that your answers will not be identified, please do not write your name on the form.

Definitions:

    SD: Strongly disagree
     D: Disagree
     A: Agree
    SA: Strongly agree

		SD	D	A	SA
1.	I have a clear idea of what I am supposed to do.	1	2	3	4
2.	I really care about what happens to this company.	1	2	3	4
3.	The company sets very high standards of performance.	1	2	3	4

		SD	D	A	SA
4.	Everything I do is checked by my boss.	4	3	2	1
5.	If you make a mistake around here you will definitely be criticized.	4	3	2	1
6.	There is a warm feeling between management and employees.	1	2	3	4
7.	Things are pretty organized around here.	1	2	3	4
8.	The things that I do are really important to the success of this company.	1	2	3	4
9.	I feel continually pressured to improve my performance.	1	2	3	4
10.	I am encouraged to take on additional responsibility.	1	2	3	4
11.	We have a promotion system that helps the best person rise to the top.	1	2	3	4
12.	I can count on support from my boss when things get tough.	1	2	3	4
13.	I understand the objectives of this company.	1	2	3	4
14.	My boss and I agree on what good performance means.	1	2	3	4
15.	The standards around here mean that I must expend maximum effort in my job.	1	2	3	4
16.	If I stick my neck out, I will be rewarded for it.	1	2	3	4
17.	We are rewarded in proportion to how well we perform.	1	2	3	4
18.	I trust management.	1	2	3	4
19.	I understand the policies of this company.	1	2	3	4
20.	What they expect me to do is fair.	1	2	3	4
21.	There are people in my work group who don't have enough to do.	4	3	2	1
22.	Management trusts my individual judgment.	1	2	3	4
23.	Good performance is recognized pretty quickly around here.	1	2	3	4
24.	The people in my work group perform as a team.	1	2	3	4
25.	When I am given a job, it is thoroughly explained to me.	1	2	3	4
26.	I have a say about decisions that affect my job.	1	2	3	4
27.	Management sets challenging goals.	1	2	3	4
28.	I can start projects I think are important.	1	2	3	4

		SD	D	A	SA
29.	There is not enough reward in this company for doing good work.	4	3	2	1
30.	I would encourage my friends to get a job here.	1	2	3	4
31.	Lack of organization and planning sometimes reduces our productivity.	4	3	2	1
32.	My boss gives me information about my performance that helps me do a better job.	1	2	3	4
33.	Management doesn't push me much to improve my performance.	4	3	2	1
34.	I am encouraged to solve problems for myself.	1	2	3	4
35.	There is a great deal of criticism in this company.	4	3	2	1
36.	I feel a great deal of loyalty to this company.	1	2	3	4

Scoring

Questions 1, 7, 13, 19, 25, and 31 are concerned with clarity; 2, 8, 14, 20, 26, and 32 deal with commitment; 3, 9, 15, 21, 27, and 33 cover standards; 4, 10, 16, 22, 28, and 34 are about the level of responsibility; recognition is covered by questions 5, 11, 17, 23, 29, and 35; and teamwork is dealt with in questions 6, 12, 18, 24, 30, and 36.

Score the responses and add up the tallies. On each scale there is a maximum score of twenty-four and a minimum score of six.

THE SURVEY: MANAGEMENT

This survey, to be completed by each department manager, will help you determine the type of organizational climate that your work group needs to maximize productivity and customer service.

Your responses should reflect the type of climate that your group needs, not the type of climate that currently exists in your work group.

You will receive feedback comparing your responses to these questions (your definition of desired climate) with a summary of the responses of your work group (the actual climate, as perceived by them). This will enable you to compare what you want with what your employees perceive you have.

The results are for your use only. The more candidly you can answer these questions, the more valuable the results will be.

DA: Definitely agree
A: Agree
D: Disagree
DD: Definitely disagree

		DA	A	D	DD
1.	It is important that employees have a clear idea of what they are supposed to do.	4	3	2	1
2.	Employees should really care about what happens to this company.	4	3	2	1
3.	The company should set very high standards of performance.	4	3	2	1
4.	I should check everything my employees do.	1	2	3	4
5.	Employees ought to be criticized if they make a mistake.	1	2	3	4
6.	A warm feeling should exist between management and employees.	4	3	2	1
7.	Things should be pretty organized around here.	4	3	2	1
8.	It is important that employees feel what they do is important to the success of the company.	4	3	2	1
9.	Employees should feel continually pressured to improve their performance.	4	3	2	1
10.	I should encourage employees to take on increased responsibility.	4	3	2	1
11.	We ought to have a promotion system that helps the best person rise to the top.	4	3	2	1
12.	I should give support to my employees when things get tough.	4	3	2	1
13.	Employees should understand the objectives of the company.	4	3	2	1
14.	It is important that my employees and I agree on what good performance means.	4	3	2	1
15.	Standards should be set that are so high that employees should expend maximum effort to reach them.	4	3	2	1
16.	Employees should be rewarded for sticking their necks out.	4	3	2	1
17.	Employees ought to be rewarded in proportion to how well they do.	4	3	2	1
18.	Employees should trust management.	4	3	2	1
19.	Employees should understand the policies of the company.	4	3	2	1
20.	Employees should feel that what is expected of them is fair.	4	3	2	1
21.	There should be people in the work group who do not have enough to do.	1	2	3	4

		DA	A	D	DD
22.	It is important that I trust the individual judgment of employees.	4	3	2	1
23.	I should recognize good performance pretty quickly.	4	3	2	1
24.	My employees should perform as a team.	4	3	2	1
25.	Employees ought to have jobs thoroughly explained to them.	4	3	2	1
26.	Employees should have a say about decisions that affect their jobs.	4	3	2	1
27.	It is important that management sets challenging goals.	4	3	2	1
28.	Employees should be able to start projects they think are important.	4	3	2	1
29.	Employees should be rewarded for doing good work.	1	2	3	4
30.	Employees should want to encourage their friends to get a job here.	4	3	2	1
31.	Things should be well planned and organized.	1	2	3	4
32.	I ought to give my employees information about their performance.	4	3	2	1
33.	I should push my employees to do a better job.	1	2	3	4
34.	I should encourage my employees to think for themselves.	4	3	2	1
35.	I should criticize my employees when they do something wrong.	1	2	3	4
36.	It is important that employees feel a great deal of loyalty to this organization.	4	3	2	1

Scoring

Questions 1, 7, 13, 19, 25, and 31 are concerned with clarity; 2, 8, 14, 20, 26, and 32 deal with commitment; 3, 9, 15, 21, 27, and 33 cover standards; 4, 10, 16, 22, 28, and 34 are about the level of responsibility; recognition is covered by questions 5, 11, 17, 23, 29, and 35; and teamwork is dealt with in questions 6, 12, 18, 24, 30, and 36.

Score the responses and add up the tallies. On each scale there is a maximum score of twenty-four and a minimum score of six.

SURVEY RESULTS

Completed surveys are mailed to an independent data-processing firm for tabulation and analysis. After the data has been analyzed, the survey forms will be destroyed. By using a data processor outside the company, survey participants will feel more comfortable in filling out the forms.

Based on the employee responses, managers are given a feedback package by work group. Responses are grouped in combinations of five or more so that managers are unable to identify individual answers. If fewer than five people are supervised, responses are combined with those from a related area. Examples might be:

- Primary contact employees: guest service, banquets and catering, front office, restaurant and lounge
- Secondary contact employees: housekeeping, kitchen, accounting, personnel

Department heads will receive a climate profile illustrating the relative climate perceived by their employees, compared to the property's overall climate. They also will be able to compare their employees' perceptions of what exists with their own perceptions of what should exist. In this way, problems within each individual department are highlighted against the backdrop of how one department is perceived compared to the property as a whole.

INTERPRETING RESULTS: AN EXAMPLE

The graph presented in figure 6–4 can be used as a guide to interpreting the results. The average scores for the various dimensions are as follows:

DIMENSION:	A	B	C
Clarity	20	22	16
Commitment	18	19	18
Standards	22	18	19
Responsibility	10	6	14
Recognition	17	22	23
Teamwork	23	22	23

A represents the collective climate within the property, as perceived by the employees.
B represents the desires of the manager in a specific department.
C represents the climate as perceived by that department's employees.

Several differences exist between what the department manager wants and what the employees feel. It appears that although there is relative agreement on standards, commitment, recognition, and teamwork, there are problems with clarity and responsibility.

Closer examination of the questions relating to these activities reveals specific problems. The percentages of employees who disagreed or strongly disagreed to the questions on clarity were:

FIGURE 6–4 ORGANIZATIONAL CLIMATE: AN EXAMPLE.

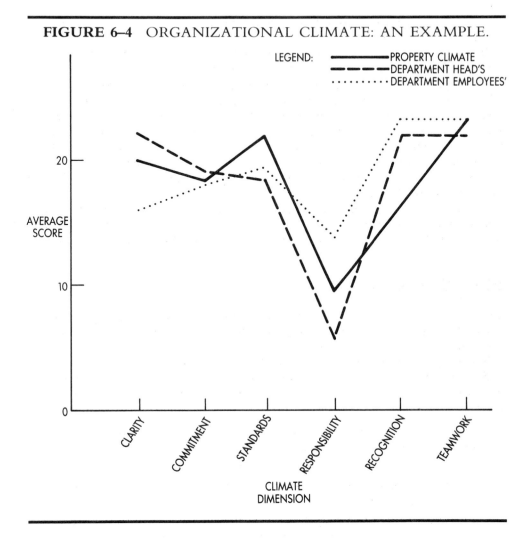

1. I have a clear idea of what I am supposed to do: 70 percent
7. Things are pretty organized around here: 50 percent
13. I understand the objectives of this company: 40 percent
19. I understand the policies of this company: 30 percent
25. When I am given a job, it is thoroughly explained to me: 80 percent
31. Lack of organization and planning sometimes reduces our productivity: 75 percent

While there is a danger in assuming that these questions represent everything related to the clarity of the job, they are a reasonable starting point for departmental meetings and discussions.

A similar analysis of questions would be performed for the section on recognition.

It would appear that this manager would have to work on installing management by objectives and job redesign to reduce these problems.

The figures also show how this particular department compares to the property climate as a whole. The employees' perceptions of clarity, standards, and responsibility are all seen as being less than that of the property as a whole, while recognition is higher in this department. It can be interpreted that although this department head and the department's employees have similar perceptions about the correct level of standards, for example, they are seen as being lower compared to the entire operation. This department head should increase his or her perception of what is required in this area.

Clarity and responsibility are seen as problems not only within the department, but relative to the operation as a whole. On the brighter side, this department head seems to give more positive recognition than other supervisors do.

FEEDBACK MEETING

The survey highlights areas that affect how well the work group is performing. This allows managers to focus on issues for later concentration. This is best done in a feedback meeting with employees.

The purpose of such a meeting is to share survey results with the employees, and to use this information to identify issues that the work group needs and wants to resolve. There are several useful guidelines for conducting such a meeting:

Prepare for it. Familiarize yourself with the feedback results and note any you find surprising.

Begin the meeting by stating its purpose.

Illustrate results clearly for employees. Make copies or use overhead transparencies.

Encourage employees to ask questions and make comments. Listen for their comments and ideas before offering yours.

Ask questions only to clarify results or to help explain surprising results. Do not discuss causes or solutions at this meeting.

Conclude the meeting with information on the items needing improvement. Ask employees to prepare to discuss causes and solutions at subsequent meetings. Schedule the next meeting for a week later.

Recap the meeting, covering both the strengths and the areas needing improvement. Thank the employees for their ideas. Positively discuss your next steps.

Both you and your employees are likely to experience a wide variety of emotions to a feedback meeting, including anxiety, because you and they do not know what to expect, and defensiveness, if it is felt that the purpose is to reveal negative information about you or them. You can influence the reactions of your employees in several ways:

Talk about situations and behavior, not personalities.

Be positive about survey results; view the results as information that will help the group work better.

Encourage people to make comments and ask questions.

Be realistic; do not make promises that cannot be kept. These results can help solve some, but not all, issues.

7 | IMPROVING PRODUCTIVITY: MANAGEMENT BY OBJECTIVES

DEFINING MBO

The first time the term *management by objectives* was widely used was in Peter Drucker's book *The Practice of Management* in 1954. Since then, many companies have attempted to implement such a concept. There have been proponents and critics of the idea that such a program can improve operations.

Management by objectives can be defined as a managerial process in which managers and employees join in pursuit of specific, mutually agreed on goals of limited duration, through a plan of action that is monitored in appraisal sessions following mutually determined standards of performance.[1]

The Process

It is clear that there are several steps involved in this process. First, at each level within the organization, manager and subordinate agree on company and personal objectives for the subordinate for a specified period of time, usually a year. These objectives should be specific, defined in measurable terms, linked to the goals of the company, reviewed periodically, quantifiable, and changeable as conditions warrant. Experts are divided on whether weights should be assigned to the various objectives; doing this can provide a valuable guide to how an employee should spend his or her time.

Next, the subordinate prepares a plan of action, which the manager may review. At the end of the set time period, both manager and subordinate review the progress made toward achieving the objectives. This is the formal appraisal session, though periodic reviews during the year are desirable. The cycle is then repeated.

Does It Work?

A review of the literature indicates support, though not conclusive proof, for the effectiveness of MBO. It appears from past efforts that the less sophisticated the research approach, the more likely the study is to show MBO is effective. It seems to be more effective in the short term (less than two years) than over

138

a longer period, although most experts agree it takes two to five years to implement it fully in an organization. It must be noted, however, that the longest study available was only over a three-year period. Neither is it clear to what extent a lack of long-term results came from reduced commitment once the initial excitement of the program wore off. MBO also seems to be more effective in the private sector than the public sector and in organizations removed from direct contact with the customer. Yet, while there are studies of its effectiveness in hospital settings, there are no studies of its results in the hospitality industry.

There does seem to be general agreement that setting goals improves performance. It may be, then, that the failure to prove MBO is successful comes from poor implementation of the concept rather than from the concept itself. Properly implemented, it can reduce the ambiguity employees may feel toward what is expected of them, promote communication between superior and subordinate, and focus efforts toward the goals considered important in the company.

On the negative side, MBO can attempt to overquantify job objectives and ignore other important aspects that may be difficult to measure objectively, such as discretion and judgment. By emphasizing results over behavior, it can lead employees to meet individual objectives through behavior that may be negative. A waiter, for example, may seek to meet the objective of wine sales by using high-pressure sales techniques that offend customers. There is also the chance that employees may ignore areas for which objectives have not been set.

USING THE CONCEPT

A program of management by objectives is most appropriate when there are problems with clarity, commitment, or standards. Clarity indicates how well employees understand the company's goals and policies and feel that things are organized and run smoothly, not confused. The extent to which this is a problem can be seen by asking: Do employees understand what is expected of them? Is there evidence of activity that is planned and organized? Is there a smooth flow of information?

Commitment indicates how strongly employees feel about achieving company goals. To what extent do they accept these goals, see them as realistic, get involved in setting them, and have their performance evaluated against them? Questions to ask include: Are there regular goal-setting and review meetings? Are goals meaningful and realistic? Is there a personal commitment to achieving company goals?

Standards indicates the emphasis that management puts on a high quality of performance. How much pressure exists to improve performance? Suitable questions would be: Is there evidence of pressure to improve performance? Do employees feel pride in doing a good job? Does management set tough, challenging goals?

If the answer to these types of questions is no, a program of management by objectives would seem called for. For such a program to work, its motivational assumption must be understood. MBO assumes that people will work toward objectives to which they are committed, which results from involving employees in the process.

Setting the Goals

Numerous studies have shown the importance of setting a goal. We all like to have something to strive for. Performance is directly related to the goal. In order to work, goals must be SMART: Specific, Measurable, Achievable, Realistic, and Time-bound.

A goal that is specific gives something definite to shoot for. "Let's sell more wine" is not as effective as "Let's sell twenty bottles of wine this week." A goal must be measurable so employees can know if and when the goal is reached. We all like to keep score. If employees feel that goals are not achievable or realistic, they will not even try to meet them. It has been shown that challenging goals of a specific duration lead to better performance than easy ones. Even more important, however, is that a goal be set, rather than no goal at all or the vague "Do your best."

There are mixed opinions about whether individual or group goals should be set. It could be argued that group goals encourage cooperation and team spirit. Others feel individual goals better promote individual responsibility and make it easier to appraise individual performance. The key is the extent to which the task to be accomplished requires the cooperation of others. The more the job requires interdependence, the greater is the argument for group goals. Selling banquet space to businesses or increasing wine sales in the restaurant, for example, should be individualized. Getting the food for that banquet out of the kitchen within a certain amount of time should be a group effort.

Goals can be set in several different ways. Frederick W. Taylor's scientific management approach used time and motion studies to determine how much should be done within a given period. This method of goal setting is appropriate for tasks that are repetitive and standardized—such as the number of potatoes that can be peeled in an hour. There is, however, the difficulty of employee resistance when new standards are set that are considerably higher than previous ones or there are frequent changes in what is expected.

Second, goals can be set based on the average past performance of employees. While this method is less scientific, most employees readily accept it as fair. Difficulties arise when past performance is below what management feels should be accomplished. Goals may be set that are easily accomplished with less than maximum effort.

Third, goals can be set jointly between supervisor and employee. A fair amount of research indicates that the importance of participative rather than assigned goals is that the former leads to the setting of higher goals and, in turn, to higher performance. In particular, some studies indicate participative goal setting has produced higher goals among minorities and the less educated. These results were counter to what researchers expected. In other situations, however, it was found that specific and challenging goals produced better results than vague, easy ones, whether they were assigned or came through joint participation.

External events often influence the setting of goals. A health inspection the following week determines what has to be done to pass muster. Competitive price cuts may dictate company objectives. The problem at this point may not be the goal so much, but rather how to reach it within a certain time limit.

Last, goals set by upper management will influence goals set at lower levels. If upper management wants a 10 percent increase in sales for the next year, then the objectives of the various units or departments must be oriented to setting their own objectives to ensure that the 10 percent increase is gained.

Communicating Company Goals

Typically, management in the hospitality industry has done a very poor job of communicating the goals that are important to the organization.

A national study of foodservice supervisors identified some good news and bad news about communication between manager and supervisor.[2] The good news was that formal communication, not the grapevine, was the major source of information for the supervisor. Twenty-nine percent of foodservice supervisors (compared to 17 percent of first-level supervisors from all industries) identified formal communication as their main source of information, while 17 percent identified the grapevine as their major source (compared to 29 percent of all supervisors). The bad news is that only 44 percent of foodservice supervisors, compared to 55 percent of all supervisors, got most of their information from their boss. Clearly, managers are missing an opportunity to take more control over the amount and type of information given their supervisors.

The manager or supervisor is the key link between the company and the employee. The objective of the company is to maximize productivity; the employee is increasingly seeking satisfaction from the job. How are these brought together? To increase productivity, the company must determine the key areas of results that should be emphasized; what employee behavior is necessary in those key areas; whether employee performance matches the behavioral objectives set; and how to communicate to employees the results of their efforts, following up with praise, coaching, or remedial actions.

At the same time, the employee has several questions: What is really expected of me? How far am I expected to go? How good is good? How am I doing?

Recent studies have indicated that there is less than total agreement on what the content of an employee's job is. Interviews with manager-employee pairs discovered approximately 75 percent agreement regarding the content of an employee's job. In other words, 25 percent of the time the employee is spending time and effort on areas that are not important at all. Equally, 25 percent of the job is important to the manager but not receiving the employee's attention. It seems that the best performance and highest degree of goal attainment exist when there is agreement between manager and employee as to the content of the employee's job. One way of working this out is by identifying areas of disagreement. This can be done through a manager's letter to the employee, outlining the job responsibilities of both. Employees cannot fully understand their own job until they understand their supervisor's.

Dimensions of Service

William Martin has suggested sixteen important results areas for high-quality food and beverage service, divided into procedural and convivial dimensions of service.[3]

The *procedural dimension* refers to the technical systems involved in getting products and services to customers. This dimension consists of seven facets:

1. Flow of service: This ensures that at any one time, no part of the service system is overextended, by spreading the load among server sections, among stations in the kitchen, and between the bar and the dining room.
2. Timeliness: This means providing service when the customer wants it.
3. Accommodation: This involves designing procedures to accommodate the customer's needs and wants rather than the operation's. A refusal to give separate checks, for example, is meant for the benefit of the operation, not the customer—even though research has demonstrated that when a large party pays by separate checks, the tips are larger than when the checks are combined into one.
4. Anticipation: This means providing services before the customer asks for them. This may involve extra napkins for messy foods, high chairs for little children, or two forks for a couple wishing to share a romantic dessert.
5. Communication: This ensures that messages among customers, employees, and management are communicated effectively. This may encompass the server's getting the customer's order right as well as the cook's being able to read the server's written order.
6. Customer feedback: This means finding out from the customer whether the service has met expectations.
7. Supervision: This element ensures the effective coordination of the above points.

The *convivial dimension* refers to the server's ability to relate to customers as people instead of just covers. It consists of nine aspects, according to Martin.

1. Attitude: the way a server communicates feelings through both behavior and words
2. Body language: the nonverbal actions that communicate as much as two-thirds of the message intended
3. Tone of voice: the way in which the words come out
4. Tact: knowing what to say at the right time
5. Naming names: an excellent way of letting guests know that the server is communicating with them as people, but rarely done, even

when customers give their name while making a reservation, writing a check, or paying by credit card
6. Attentiveness: being tuned in to the needs of the customer—and demonstrating it
7. Guidance: providing helpful suggestions to customers who need them
8. Suggestive selling: describing food and beverages in ways designed to enhance their appeal, thereby increasing their sales
9. Problem solving: letting guests know their complaints are welcome, will be properly received, and will be handled effectively

Obtaining Goal Commitment

Management's responsibility is to determine the areas considered vital for the proper operation of the business and to communicate these areas to employees. Behavioral objectives must now be set to put these sixteen points into operation. The company's responsibility is to let employees know what behavior is expected of them in order to meet the service goals.

The employee wants to know, "What is really expected of me?" and "How good is good?" How best to obtain employee commitment must be considered.

Generally, employees resist making commitments to goals for two reasons: they do not feel that they are capable of reaching a goal because they lack confidence, ability, or knowledge or because they see no personal benefit or gain in terms of money, promotion, recognition, or personal pride.

There are various ways to overcome these obstacles. The manager is responsible for communicating to employees just how their objectives and the operation's mesh. This means more than saying, "Work—or be fired." It means demonstrating that when the company wins, the employees win; when more customers are served, there is more work, better shifts, and bigger tips. It also means providing a supportive atmosphere. Support can be given in the form of training to give employees the skills and knowledge necessary to reach the company objectives. Support is also shown by involving employees in the setting of behavioral objectives to reach company goals.

Participation in setting objectives has been shown to be particularly effective in obtaining commitment from less educated and minority employees. This may be true because it gives employees a feeling of control over the process that they might not ordinarily have had in their lives. There are those who fear that allowing employees to participate will result in objectives that are far less than what management desires. There is evidence, in fact, that when employees are allowed to participate in the setting of objectives, the standards set are higher than they would have been if management alone set them.

Steak and Ale officials recently concluded from a study of its operations that commitment is highest when:

- Decisions are made as far down the company ranks as possible.
- People are told the whys and hows of change.
- People are informed about how well the company is performing.
- Employee input is sought.

- Employees' individuality is respected.
- The focus of leadership styles is on helping people perform.

Although employees may be able to assist in determining key areas of service such as Martin described, management probably will have to take prime responsibility for this. However, employees can be heavily involved in helping set objectives for those key areas. This involvement gets to the nub of what management by objectives is all about. Douglas McGregor, known for the concept of *theory X* and *theory Y* managers, emphasized that the aim of MBO should be to achieve management by integration and self-control. It should not be used as another method of directing and controlling employees; rather, it should be a strategy for managing people in a way that helps employees see how their objectives mesh with those of management, so that ultimately the employees take more responsibility for controlling their actions as they move toward achieving company goals.

As an example, let us consider one of the key areas mentioned above. Suggestive selling was identified as one of the convivial dimensions of service. Objectives could be set in one of two ways. The manager could come in one morning and announce to the servers, "I want you to concentrate on selling rather than on just taking orders. From this day on, I expect you all to sell ten bottles of wine and twenty appetizers a week." Will servers get involved? It may be that some will see this as an opportunity to please the manager. Perhaps some who fear they will lose their jobs if they do not achieve these objectives will push wine and appetizers. It is unlikely, however, that all the servers will get involved. The objectives are the manager's, not the employees'. Employee acceptance of and commitment to these standards is liable to be low.

On the other hand, the manager could hold a staff meeting to announce the importance of suggestive selling, pointing out how selling more affects the servers. Ideas then could be solicited from the employees about how to measure who was actually putting this into practice. The manager's role is to ensure that the group comes up with objectives that are in fact measurable and acceptable to the company. One measurable way to identify suggestive selling would be to have at least one additional item—appetizer, dessert, or after-dinner drink—sold with each entrée ordered. By involving employees in setting objectives, the goals are more readily accepted because the employees have partial ownership over them. Because they are "our" goals, employees are more committed to achieving them. They do, however, take longer to set this way. Rather than announcing objectives to employees—a process that might take two minutes—it may take a half hour for servers to agree on objectives in one area alone. The commitment gained, however, compensates for the extra time spent.

The Hospitality Clinic

Employees may be reluctant to make suggestions or may lack, or feel they lack, the experience to add ideas. One tool to get discussions started is the hospitality clinic. Employees are given a form that identifies various aspects of the meal experience and asked to fill it out from the perspective of a customer the next time they eat out. The results of their experiences form the basis for discussion at the next staff meeting. By looking at other operations, they view the service with a critical eye and in a way that is not threatening to them. Instead of the manager's stressing the importance of not keeping customers waiting and saying that things must be improved, it is employees who identify how long they were kept waiting when they went out to dine, note how they felt as customers, and agree on the importance of these factors. A hospitality clinic form might look at the following:

Waiting time: How long did you wait? Why were you kept waiting? Was your presence acknowledged?

Approach: Friendly and cheerful? Wanting to help you? What were the server's first words?

Attitude: Friendly, cheerful, helpful? Bored or indifferent? Interested, trying to help?

Knowledge: Stated the difference between choices, prices? Gave the impression that value exceeded price?

Suggestive selling: Suggested items? Did you buy? Why, or why not?

Thank you: Thanked you for business? Mechanically or with feeling?

Asked back: Asked to return?

Reaction: Would you make an effort to return?

Evaluating Employee Performance

Once set, the objectives become the performance standards against which employee performance will be evaluated. The next stage in setting up a system of MBO is to monitor the employees' performance. In selecting a method, several criteria should be kept in mind. First, the method should validate the selection techniques used. If employees themselves have been properly selected, then an effective appraisal method should show a significant percentage of employees meeting the performance objectives of the job. If this does not happen, it may indicate that we are not selecting the right kind of employees in the first place.

Another purpose of an appraisal method is to provide a rationale for making personnel decisions. In this regard, it is important that the method selected be legally defensible. W. Terry Umbreit et al. suggest the method chosen should meet ten tests.

1. Performance standards must be based on an analysis of job requirements.
2. Evaluations should be based on specific dimensions of job performance, not on a single "global" dimension.
3. Performance standards should be objective and observable.
4. Ratings should be documented.

5. The validity of individual raters' evaluations should be assessed.
6. Performance standards should be communicated to and understood by the employee.
7. Specific instructions for evaluation should be put in writing.
8. Use more than one evaluator whenever possible.
9. The evaluator should review the appraisal results with the employee.
10. The employee should be able to have a formal appeal procedure.[4]

A third requirement of an appraisal method is that it measure performance accurately. It should also provide a mechanism to help employees with feedback and development. Appraisal methods are also useful in suggesting the need for training programs. When a majority of employees are performing poorly on certain aspects of the job, the fault may not be with the employees but, rather, with inadequate training. Appraisal methods also are used to decide how rewards should be allocated.

Methods of Appraisal

A variety of methods are commonly used. Performance can be evaluated through *direct indices* or *personal traits,* against *set objectives* or *behaviorally anchored rating scales.*

Direct indices are objective and can be well documented. For example, hotel managers can be evaluated on such things as the ratio of payroll to room sales, or housekeepers on the number of rooms cleaned to the standards per day. They cannot, however, take into account how well employees deal with guests or subordinates (if that is an important part of the job).

In the personal trait method, characteristics are identified that are considered an important part of the job—such as creativity, dependability, and initiative—and the employee evaluated on the extent to which he or she possesses them. A major problem here is the subjectivity involved. The extent to which an individual is creative is open to a great deal of interpretation and argument.

Behaviorally anchored rating scales are very compatible with—and arguably a necessary prerequisite for—a program of MBO. While management by objectives focuses on the end result, BARS stresses the means to reach the end. In the example given above of selling one additional item per entrée sold, there are potentially several problems. An employee may adopt a "sell at any cost" attitude, pressuring customers to order certain items. The result may be a guest turned off by the heavy-handed sales approach. Second, an employee may not know how to sell additional items. The manager must be responsible for giving training and, where necessary, confidence to the employee to help him or her meet the objective. Last, an employee may fail to meet the objective through no fault of his or her own. Perhaps the customer just would not buy more, no matter how persuasive the employee is.

These problems can be addressed through a BARS program. In this appraisal method, the behavior necessary to reach the final objective is specified and the employee evaluated on the extent to which the behavior is displayed.

To implement this method requires identifying the dimensions of the job: the broad areas that describe what duties, skills, responsibilities, or activities are performed. For the server, suggestive selling may be one such dimension. Within that dimension, the behavior necessary for success is identified. At this point, the employees can be involved in determining behavioral objectives. What would employees be doing that would cause us to say, "They are really doing an excellent job of selling?" Success in selling probably comes from suggesting items to every customer (the more times we ask for the sale, the more sales will be made); displaying a knowledge of the items on the menu; and describing those items using language that paints a desirable picture. Given a few minutes and some encouragement, employees can come up with several types of behavior that would represent an excellent level of performance for this dimension. They could also identify behavior that would represent adequate and unacceptable levels of performance. These behavioral objectives, or anchors, become the standard against which employees will be measured. The key point is that the employees have been involved in setting the behavioral objectives.

The ratings scale is typically displayed on a single page with the word *excellent* at the top and *unacceptable* at the bottom. In between are a number of scale points, usually five, seven, or nine in number. Behavioral statements, or anchors, that represent the level of performance intended are developed at or between those scale points.

By observing an employee's behavior, the evaluator can give the employee a score reflecting how well the objective was met.

BARS are useful for several reasons. They focus on behavior—what employees actually do in their jobs. They stress only those things over which the employee has control. Employees have no control over whether a customer buys dessert; they do have control over whether they ask the person to buy. Specifying behavior tells employees what to do in order to be given a rating of excellent; employees then can adjust their performance accordingly. If they do not perform as desired, managers can also be specific about what the employees did wrong. The BARS method permits employee participation in setting behavioral objectives, which makes employee commitment more likely than having management alone set standards. Because behavior is anchored to scale points, employees are given a quantitative rating. This makes it easy to make decisions about rewards such as merit raises.

On the other hand, this method is time-consuming and costly to develop. For this reason, relatively few companies have developed it as their employee appraisal system. By offering measurable and observable behavioral objectives, however, BARS makes it easier for managers to implement the last part of the MBO process: providing employee feedback.

Providing Employee Feedback

It is very important for employees to know how they are performing in the eyes of the manager. Psychologists talk of feedback in three ways: praise, punishment, and extinction—which means no feedback. The employee is not told how management views performance. Extinction, in fact, can be more punishing to the employee than punishment.

Many managers view the appraisal session with as much trepidation as the employee. It is viewed as a win-or-lose situation. Either the employee has performed well, in which case the appraisal becomes an enjoyable, winning experience for both, or performance has been subpar, in which case the session results in a losing one for the employee. Many find it difficult and uncomfortable to criticize others, particularly if the subordinate is older or has more experience than the manager.

There are several useful steps the manager can take to plan for the appraisal session. The first thing is to confront one's fears about the interview, by asking oneself: "How do I really feel about evaluating this person? Why do I feel this way? What is the worst possible thing that could occur as a result of this interview? What is the best possible outcome that could occur? How likely is it that something negative, or something positive, will occur?" Thus, the manager is likely to find that if an employee is not performing well or is difficult to work with, facing the situation would not make it worse and, indeed, is likely to improve it.

It has been found that allowing employees to evaluate themselves prior to the appraisal interview with the manager provides a basis for discussion of any differences in the ratings. Employees are also exposed to the appraisal method used and may have a better idea of the difficulties involved in evaluating performance. In some cases, managers may be surprised how perceptive employees are regarding their own shortcomings. It is also a good idea to give the employee the manager's basic evaluation one to three days prior to the appraisal interview. This allows the employee to get over the initial defensiveness that comes from a negative appraisal and approach the interview more objectively.

Some people feel a formal, annual appraisal interview is of questionable value. Some research is available to show that in annual interviews, praise has no effect while criticism brings on defensive reactions that in some cases result in decreased performance in the future. For this reason, it is suggested that coaching be a day-to-day activity, not once a year. Employees accept suggestions for improved performance if they are given in a dispersed form rather than concentrated in an annual appraisal. Each person has a certain tolerance level for criticism. Once this level has been reached, the person will reject additional criticism out of hand. In addition, managers tend to stock up on criticisms of employees in order to have enough to discuss in a formal appraisal session. This, of course, negates the whole purpose of appraisal: giving feedback to the employee sufficiently soon after the performance that the employee can see a link between performance and reinforcement.

Interview Formats

The actual interview can take one of three formats. In the *tell and sell* interview, the objective is to communicate the manager's evaluation of the employee and persuade the employee to improve. Behind this is the assumption that employees want to know their weaknesses and a person can choose to improve. The manager acts as judge and, in conducting the interview, also must call upon such skills as salesmanship and patience. The employee is expected to suppress defensive behavior and attempt to cover any feelings of hostility. This approach is most likely to work when the employee respects the manager and feels the manager is, in fact, qualified to pass judgment on his or her performance.

There are certain risks involved. The manager may lose the loyalty of the employee. A greater potential problem is that employees will not grow. If the manager is always the one to evaluate performance, the employee need never take any responsibility for doing a good job. The manager, after all, will be the judge of that.

A second approach is the *tell and listen* interview. In this situation, the task is to communicate the evaluation while giving the employee an opportunity to react to it. The feeling inherent in this method is that people will change if defensive feelings are removed. The manager still takes the role of judge but spends time listening to the employee and attempting to summarize the employee's reactions. Given a chance to express any defensive feelings, the employee is likely to feel accepted, reducing the employee's resistance to change. In this type of interview, however, the need for change may not be developed.

In the *problem-solving* interview, the approach is not to focus on past employee behavior but rather to stimulate growth and development within the employee. Improved performance stems from an open discussion of job problems. In the role of helper, the manager uses exploratory questions to identify new ideas from the employee on how performance can be improved. This does not mean that performance is not evaluated. It does mean, however, that the focus is not on how the employee has failed, but rather on how the employee can succeed.

While the potential for change is great and both manager and employee learn as views are exchanged, the interview is unsuccessful if the employee is unable or unwilling to bring forward ideas. This is where the manager must coax ideas from the employee. Additionally, the discussion may not go the way the manager thought. The employee may identify changes the employer is unwilling or unable to consider.

SUMMARY

Management by objectives is not a cure-all. Its shortcomings have been due to the way it has been implemented. It must be developed as a method of managing, fully supported in an active manner by top management. It should not be thought of as a paper mill in which everything is reduced to writing. The emphasis, strangely enough, should not be on the objectives.

Implementing a program of management by objectives can improve employee productivity if it is seen as a way of getting workers to take more responsibility for controlling their actions as they move toward achieving company goals.

Employees can be involved in helping determine what is really important in fulfilling their jobs and in setting standards they should adhere to in order to perform their jobs well.

Once types of behavior are defined and observed, managers can sit down in an open atmosphere with the employees they supervise to highlight their key strengths and the areas that need improvement. Future improvement is ensured through an ongoing program of coaching.

Properly implemented, an MBO program will let employees know what they are responsible for while increasing their commitment to higher goals.

NOTES

[1]McConkie, M. C., "A Classification of the Goal-Setting and Appraisal Process in MBO," *Academy of Management Review* 4, no. 1, 1979, 29.

[2]Bilon, John J., and Jackson F. Ramsey, "Supervisory Attitudes in Foodservice," presentation at the National Restaurant Association Show, Chicago, 1982.

[3]Martin, William B., "Defining What Quality Service Is for You," *Cornell Hotel and Restaurant Administration Quarterly* 26, no. 4, February 1986, 32–38.

[4]Umbreit, W. Terry, Robert W. Eder, and Jon P. McConnell, "Performance Appraisals: Making Them Fair and Making Them Work," *Cornell Hotel and Restaurant Administration Quarterly* 26, no. 4, February 1986, 59–69.

SUGGESTED READINGS

Barton, Richard F., "An MCDM Approach for Resolving Goal Conflict in MBO," *Academy of Management Review* 6, no. 2, 1981, 231–41.

Beatty, Richard W., and Craig Eric Schneier, *Personnel Administration: An Experiential Skill-Building Approach,* Reading, Mass., Addison-Wesley Publishing Company, 1981.

———, "A Case for Positive Reinforcement," *Business Horizons,* April 1975, 57–66.

Benford, Robert J., "Found: The Key to Excellent Performance," *Personnel,* May–June 1981, 68–75.

Education Research, "Motivation," Warren, N.J., 1981.

Farrell, Thomas, "Communication in Foodservice Establishments," *Cornell Hotel and Restaurant Administration Quarterly* 5, no. 3, November 1964, 15–24.

Kent, William E., "Taking the Dread out of Employee Evaluations," *Cornell Hotel and Restaurant Administration Quarterly* 22, no. 1, May 1981, 47–51.

Klein, M. G., and S. P. Himburg, "The Effect of a Public-Posting Feedback Mechanism on Employee Performance," *Journal of Foodservice Systems* 2, 1982, 75–84.

Kondrasuk, Jack N., "Studies in MBO Effectiveness," *Academy of Management Review* 6, no. 3, 1981, 419–30.

Latham, Gary P., and Edwin A. Locke, "Goal Setting—A Motivational Technique that Works," *Organizational Dynamics,* 7, Autumn 1979, 313–24.

Maddux, Robert B., *Effective Performance Appraisals: A Fifty-Minute Guide,* Los Altos, Calif., Crisp Publications, Inc., 1986.

Martin, Robert A., and James C. Quick, "The Effect of Job Consensus on MBO Goal Attainment," *M.S.U. Business Topics,* Winter 1981, 43–48.

Martin, William B., *Quality Service: The Restaurant Manager's Bible,* Ithaca, N.Y., Cornell University School of Hotel Administration, 1986.

"Participative Management Training," *Lodging* reprint, East Lansing, Mich., American Hotel and Motel Association, undated.

Training Resource Corporation, "Avoid Common Rating Errors," Session Builder 210, Harrisburg, Pa., 1986.
———, "Behaviors or Attitudes," Session Builder 245, Harrisburg, Pa., 1986.
———, "Coach vs. Judge," Session Builder 238, Harrisburg, Pa., 1986.
———, "How Shall I Handle It?" Session Builder 108, Harrisburg, Pa., 1982.
———, "Setting Objectives and Standards," Session Builder 113, Harrisburg, Pa., 1982.

APPENDIX: IMPLEMENTING AN MBO PROGRAM

There are several steps in developing and implementing a program of management by objectives. It is necessary first to determine the major results areas—the aspects of the business for which objectives should be set—and then to set specific objectives. Performance is then measured and feedback is given in an employee appraisal session to the person responsible for attaining the objectives.

It should be stressed throughout that the philosophy of an MBO program is the development not only of business objectives but also of employees, toward what Douglas McGregor called "management by integration and self-control."

MAJOR RESULTS AREAS: HOTEL SERVICE

A common tendency in the first stage is for hotel employees to feel that the major results areas are financial: the generation of sales, minimization of costs, and maximization of income. Although every business seeks these things, it is the pursuit of guest satisfaction that will produce the financial successes here. In marketing, this is the difference between product orientation and customer orientation. Product orientation focuses on the product being offered—the hotel room, the meal, the drink—while customer orientation focuses on the needs and wants of the customer. The latter realizes that products and services should be developed only in response to those needs and wants. Thus, in addition to setting objectives in the traditional areas of business, it is necessary here to set objectives that deal with guest satisfaction.

Guest-Oriented Results

The procedure for ensuring customer orientation as key results areas are determined is to answer some questions: What do guests need and want? What facilities and services should be provided to satisfy those needs and wants? With what attitude and manner should we serve guests?

Inter-Continental Hotels has developed a process for answering these questions. Sessions typically include twelve people led by two trainers. The general manager may participate but has no veto power over others' suggestions.

Participants are divided into three groups of four, and each group is assigned one of the three questions above. Each group selects someone to record and report on everyone's answers, and participants are asked to put themselves in the role of guests in developing responses.

152

The training manual for these exercises lists numerous possible responses to the question, "What do guests need and want?" These include a clean room, comfortable bed, good food, dependable reservation, responsible front desk, bath or shower, restaurant, bar, meeting rooms, courteous and prompt attention, newsstand, cigar counter, shops, coffee shop, telephone or telegraph, laundry or valet, car park, local information, mailbox, and ballroom.

In an actual group situation, participants came up with the following suggestions of what guests are looking for: value for their money, comfort in the guest room, entertainment, quick service, personal recognition, friendliness, staff people who listen, good laundry service, barber and beautician, travel information, shopping, responsible reservations handling, banking facilities, good valet service, massage, good food, telex, credit, security, car service, travel arrangements, and pool with sauna.

By helping to determine what is important from a guest's point of view, rather than relying on the training manual suggestions, the employees are more likely to accept these areas of concern as their own.

In answer to the second question, "What facilities and services should be provided to satisfy those needs and wants?" the training manual suggests several responses: rooms with baths, a front service desk, cashier, bar, restaurant, coffee shop, garage, reservations, meals served in the room, messages and telephone service, baggage handling, valet, credit, information, wine cellar, meeting rooms, news and cigar shop, pool, courtesy car, laundry, sauna, registration, vault for valuables, catering, theater tickets, sightseeing tours, meeting equipment, checkroom, and travel service.

The group, on the other hand, suggested a guest information desk, global reservations, next-destination arrangements, secretarial service, multilingual services, fast laundry, flowers, security, hair dressing, shops, banking, responsible message service, sports arrangements, car rental, dependable room service, TV with in-room movies, a variety of restaurants, nursing, baby-sitting, parking with a car valet, newspapers from other cities, deluxe rooms, air-conditioning, banquet facilities, conference facilities, and outside catering.

At first glance it would appear the writers of the training manual underestimated the ability of this group to match the provision of facilities to the determination of guest needs.

The third part of this exercise seeks to answer, "With what attitude and manner should we serve guests?" Typical manual responses are to regard the guest as boss, be polite, cordial, pleasant, tactful, respectful, hospitable, friendly, courteous, patient, efficient, thorough, gracious, good-natured, considerate, and thoughtful, respond promptly, anticipate needs, hold guests in high regard, and provide individual attention.

Group participants countered with their own, smaller list, with suggestions to recognize guests and to be professional in doing one's job, happy, calm, available to guests, punctual, respectful, an understanding listener, sales oriented, and positive.

Financially Oriented Results

If the hotel is successful in meeting the needs of its guests, the results will show up in better financial performance. However, satisfying all guest needs may also result in a loss to the hotel. In order to determine the extent to which the business has met the needs of the guests at a profit to itself, objectives must be set in financial areas.

Objectives will vary depending on the size of the property, but the following listing of corporate results areas from Inter-Continental Hotels will serve as a guide.

1. Marketing objectives in such areas as sales, industry position, corporate position, and the identification and development of prime markets. Examples include an increase in sales, occupancy, the average room rate, food and beverage sales, average sales per cover, store rentals, inter-hotel sales (for chains), in-hotel sales, and local sales.
2. Production and operating objectives in the areas of quality, productivity, and cost. Examples include the ratio of payroll to sales and room costs to other expenses, food and beverage costs and other expenses, administrative and general expenses, utility costs, and sales per employee-hour.
3. Financial and control objectives in the areas of cash and inventory turnover, credit, and employment of resources. Examples include the ratio of gross operating profit to sales, profits for the room, food and beverage, and minor operating departments, the ratio of current assets to current liabilities and of sales to inventories, the average collection period, number of times taxes were earned, and times the average room rate was earned.
4. Personnel objectives in recruitment, organization, and development. Examples include development of a training program to provide career advancement opportunities for key personnel, and lower labor turnover.
5. Community and company relations objectives relating to community involvement. Examples include improving the local image and local acceptance of the hotel.
6. Research, development, and technical objectives in the areas of product, services, and process improvement, new product and new service development, and preventive maintenance. Examples include conducting market research of the community, investigating and reporting on national and international tourism trends, and developing and implementing a program of preventive maintenance.

Remember that employees will relate to objectives involving guest satisfaction much more than to financial objectives. Employees also will be more dedicated to achieving those objectives if they are involved in setting them.

Setting Objectives

Once the major results areas are understood, objectives can be set and employees involved in the process.

First, the general manager prepares guest and financial goals for the hotel. These goals are distributed to department managers and supervisors.

Next, supervisors and department managers are asked to list the hotel goals and performance indicators that apply to their department and then list proposed departmental goals, preparing a worksheet for each. (Examples of key performance indicators and a worksheet for departmental goals are given in figures 7–1 and 7–2.)

The entire group then divides into smaller study groups consisting of people from one department or related departments. One person is elected to speak for each subgroup. Through discussion, a consensus is reached about the hotel goals that relate to that department and the best performance indicators that apply. The two departmental goals that the subgroup considers the most productive are selected.

Finally, the results of all subgroup discussions are reported back to the entire group.

MAJOR RESULTS AREAS: RESTAURANT SERVICE

There is a procedural and a convivial dimension to delivering excellent restaurant service. The procedural part involves the mechanics of selling and serving a meal; the convivial part refers to the way in which it is served. The concentration in the latter is on the attitudes, behavior, and verbal skills the employees use in presenting the food and beverages ordered.

The Procedural Dimension

In *Quality Service: The Restaurant Manager's Bible*, William Martin identified seven facets of the procedural dimension of service. These were defined earlier in this chapter as:

1. Flow of service: making sure there are no bottlenecks in one part of the restaurant that would slow down overall service
2. Timeliness: giving service when the customer is ready for it
3. Accommodation: designing procedures for the convenience of the customer rather than the restaurant
4. Anticipation: providing service before the customer has to ask for it
5. Communication: ensuring that communication among employees, customers, and management is accurate, thorough, and timely
6. Customer feedback: actively seeking comments from the customers
7. Supervision: coordinating the service to ensure customer satisfaction

FIGURE 7–1 KEY INDICATORS OF PERFORMANCE IN HOTELS.

1. Quality of service. Methods of measurement include inspections, responses to guest questionnaires, and studies of complaint files and complimentary files.
2. House profit before repairs and maintenance.
3. Operating results compared to forecasts.
4. Departmental results compared to previous year.
5. Number of rooms occupied.
6. Percentage of rooms occupied.
7. Percentage of double occupancy.
8. Average daily rate per room.
9. Number of times average room rate earned.
10. Total covers served.
11. Covers served per paying overnight guest per outlet.
12. Covers or rooms serviced per employee day.
13. Average check per cover, by outlet, or per meal period.
14. Comparisons of operating results with economic indicators, price level, or currency exchange; adjusted indices for the country and the city.
15. Sales growth by category. Rooms sales, in total and subdivided by category; conferences, food and beverage, outside catering, garage, casino, shops, swimming pool, etc.
16. Sales growth by category compared to total sales.
17. Sales by category or department compared to room sales.
18. Contract sales by category: airlines, local companies, etc.
19. Sales per outlet or on basis of average employee per day.
20. Ratio of accounts receivable to total credit revenue.
21. Average collection period.
22. Accounts written off as bad debts compared to sales charges.
23. Effectiveness of manpower productivity control system.
24. House profit before repairs and maintenance per employee-day.
25. Payroll percentage for the entire hotel and for each department. For operating departments, compare to each department's sales; for nonoperating departments, compare to total hotel sales.
26. Number of employees (employee-day basis), in total and by department.
27. Waiting time at outlets for service.
28. Number of guest questionnaires received per thousand guests.
29. Total value of inventories.
30. Inventory turnover and trends in increases or decreases.
31. Heat, light, and power costs per occupied room.
32. Maintenance and security of property and equipment using standardized checklists.
33. Testing, evaluating, and reporting on new products, services, facilities, and techniques.
34. Effects on guests and staff of internal and external building and rehabilitation programs as measured by sales, covers, productivity, guest questionnaires, and letters.
35. Return on assets utilized.
36. Improvement in scores in annual executive evaluations of department heads.
37. Promotion records.
38. For chain operations, evaluation of marketing cooperation and records of guest referrals.
39. Number of employees completing manpower development and training programs.
40. Extent of staff involvement in professional and trade associations and charitable and civic groups.

(*Source:* "Participative Management Training," *Lodging* reprint, American Hotel and Motel Association, updated, 32, courtesy of Inter-Continental Hotels.)

FIGURE 7–2 WORKSHEET FOR DEPARTMENTAL GOALS.

1. Hotel or corporate goals that apply to my department:
    1. _____
    2. _____
    3. _____
    4. _____
    5. _____
    6. _____
2. Key performance indicators that apply to my department:
    1. _____
    2. _____
    3. _____
    4. _____
    5. _____
    6. _____
    7. _____
    8. _____
3. Proposed department goals:
    1. _____
    2. _____
    3. _____
    4. _____
    5. _____
    6. _____
4. Specifics for accomplishing each proposed department goal:
    Goal No. _____ Statement _____
    Key indicators of performance for this goal _____
    _____
    Who is responsible _____
    What must be done _____
    How it will be done _____
    When (schedule) _____
    Indicated costs _____
    Indicated savings _____

(*Source:* "Participative Management Training," *Lodging* reprint, American Hotel and Motel Association, undated, 35, courtesy of Inter-Continental Hotels.)

The Convivial Dimension

Martin identified the nine parts of the convivial dimension of service as:

1. Attitude: the way the server communicates through behavior and words
2. Body language: the use of facial expressions and body movements to express attitude
3. Tone of voice: the manner in which words are used
4. Tact: knowing what to say under different circumstances
5. Naming names: calling the customer by name

6.   Attentiveness: being tuned in to the needs of customers
7.   Guidance: exhibiting a thorough knowledge of the menu by offering assistance to indecisive customers
8.   Suggestive selling: describing menu items in such a way that the appeal is enhanced
9.   Problem solving: gratefully acknowledging a complaint and dealing with it in a way that will ensure its resolution

It is certainly possible to involve employees at this stage by having them assist in defining the areas that result in excellent service. However, if management feels that it is its prerogative to set the areas of prime concern, employees can be actively involved in the next stage, the setting of objectives.

Setting Objectives

In Table 7–1, the dimensions of service are listed, together with sample behavioral objectives. In all likelihood, management will find that employees who are involved in setting objectives will impose higher standards than if management set the standards itself. Additionally, employees are more likely to accept and meet these objectives if they have been part of the process in setting them.

PERFORMANCE APPRAISAL

There are four parts to the appraisal of an employee's performance. They are: preparation by both manager and employee; the appraisal discussion itself; the closing of the discussion; and the follow-up.

Preparation

To prepare effectively for an employee appraisal interview, the supervisor must review first the requirements of the job, in order to be familiar with them, and then the previously discussed and agreed-on objectives, or goals, and standards, or behavior to reach those goals.

The employee's history is then reviewed, including the employee's job skills, training, experience, special qualifications, and past jobs and job performance.

Next, the supervisor evaluates job performance relative to expectations for the period under review, rating it between unacceptable and outstanding. The supervisor must be wary of differentiating between attitude and behavior. Behavior can be observed; attitude, which involves subjective judgments about an observed situation, cannot itself be observed, measured, or objectively discussed, yet it finds its way into appraisal discussions.

Some examples of attitude statements are:

Sarah is very sensitive to the needs of our guests as they check in.

Cindy has the potential to grow with us and is what we are looking for in a manager.

TABLE 7–1:	BEHAVIORAL OBJECTIVES FOR RESTAURANT SERVICE
Results Areas	*Behavioral Objectives*
Flow of service	Hostesses alternate customers when seating sections.
Timeliness	Customers are greeted within one minute of sitting down.
Accommodation	Menu items can be substituted and combined.
Anticipation	Customers with small children receive booster chairs without having to ask.
Communication	Every customer receives exactly the items ordered.
Customer feedback	The server checks back with the party at least once during the meal.
Supervision	A supervisor makes contact with each table once during a shift.
Attitude	Smiles are visible on employees' faces.
Body language	Eye contact is made when talking to customers.
Tone of voice	Servers speak with a smile in their voice.
Tact	Servers avoid slang.
Naming names	All guests are called by name at least once during their visit.
Attentiveness	Customers ask for specific servers.
Guidance	Servers communicate complete and accurate menu knowledge to every table.
Suggestive selling	One additional item (e.g., dessert, appetizer) is sold with each entree ordered.
Problem solving	All complaining customers leave happy.

Source: **William B. Martin,** *Quality Service: The Restaurant Manager's Bible,* Ithaca, N.Y., Cornell University School of Hotel Administration, 1986, 85–87.

Bob is obviously not interested in the job, and his attitude affects the other employees negatively.

How could they be rewritten into behavioral statements appropriate for discussion with the employee?

Sarah welcomes guests to the hotel, smiles her greeting, and maintains eye contact while getting them a room appropriate to their needs.

Cindy has completed her delegated assignments on time and in an accurate manner. She has accepted projects beyond her normal job responsibilities and has completed them to the satisfaction of her supervisor.

Bob has been absent six times this year and late fourteen times and has failed to complete two assigned reports within the agreed-on deadline. His absences and lateness mean that other employees have to cover for him.

Behavioral variations in the employee's performance can be noted for discussion. It is important to provide specific examples of both positive and negative behavior. Discussion should be limited to important areas.

It is a good idea at this stage to prepare a preliminary determination about the employee's future career opportunities or limitations, as well as the major areas of concentration for setting objectives and standards for the next appraisal session.

The result of your evaluation will determine the employee's likely future, which in turn will determine the objective of the discussion.

For example, if the employee is rated outstanding, several options may be available. The employee may be a candidate for promotion, in which case the interview should consider the opportunities available. The employee's present job may be redefined and new responsibilities added to it. In this case, development plans must be made. A major difficulty arises with an employee evaluated as outstanding for whom no change in job duties is planned. In this situation, the discussion should end on ways to maintain the existing performance level.

For an employee rated satisfactory, it is unlikely promotion will be considered. New responsibilities may be added if it is felt that better performance will result. If no change in job duties is envisioned, the major result will be to maintain, and preferably improve, the employee's performance level.

When a worker is perceived as performing in an unsatisfactory manner, the supervisor has to determine whether the performance is correctable. If it is, then the interview should culminate with a corrective plan to which the employee will be committed; if not, then reassignment or, as a last resort, termination must be considered.

The point is that a manager must think all this through before the interview. At the same time, it is important that the manager is open to new information that may surface in the interview and change the previously thought-out options.

Once the employee gets advance notice of the meeting and an opportunity for self-evaluation, an interview site can be chosen that will help ensure a relaxed interview. A neutral office may be the best place for this. Finally, it is crucial that sufficient uninterrupted time be scheduled for the session.

Two other items sometimes give appraisers particular problems. One is the approach to take with the employee; the other is the tendency to fall into common traps affecting evaluators.

Taking the Right Approach

A supervisor can take one of several approaches to the interview. The traditional approach has been to take on the role of judge over the employee. A better approach is for the manager to act as coach. The differences between the two can be understood if the reader attempts a word association exercise.

On a blank piece of paper, the reader should write down all the words that come to mind when *coach* and *judge* are mentioned.

When the two lists are compared, it is generally found that the words associated with *coach* are more positive, development-oriented, supportive, and focused on the future, while those associated with *judge* are more negative, reactive, judgmental, and focused on the past. Which one would you prefer to have as a supervisor, a coach or a judge? Perhaps your employees—present or future—would prefer the same.

Certainly what happened in the past is an important consideration in planning for the future. An overemphasis on the past, however, creates a report card mentality and adds stress to an already stressful situation. This does not mean that poor past performance should be glossed over. It does mean that the primary focus should be on what management and employee can do to improve the latter's future performance. Acting as coach, the manager will help ensure that the employee is given the help and encouragement needed to perform to the agreed-on standards and achieve the company's objectives.

Avoiding Common Rating Errors

Most supervisors strive to be objective when evaluating their subordinates' performance. Even for the most diligent of people, however, it is easy to fall into one or more traps when it comes to performance appraisal. Mentioned below are some common errors in rating the performance of employees, a definition of each, and suggested strategies on how to avoid them.

The *halo effect* means letting one factor in the individual positively or negatively affect your opinion of other factors. For example, "This person is pleasant to the guests as they check in; therefore he/she must get along well with fellow employees."

Avoid this by looking for both strong and weak points in the individual, focusing only on job-related factors.

Recency means evaluating only recent performance. When evaluations are conducted formally only once a year, there is a tendency to forget about one until only a few days or weeks before the interview. Then the tendency is to concentrate on the employee's performance during those few days or weeks, to the exclusion of what went on before.

Avoid this by keeping an ongoing file of each employee's performance and reviewing that file in preparation for the evaluation.

Central tendency means checking all the middle or average boxes as an easy way out. This is an example of management by abdication and is symptomatic of managers who have little confidence in their own ability to make decisions.

Avoid this by eliminating a middle choice. On evaluation forms have categories such as excellent, above average, below average, and unacceptable that force a decision. Managers should also actively look for both strong and weak points, building on the employee's strengths while coaching the weaknesses.

Grouping means attributing poor performance to group characteristics, such as saying, "Everyone does it."

Avoid this by focusing on the individual.

Holding a grudge means penalizing the employee for something that happened a long time before.

Avoid this by actively looking for any positives in such an employee's performance. Face up to the fact that you are harboring a grudge, discuss it with the employee, then get rid of it.

Prejudice is unjustified bias against a person, such as the feeling that women should not be managers because they cannot handle the stress of the job.

Avoid this by looking for strong performance areas and focusing on performance targets and job-related issues.

Favoritism means overlooking the poor performance of employees you personally like.

Avoid this by looking at factors related to the job.

The *sunflower effect* means giving everyone high ratings in order to make yourself look good. The implied assumption is that if all your employees are performing well, then as their supervisor you also must be performing well.

Avoid this by focusing on the individual development of your employees rather than how they rate; concentrate on helping them become better than they already are. Perhaps higher performance targets need to be set.

The Appraisal Discussion

Managers must begin the appraisal discussion by creating an open, friendly, and sincere atmosphere. This can be done by outlining the purpose of the meeting and putting the employee at ease.

While most people want to know where they stand and how they are doing, the main objective in any appraisal interview with an employee who is not performing as desired is to develop a plan to upgrade the performance. It would be difficult to cover all of the employee's strengths and weaknesses, and both wrong and threatening to focus solely on the employee's weaknesses. In preparing for the interview, the manager must identify only the major strengths and weaknesses of the employee—those that most directly affect job performance. The key must always be the job the employee does and how the employee can become more effective in performing that job.

How can you put the employee at ease? A certain amount of small talk and pleasantries may be appreciated, but this should be kept to a minimum. Both parties know why they are there. An extensive period of chitchat will only heighten the tension.

The session quickly moves to the evaluation. Two starting points are possible. One is to discuss first a specific job achievement. This will further put the employee at ease while emphasizing that the interview's purpose is to examine both positive and negative variations from stated objectives.

A second method is to allow the employee to review his or her own accomplishments for the period under review. In this situation, the employee can select where to begin and what he or she considers important. Some managers may fear this supposed lack of control, while others may think the employee will exaggerate any achievements. But most employees appear to be surprisingly hard on themselves, often more so than their supervisor. As long as the objectives and standards have been well defined, it is difficult to overstate the extent to which they have been met. A further bonus for this approach is that it allows the manager to compare what he or she thinks are important contributions to what the employee thinks. The employee may be focusing on areas of the job that are not important to the manager.

At some point, there will be differences of opinion as to what the manager and the employee each thinks the latter has accomplished. Such differences can be arbitrated by referring to the stated objectives. The important consideration is to determine what the variations are and why they occurred. This can effectively lead to a joint discussion of what can be done to improve performance.

It is easy for the manager to discuss the positive aspects of an employee's performance, even though managers tend not to give sufficient feedback on what employees did right. Major difficulties arise when it is necessary to talk about performance deficiencies. The problem may not be so much bringing up the problems; rather it is the way the problems are discussed. The key is to discuss the shortcomings in such a way that the performance will improve.

If employees feel the job situation is nonthreatening, they are more likely to bring up areas in which they need to improve. Given this opening, a supervisor can ask, "What can we do to correct this situation?"

If an employee does not recognize poor performance, the manager must bring it up. It helps to discuss the effect on the hotel or restaurant. How does what the employee is doing, or not doing, affect the performance of the property? It is important that the employee be given specific instances of behavior that was not as desired, for example, "You have been late five times in the past month," or, "Your sales forecast exceeded company tolerances in four out of twelve months last year."

The manager then can go on to review what is expected of the employee. The employee may not know what is expected of him or her; point out what the expectations are and get a commitment to meet those expectations.

If the employee is aware of what is expected but is still not performing, it is necessary to find out why. If the supervisor does most of the talking, the session will not be productive. It is important to get the employee to talk. In so doing, the employee is likely to come to realize what is wrong and, having been involved, is more likely to be committed to correcting the situation. Four approaches are useful in creating the desired nonthreatening atmosphere.

Be descriptive rather than judgmental. Say, "What caused you to lose your temper when dealing with the guest at the front desk?" rather than, "How could you do something so stupid?"

Be supportive rather than authoritarian. Say, "How do you suggest we reduce turnover in your department?" rather than, "You must reduce turnover in your department."

Emphasize equality rather than superiority.

Say, "This is how I learned to develop a forecast. Do you have any ideas of how it can be improved?" rather than, "This is how we forecast around here. Do it this way."

Be accepting rather than dogmatic. Say, "This is the best way I can see to improve things. Do you see any other possibilities?" rather than, "This is the best way."

Planning Future Performance

Having moved through the introduction, strengths, and weaknesses or areas that need improvement, the manager then turns to the employee's plans for future improvements.

The employee should be encouraged to develop self-improvement plans before the manager offers any suggestions. The manager's role may very well be one of scaling down the employee's over ambitious objectives. If, however, the employee cannot come up with any ideas for improvement, or if the ideas mentioned are unacceptable to management, then direct involvement is required.

It is up to the manager to suggest a course of development that the employee can realistically attain. Develop objectives that will require the employee to stretch but that the employee feels are possible. The objectives should require actions by both the employee and the manager, acting as coach.

For example, assume that we have a front-office manager responsible for rooms forecasting. Among other things, the forecast serves as the basis for scheduling housekeepers. While excellent in other respects, reports are periodically late in reaching the head housekeeper, with the result that overscheduling occurs.

The best goal for the front-office manager might be to complete all forecasts on time for the next month. This objective is specific, results-oriented, and realistic. The role of the supervisor in assisting the front-office manager reach this goal depends on the subordinate. One who is self-directed and has shown a willingness in the past to ask for help would appreciate an offer of help when needed. But if the employee has demonstrated an unwillingness to seek help when a problem arises—some employees see this as a sign of weakness—a more direct approach is called for. The supervisor must participate without being seen as taking over. The supervisor initially may have to approach the front-office manager to ask if any problems are foreseen in getting the forecast in on time, and if there are, what the supervisor can do to assist.

At this point, the employee may agree, or appear to agree, in order to end the interview. To ensure employee commitment, several strategies are in order. By asking, "What do you feel will be most difficult for you in getting your forecasts in on time?" the manager focuses on implementation of the plan. This question also allows the supervisor to gauge the employee's attitude while finding out where a potential problem may lie. If the feeling persists that the employee does not fully support the plan, ask, "What parts of the plan would you like to change?" This will involve the employee while verifying whether any problems exist in his or her mind. This plan can be reinforced by having the employee summarize the interview in writing. A brief report will show any differences in understanding, and putting the plan in writing will further commit the employee to it.

In closing the interview, the manager should summarize what has been discussed, enthusiastically endorse the employee's future efforts, give the employee a final opportunity to add any suggestions, and end on a friendly and positive note.

Now comes the coaching to ensure that the plan agreed to is adhered to. Some employees may need constant supervision after each forecast to ensure it is on time. Others work best with a less overt style of supervision. For the latter it is better to review the employee's work over the next few weeks but not take any action until a pattern of improvement or failure emerges. Whatever follow-up is deemed best, it is important to let the employee know what those plans are. This way everyone knows the rules of the game.

8 | IMPROVING PRODUCTIVITY: JOB DESIGN

Job design—or redesign, when changes in existing jobs are involved—consists of three elements. It involves determining the duties and responsibilities inherent in a job, which methods should be used in carrying out that job, and what relationships should exist between the person doing the job and the supervisor, any subordinates, and fellow employees. The objectives are to design jobs in order to help the company perform required tasks in the most productive way possible while also satisfying employee needs for interest, challenge, and accomplishment, thereby contributing to their quality of work life.

Redesigning jobs can be appropriate when employees feel they are being given insufficient responsibility. It has been found to work best with jobs that are extremely monotonous, segmented, and routine.

It is important to distinguish between two common job design strategies: job enlargement and job enrichment. Job enlargement consists of adding more tasks to an individual job to provide the person doing it with a greater variety of work. It can be thought of as horizontal job loading. It has been suggested, however, that such an approach can merely enlarge the meaninglessness of the job. Adding one meaningless task to another is like adding zero to zero; the result is still zero. Similar analogies can be developed for substituting one task for another.

Job enrichment is concerned with vertical job loading. Typically, work is planned by management, performed by workers, and controlled by management. Job enrichment seeks to build into people's jobs some planning or control or both. In this way, employees perform more challenging work.

In their book,[1] W. J. Paul and K. B. Robertson saw the goal of job enrichment as improving both task efficiency and human satisfaction. This could be achieved, they felt, by building greater opportunities for personal achievement and recognition into people's jobs.

THEORETICAL BACKGROUND

Classical Approach

In *The Wealth of Nations* (1776), Adam Smith wrote about the economic advantages of a division of labor. He argued that a person's skill and dexterity were

166

improved by repeatedly performing a task; that the less frequently employees change activities, the greater the time and production savings; and that work-related inventions take place when job specialization occurs. His concern, then, was in designing jobs that consisted of a limited number of tasks.

In 1832, Charles Babbage saw job design as a way of paying for the exact skills used. By simplifying jobs so that the tasks involved in any one job were of the same level of complexity, management could avoid paying for a difficult skill that was used only sparingly in the performance of a piece of work. In this way, employees would use one skill repeatedly in the performance of a job. Management would pay the worker according to the difficulty of the task performed.

In 1911 Frederick W. Taylor focused on dividing managers' tasks from workers'. He contributed to both vertical and horizontal specialization. Vertical specialization involves removing planning and controlling activities from those who perform the tasks. Horizontal specialization involves the creation of repetitive jobs that require low levels of skill.

Through these methods production was increased, efficiency was maintained, and there was greater control and standardization of the completed work. To what extent this was a result of the way jobs were designed, or of external factors such as new technologies, is difficult to ascertain.

Neoclassical Approach

In the 1950s, writers such as Chris Argyris and Douglas McGregor suggested more of a humanistic approach to job design. They wrote that employees who perform low-skill, simplified jobs will eventually find them monotonous. This will lead to boredom and job dissatisfaction, they argue, which will translate into lateness, absenteeism, and less than desirable performance on the job.

To achieve maximum benefits for the organization, job design must take into account the feelings, needs, and motives that employees bring to the workplace. Unless these needs are met in the design of jobs, employee productivity will suffer.

Modern Approach

Integration of the neoclassical perspective has led to the development of job enlargement and job enrichment programs. Several theoretical models have been developed to explain the relationship between the employee and the job being performed. Job enrichment, for example, can be viewed as an outgrowth of Frederick Herzberg's two-factor theory of motivation.

Herzberg's research indicates that over 80 percent of the factors contributing to job satisfaction come from the job itself: achievement, recognition, and responsibility. On the other hand, two-thirds of the factors contributing to job dissatisfaction involved organizational policy and administration, supervision, and working conditions. Success with these factors would not ensure job satisfaction, but their absence would prevent it.

The behaviorists, led by B. F. Skinner, believe that reinforcement is the key to achieving performance. They view job design as a way of making the task more intrinsically reinforcing, thus leading to higher levels of performance.

William Scott offered an activation theory based on physiology to explain motivation. He holds that cues received from the environment are diffused over areas of the brain to arouse and activate the individual. The greater the variety and stimulation in a task, the higher the state of arousal. Thus, enriched jobs led to more cues from the environment, which lead to more arousal, which leads to more motivaton. The reverse is also true.

A fourth theoretical explanation of why complex task design will lead to more motivated employees is based on V. H. Vroom's expectancy theory. This is based on the idea that behavior is determined by an individual's perception of what he or she expects to happen, in conjunction with how important that outcome is to the individual. An individual will behave in a certain way if he or she believes that will result in an important outcome. This theory holds that the worker perceives an enriched job will lead to an intrinsic reward, so the employee is more committed to the job and performs better.

Researchers have approached the subject from different directions, but there seems to be agreement that extreme job simplification leads to boredom, job dissatisfaction, and decreased productivity. Resulting programs have three common elements: workers should be given as much freedom as possible to control their work while developing their skills; jobs should be made up of tasks that are varied, challenging, and meaningful; and a sharing, team concept should replace the vertical breakdown of jobs, in which a supervisor does all the planning and controlling while the worker performs all the tasks.

ROADBLOCKS TO IMPLEMENTATION

Several barriers exist to implementing job redesign programs. Prominent among these are incompleteness of the evidence, the attitudes of top management, reluctance of first-level supervisors, union influence, and the restrictiveness of industrial engineering.

Incompleteness of the Evidence

Job redesign programs have been criticized as being poorly designed and lacking in empirical validity. Most of the studies present indirect evidence at best of the effects of job design on productivity. There is also the problem that certain jobs cannot be enriched beyond a limited point. Dishes have to be washed; pots have to be scrubbed; potatoes have to be peeled.

Perhaps the most damning criticism is that many workers do not feel alienated from their jobs and desire no additional responsibility or involvement in the workplace. Job enrichment assumes that intrinsic motivation is crucial in the long run and is sought from work. This will not work, however, for employees who are more interested in extrinsic motivation such as a higher paycheck or who seek their intrinsic motivation in hobbies or their pursuits off the job. The predominant issue in collective bargaining is still wages. For many, the standard of living may be more important than the quality of work.

Managerial Attitudes

The philosophy that supports job design is a belief in worker participation in controlling job functions. This requires an organizational climate in which employees are valued and respected. The implementation of such a climate entails having managers who hold a *theory Y* set of assumptions about employees. Douglas McGregor developed the idea that theory Y managers believe that employees enjoy their work, act in a responsible manner, and are genuinely interested in contributing toward the goals of the company. Some research exists that in fact many organizations are still structured and run by *theory X* managers, who assume that workers are inherently lazy, lack responsibility, and require close supervision. One major study of three thousand managers found that although a majority supported the idea of participative decision making, most maintained that employees are not capable of initiative or leadership, avoid responsibility, and prefer to be led.[2]

For others it is illogical that managers should support this program. Job redesign has those with power make concessions to those without power. The common tendency is for those at the top of an organization to make their job as easy as possible, thereby making the jobs of those below them more difficult. It is difficult for some to assume that managers will reverse this tendency willingly.

First-Level Supervisors

Implementation of any job design program, and therefore its success, depends on the support of first-level supervisors. There are good reasons supervisors would resist such a program and either overtly or covertly work for its failure. Over the years, the amount of discretion in the supervisor's job has declined. As organizations have grown, specialists have taken over functions that were in the supervisor's purview. Chief among these is the personnel function. In large part because of the increasingly difficult legal environment surrounding how employees can be dealt with, specialists now perform many of the activities that supervisors formerly dealt with.

Associated with this is the need to treat employees fairly. Uniformity of treatment is assured by centralizing the formation of company rules and control of their appplication. This dilutes the power, discretion, and amount of enrichment inherent in the supervisor's job. Job design puts pressure on supervisors to give employees more autonomy and responsibility; but doing that reduces the autonomy of the supervisor. It is argued that many employees seek greater autonomy. But surely so do supervisors! The result may be less than full supervisory support for any job redesign program.

In fact, research has shown in one case that supervisors of workers who experienced job enrichment experienced less satisfaction themselves regarding job security, job challenges, interpersonal relations, and the meaningfulness of work.

Union Influence

Many union officials resist job design programs on the grounds that they are no more than efforts to increase productivity at the expense of jobs and wages. In a way, of course, they are correct. The task is to increase productivity. Designing jobs that are intrinsically rewarding also reduces the need for a union or any other body to attend to the needs of employees. Some union officials refuse as a matter of principle to support anything management proposes.

Industrial Engineering

The techniques of industrial engineering and quality of work are different. Industrial engineering emphasizes task fragmentation and specialization, with little employee input. Proponents of the quality of work are interested in changing jobs in order to increase worker involvement and responsibility.

The evidence to support these two opposing positions varies. Industrial engineers are capable of presenting top management with facts and figures to justify their proposals. Those who support the quality of work have, in the past, relied too often on subjective appeals based on the humanization of work.

THE JOB DESIGN MODEL

A model of job design is presented in figure 8–1. This model incorporates the basic managerial concepts, critical dimensions of the job and psychological states, and expected outcomes. Understanding the motivational assumption behind this model and the program's expected consequences will permit an examination of the desired changes; then we can explore what steps management can take to effect those desired changes and create the desired outcomes.

Motivational Assumption

The assumption behind the successful application of this tool is that intrinsic, rather than extrinsic, motivation works best in the long run, and proper application will result in more productive workers. The ultimate reward for an employee who is motivated intrinsically is completing a challenging piece of work and knowing he or she did a good job.

Consequences

If job redesign is properly applied, it will result in the creation of more interesting jobs. Employees will enjoy the work more. Productivity, in terms of quality

FIGURE 8–1 A MODEL OF JOB DESIGN.

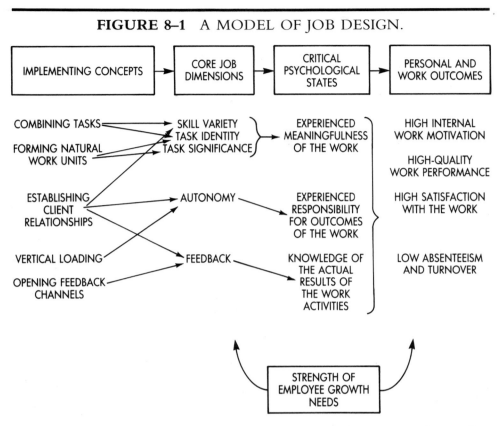

(*Source:* Craig Eric Schneier and Richard W. Beatty, *Personnel Administration Today*, Reading, Mass., Addison-Wesley Publishing Company, 1978, 383.)

and perhaps quantity, will increase while turnover and absenteeism will be reduced.

On the other hand, not all employees want more challenging jobs. For those who are primarily motivated by money and other external factors, designing more interesting and challenging jobs may actually produce confusion and concern. Productivity is likely to go down. Some employees also may lack the ability to handle more complicated jobs. For them, the results in terms of production are liable to be negative. Some managers believe that employees who are involved in redesigning jobs may also feel they should be able to exert more influence over the workplace than the managers want or are willing to allow. In addition, if we redesign jobs to make them more challenging and complex, presumably we will need to hire more educated and experienced people to staff them. This will tend to increase the wages paid for those positions.

Psychological States

Behavioral scientists have found that three factors are critical to satisfaction and motivation on the job. First, employees must feel that what they are doing is meaningful in terms of their own set of values. The waiter who feels that serving food is demeaning will be satisfied with neither himself nor his job. Second, employees must feel personally responsible for the outcome. Third, employees must learn fairly regularly how well their jobs are being performed. When employees are not told, they feel as if they are in a vacuum. They are given no chance to improve because they do not know whether they need to improve. For maximum satisfaction, jobs should be ranked high in all three of these areas.

Core Job Dimensions

Five core job characteristics have been identified that affect the three psychological states to produce positive or negative outcomes.

How meaningful a job appears to the person doing it depends on three of the job dimensions: the *variety of skills* used, the extent to which the job entails doing something from beginning to end, or *task identity,* and the extent to which the job affects others in a substantial way, or *task significance.*

The more skills are called into use in performing a task, the more meaningful the task is to the employee performing it. The job seems more important because it requires more skills. It also is less boring because of the variety of skills required.

With task identity, it is more meaningful for an employee to be responsible for the preparation of a complete dinner salad than to be given the task of solely preparing lettuce for all salads. Similarly, employees who feel that what they do has an impact on whether guests enjoy themselves will think their jobs are more significant than employees who perceive that customers will not notice their efforts.

A fourth core job dimension deals with the amount of *autonomy* in the job. The more autonomy workers experience, the more personal responsibility they will feel for the outcome of the work. Employees in highly autonomous jobs know that they are responsible for success or failure. The management trainee who is urged to consult the manual for the answer to problems can use the book as a crutch in place of initiative and judgment. The manager then is not responsible for guest satisfaction or dissatisfaction; the manual is.

The fifth core characteristic of the job is *feedback.* The more feedback employees have, the better they know how they are performing. Feedback is most effective when it comes from the work itself.

Growth Needs

Research has been conducted to determine the extent to which job satisfaction is moderated by how strong an individual's need for growth is. It was thought that for those who have a low need to grow in the job, job redesign would have little positive or perhaps even a negative impact. That is, employees who had all the responsibility and meaningfulness they could handle or wanted to handle would experience reduced productivity when jobs were enhanced. In fact, the results of the research have been mixed. While some results show that the strength of growth needs does moderate the amount of job satisfaction experienced, other studies show no effect. It appears that job satisfaction can be increased for all employees, but the increase is greater for those who have strong needs for growth.

MANAGEMENT'S ROLE
IN IMPLEMENTING JOB DESIGN

Management can take any or all of five actions in implementing a job design program (fig. 8–1). First, managers can combine tasks. Banquet waiters who, as part of a group, were responsible for setting up only the entrée knife at each place for a banquet of five hundred can be given the task of setting up the entire dinner setting for a smaller number of guests. The more tasks given the waiter, the more skills are required. Additionally, the waiter is able to identify more readily with the finished banquet setting, improving task identity.

Second, managers can form natural work units. The central idea is to establish in an employee's mind a sense of ownership over the job. This occurs when room attendants are assigned a specific floor of their own rather than getting rooms that are randomly assigned. It also happens when a hotel has three airport shuttle buses and each driver is assigned responsibility for a particular bus. When this happens, task identity and task significance both increase. The room attendant sees the results of his or her work every day and can be proud of a specific floor; the driver knows that the way the bus is handled today will affect him or her tomorrow because the driver will be using the same vehicle.

Third, managers can enrich back-of-the-house jobs by bringing out front employees who ordinarily would not come in contact with guests. For example, the server acts as an effective buffer between the chef and the customer. Occasionally bringing the chef out front affects three core job dimensions. It requires the use of an additional skill: dealing with people. It can increase autonomy, for example, if the chef is given responsibility for handling customers' complaints, perhaps by being allowed to issue a complimentary meal check if something is wrong with the food. It also improves feedback from customer to employee on the quality of the food.

Fourth, managers can vertically load jobs. Vertical loading refers to the idea of passing on to the employee some of the traditional management functions of planning and control. This is the single most crucial principle of job redesign. There are various ways to implement this. The employee doing the job may be given more discretion for setting work schedules, choosing how to do the job, checking on quality, or training other people to perform the job. Additional authority can be granted to employees. Discretion may be given over when to take breaks. Employees can be encouraged to develop solutions to problems rather than bring every concern to a supervisor. Workers can be given more information about the finances of the business. Many employees overestimate the profits a hotel or restaurant obtains; letting them know the costs involved in wastage and breakage and the thin margin the property exists on makes them feel more involved as well as more cost-conscious.

Take the position of room attendant. Typically, the attendant cleans the room; then a supervisor comes around to inspect that room, using a checklist. The incomplete items are noted and given to the attendant. The room attendant is shielded from taking responsibility; the supervisor, after all, will find any mistakes. But if we give the checklist to the room attendant and have the person doing the job also double-check whether it has been done properly, we are vertically loading the job. This does not mean the room inspections need never be done. But it places more responsibility on the shoulders of the person performing the task, which can increase the worker's motivation and satisfaction. It may also be more satisfying to let this person take a break when it seems appropriate to him or her—subject to the necessity of serving the guests, of course—rather than according to the whim of the supervisor, and also to tell the employee such relevant information as how much a torn sheet costs to replace.

All of these examples of vertical loading affect the extent to which the worker experiences responsibility for the outcome of the job.

The fifth major action management can take to implement job design is to open up channels of communication. Employees want to know how they are performing. This means more than keeping an open-door policy. It means touring the property several times a day to see what is going on and to compliment and coach where necessary. The best kind of feedback comes from the work itself, however, rather than a wait for what management may or may not notice. The tips at the end of a busy shift represent feedback; the night audit that balances also represents feedback. Often the supervisor corrects mistakes without informing the employee because the order has to go out immediately or the employee has gone home at the end of a shift. But this does a disservice to the worker as well as harms future job performance. Without feedback, the employee does not have a chance to improve, thinks that he or she has done a good job, and is likely to repeat the same error.

Leadership Style

Managers also can affect employee job satisfaction and performance through the style of leadership they adopt. A model showing how leadership style relates to the scope of the job and the growth needs of the employee is depicted in figure 8–2.

This model assumes that appropriate leadership style is dependent on the interaction of the employee's growth needs and the scope of the job being performed. When an employee has high growth needs and is performing a job

FIGURE 8–2 RELATIONSHIPS AMONG TASK DESIGN, INDIVIDUAL, AND LEADERSHIP BEHAVIOR VARIABLES.

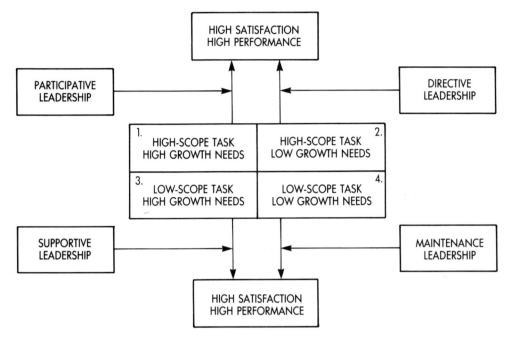

(*Source:* Ricky W. Griffen, "Relationships Among Individual, Task Design and Leader Behavior Variables," *Academy of Management Journal* 23, no. 4, 1980, 667.)

high in variety, or a high–scope job, autonomy and participative management would be appropriate (box 1).

When a job is varied but the employee does not want to cope with it (box 2), the manager should provide direction in planning, organizing, and controlling the work of the employee.

When an employee with high growth needs is performing a task that is unfulfilling (box 3), frustration and dissatisfaction will probably result. Supportive leadership will be necessary to produce a satisfied and productive employee.

An employee with low growth needs might be performing a task that is rather dull and repetitive (box 4). In this case supportive leadership is unnecessary because the employee is unlikely to be frustrated. The most appropriate style is a form of minimum interference, in which performance is monitored but the manager does not closely supervise the employee. As long as the job is being performed to the level required, little or no interaction between manager and employee is needed. This maintenance leadership behavior may be appropriate unless and until performance or satisfaction problems arose, in which case more direction or support would be given.

Limited research has been conducted on this model. For the most part, no causal relationship has been proven between leadership behavior and productivity. It may exist, but researchers have as yet been unable to prove it. The only situation in which such a relationship has been found is when an employee with low growth needs is performing a job that is low in variety, autonomy, and feedback. In this case, maintenance leadership (box 4) has produced more productivity. In all likelihood, the factors affecting productivity are more varied than the two suggested here; this may account for the lack of evidence about the model.

It appears there is less a manager can do to affect job satisfaction when there is a match between employee growth needs and job scope. When an employee high in growth needs is performing a job high in scope (box 1) or an employee with little desire for an enriched job is performing a task low in scope (box 4), satisfaction with the job appears unrelated to management style. Leadership style can and does seem to make more of a difference in the other two cases (boxes 2 and 3), along the lines suggested.

Management of Symbols

So far, this chapter has assumed a link between objective job characteristics and employee satisfaction and productivity. But individual behavior is a function of that individual's perception of a situation. Adding more tasks to a job will have no impact on the employee unless that person perceives that the job has been enriched. Managers can influence the way employees perceive their jobs through a variety of symbols. The symbols used cannot and will not substitute for substance. Calling a cleaner a maintenance engineer will have little or no positive impact on the employee if the change in job title is not accompanied by substantive changes in job assignments and rewards. On the other hand, changes in a job can be ineffective if management continues to give the employee the impression that the job is unimportant.

The words management uses, the way management chooses to spend time, and the settings chosen for various activities all can influence employee perceptions.

The language used can tell an employee how management perceives the job. Job descriptions that indicate routine duties and close supervision paint a negative picture to the employee. Of course, in some cases the employee is not given a written job description. When an employee is told to "follow Harry" for two days, and that is the sum total of the "training," the impression is that the job is not very taxing, requires little preparation or knowledge, and therefore is of little importance. That means the person performing the job is not considered very important. The Disney organization, on the other hand, calls its employees "cast members," talks about being "on stage," and stresses the importance of every position in the words and actions used. Contrast that with the food and beverage manager who wonders aloud to the dishwasher, "I don't know how you can stand this for eight hours a day." Many phrases can convey management's negative perception of a task:

- "I hate to ask you to do this, but . . ."
- "All you have to do is . . ."
- "Would you mind . . ."

Language is also used to describe the level of skill required for the job. Describing a position as unskilled or semiskilled has the same negative effect. It can help in the orientation process to let employees know the history and tradition of the job they are performing. Innkeepers have a long and rich tradition of providing refuge for the weary traveler; servers have long been regarded as artisans in Europe. Disney has each of its employees take a course entitled Traditions 1. This course starts with *Steamboat Willie*—the original Mickey Mouse cartoon—and ends with EPCOT (the Experimental Prototype City of Tomorrow). Employees see where the organization has come from and where they fit in.

If restaurant employees are told, "You start as a hostess and, if you work out and when we get an opening, we'll move you into a server's position," they learn that we do not think much of the hostess position. It's better if they are told, "We have found that you will benefit from starting out in this position. You will have a chance to work with all of our servers and see how this operation works. You set the tone for the customer's experience because you make that first impression. When you get your own station, you'll have a better understanding of the way the restaurant operates."

A story is told of two stonemasons working on a project. When asked what they were doing, the first answered, "I'm smoothing this stone"; the second said, "I'm building a cathedral." Who do you think was more motivated?

Managers can impress on all employees the important role each one plays in ensuring that a special dinner celebration is successful for a customer or that a vacation a family has saved for all year is enjoyed. In part, the quality of tools, supplies, and materials used is also a symbol of how important we consider a job. Attempts to shave costs by providing cheap substitutes for quality reflect on the importance of the job and, therefore, the person performing that job. An operator is not merely washing dishes; he or she is responsible for a piece of equipment worth several thousand dollars. Let them know.

Language also can be used to tell employees how important their job is to the profits of the hotel or restaurant. Take those who burnish the silverware up to see the banquet room when it is set up for a party. Let them see and know in words how important the job that they do is to the look of the room and how tarnished silverware can take away from the enjoyment of the meal.

Management actions also can influence employee perceptions. What managers do reflects what they consider important. The manager who does not spend time in the back of the house tells kitchen employees their jobs are less important. Managers should notice the little things employees do that make the difference between doing or not doing a job well. It is also important to know when to step in to assist.

Management also can influence employee perceptions through the work setting chosen. At the employee dining area of the Bank of England in London, the dish-washing section is placed on the third floor in a well-ventilated, brightly painted large room with a view. The effect on the employees, who are used to being sequestered in the dingy basement of a restaurant, is dramatic.

The place chosen for employee meetings can affect the way in which employees view the importance of the topic under discussion. A meeting held in the comfort of a meeting room normally used for guest business will have more attention than one held in the employees' quarters.

Symbols cannot be a substitute for substance. However, a program of job design can be made ineffective unless management ensures that positive signals about the employees' jobs are given them through management words and actions.

JOB EVALUATION

As jobs are redesigned, it becomes necessary to reevaluate their worth to the company. The process of job evaluation determines a hierarchy of job values.

Purpose

The objectives of job evaluation are threefold:

1. Establish the ranking of jobs within an organization, measure the difference in value between them, and group them into an appropriate grade in a pay scale.
2. Ensure that as far as possible, judgments about job values are made on objective rather than subjective grounds, based on analytical studies of the content of the jobs irrespective of the contributions particular job holders make.
3. Provide a continuing basis for assessing the value of jobs that is easy to understand, administer, and control and is accepted by employees as fair.[3]

Techniques

The starting point for an evaluation is a job analysis. The job is studied in terms of the tasks involved, and an evaluation is made of the overall importance of those tasks to the company.

A variety of methods exist to compare the importance to the company of one job to another. They can be broken down into two categories: nonanalytic and analytic. In a nonanalytic plan, comparisons are made between whole jobs. An analytic plan, on the other hand, breaks jobs down into their constituent parts, and the factors that make up the jobs are compared.

Job Ranking

The simplest nonanalytic method is job ranking. Each job is compared to the others and all are arranged in order of importance. Jobs may be compared on the basis of one factor, such as responsibility or skills required. In other situations, the job as a whole would be evaluated relative to several factors. Typically, this might involve such things as the difficulty of the job, the amount of decision making, the range of tasks carried out, the level of knowledge and skills the job holder requires, and the physical effort required to do the job.

Each job is analyzed and described in such a way that the criteria being used to evaluate the jobs are brought out. Key jobs are then established for the basis of comparison. These would be the most and least important jobs, as well as those midway along the scale. Jobs are then ranked around the benchmarks in order of importance and divided into grades based on similarities in duties, skills, or required training, in order to provide guidance for future placement of new jobs in the hierarchy.

Job ranking is easy to do and understand. It may be appropriate when few jobs are involved and the person doing the evaluation is familiar with them all. As the number of different jobs increases, so do the difficulties in ranking them on a consistent basis. Different evaluators may weigh the various criteria differently. It is relatively easy to establish the extremes within a hierarchy. It is more difficult to place the positions in between correctly.

Paired Comparisons

One way around this is the *method of paired comparisons*. Each job in the property is compared with each other job, one at a time. For each pair, the job that is more important—relative to the criteria decided above—receives two points. The one that is less important receives no points. If two are equally important, each receives one point. Once all the comparisons have been made, the total number of points for each job is determined and a ranking of importance developed. It is easier to compare one job to one other than one job to all.

Job Classification

The *job classification method* etsablishes several levels into which jobs will be placed. Each level is defined in terms of the skills and responsibility required. Benchmark jobs are then determined for each level, and the remaining positions within the property are slotted into the various levels based on their similarity to the descriptions of levels and the benchmark jobs. An example is given in table 8–1 of a job classification system for a hotel involving seven levels. Although this system is easy to implement and understand, there are drawbacks. When using only one factor to evaluate jobs, such as skill levels, the problem of comparison is difficult for those positions that require little skill but, for example, demand great responsibility. If different factors are used, the problem becomes determining which is more important. In addition, different evaluators will weigh factors differently.

Point Rating Method

The most widely used method of evaluating jobs is the *point rating method*. This consists of determining the factors common to all jobs, weighing the

TABLE 8–1:	HOTEL JOB CLASSIFICATION LEVELS	
Level	*Definition*	*Examples*
1	Very simple tasks of a largely physical nature.	Cleaner
2	Simple tasks carried out in accordance with a small number of clearly defined rules after a short period of training, perhaps two to three weeks. The work is checked and closely supervised.	Room attendant, bartender
3	Straightforward tasks, but involving more complicated routines and requiring a degree of individual knowledge and alertness, as the work is subject to occasional checking	Waiter
4	Tasks calling for the independent arrangement of work and the exercise of some initiative; little supervision is needed. Detailed familiarity with one or more branches of established procedure is required.	Front-desk clerk, server
5	Routine work, but involving an individual degree of responsibility for answering routine queries and/or exercising some measure of control over a small group of employees.	Maître d', assistant housekeeper
6	Nonroutine work involving coordination of several lower-grade functions, possibly some measure of control over a small group of employees. Also nonroutine work involving recognized individual knowledge and some responsibility without follow-up.	Head housekeeper Restaurant manager
7	Work necessitating responsibility for sections involved in routine tasks or where there are also individual tasks to be undertaken, calling for specialized knowledge.	Chef, front-office manager

importance of these factors to each other, then establishing the number of points at each level for each factor. There are several common factors in use, within a few broad categories:

Skill: education, experience, initiative and ingenuity

Effort: physical demand, mental or visual demand

Responsibility: for equipment or process, for materials, products, or service, for the safety of others, for the work of others

Job conditions: working conditions, unavoidable hazards

Each factor would be given a number of points relative to its importance to the company. Then, levels for each factor would be established, using the initial rating as a base, multiplied by the number of levels for each factor. It may be determined, for example, that experience is worth twenty points but working conditions only five points. At the second and third levels, the values for experience would be forty and sixty, respectively. For working conditions, the values would be ten and fifteen.

While the consideration of several factors allows for greater objectivity and consistency, it is more difficult to complete. A major difficulty is determining a list of factors that will describe all possible jobs. Additionally, some subjectivity still exists in the determination of weights for the factors.

Hay Plan

A widely used method for evaluating managerial jobs is the *Hay plan.* Know-how, problem solving, and accountability are assumed to be the most important aspects of managerial jobs. Know-how has three dimensions: the amount of knowledge required, the breadth of the job in terms of the number of activities, and the requirement for skill in motivating people. Problem solving has two dimensions: the amount of freedom called upon in making decisions without regard to previously determined standards, and the complexity of mental activity involved. Accountability refers to the freedom to act independently, the dollar figure of job accountability, and the direct or indirect impact of the job in dollars on the bottom line. A job with direct impact is considered more important than one with indirect impact.

SUMMARY

When employees who seek fulfillment from the job are faced with mindless repetitive work, productivity will go down. Job design offers a way to restructure the job so that it will provide satisfaction for the employee while raising productivity for the company. Management can play an active role in this process. More complex jobs, however, will require more compensation. It is for management to determine whether (possibly) fewer, more skilled employees performing more complex jobs will result in greater productivity.

NOTES

[1]Paul, W. J., and K. B. Robertson, *Job Enrichment and Employee Motivation*, London, Gower Press, 1970.

[2]Haire, Mason, Edwin Ghiselli, and Lyman Porter, "An International Study of Management

Attitudes and Democratic Leadership," proceedings of the CIOS 13th International Management Congress, New York, Council for International Progress in Management, 1963, 101–14.

[3] Armstrong, Michael, and John F. Lorentzen, *Handbook of Personnel Management Practice,* Englewood Cliffs, N.J., Prentice-Hall Inc., 1982, 258–59.

SUGGESTED READINGS

Abdell-Halim, Ahmed A., "Effects of Role Stress–Job Design–Technology Interaction on Employee Work Satisfaction," *Academy of Management Journal* 24, no. 2, 1981, 260–73.

Armstrong, Michael, and John F. Lorentzen, *Handbook of Personnel Management Practice,* Englewood Cliffs, N.J., Prentice-Hall Inc., 1982, 191–96.

Bazerman, Max H., "Impact of Personal Control on Performance: Is Added Control Always Beneficial?" *Journal of Applied Psychology* 67, no. 4, 1982, 472–79.

Beatty, Richard W., and Craig Eric Schneier, "A Case for Positive Reinforcement," *Business Horizons,* April 1975, 57–66.

———, "Designing and Implementing Job Enrichment Programs," in *Personnel Administration: An Experiential/Skill-Building Approach,* Reading, Mass., Addison-Wesley Publishing Company, 1981, 411–35.

Bohlander, George W., "Implementing Quality-of-Work Programs: Recognizing the Barriers," *M.S.U. Business Topics,* Spring 1979, 33–40.

Caldwell, David F., and Charles A. O'Reilly III, "Task Perceptions and Job Satisfaction: A Question of Causality," *Journal of Applied Psychology* 67, no. 3, 1982, 361–69.

Champoux, Joseph E., "A Three Sample Test of Some Extensions to the Job Characteristics Model of Work Motivation," *Academy of Management Journal* 1980, 23, no. 3, 466–78.

Derakhshan, Foad, "The Effect of Span of Supervision on Leadership Attributes of Fast-Food Restaurants," *Journal of Foodservice Systems* 2, 1985, 85–94.

Griffen, Ricky W., "Relationships Among Individual, Task Design, and Leader Behavior Variables," *Academy of Management Journal* 23, no. 4, 1980, 665–83.

Hackman, J. Richard, Greg Oldham, Robert Janson, and Kenneth Purdy, "A New Strategy for Job Enrichment," *California Management Review* 17, no. 4, 1975, 57–71.

Hamner, W. Clay, "Worker Motivation Programs: The Importance of Climate, Structure and Performance Consequences," in *Contemporary Problems in Personnel,* Kenneth Pearlman, Frank L. Schmidt, and W. Clay Hamner (eds.), New York, John Wiley & Sons, Inc., 1983, 285–312.

Moberg, Dennis J., "Job Enrichment Through Symbol Management," *California Management Review* 24, no. 2, Winter 1981, 24–30.

Mowday, Richard T., and Daniel G. Spencer, "The Influence of Task and Personality Characteristics on Employee Turnover and Absenteeism Incidents," *Academy of Management Journal* 24, no. 3, 1981, 634–42.

Pierce, Jon L., "Job Design in Perspective," in *Contemporary Problems in Personnel,* Kenneth Pearlman, Frank L. Schmidt, and W. Clay Hamner (eds.), New York, John Wiley & Sons, Inc., 1983, 325–34.

Training Resource Corporation, "Add the Missing Motivation," Session Builder 207, 1986, Harrisburg, Pa.

———, "Adding Challenge to a Job," Session Builder 214, 1986, Harrisburg, Pa.

———, "The Big Turn-Ons," Session Builder 117, 1982, Harrisburg, Pa.

Welsch, Harold P., and Helen Lavan, "Inter-Relationships Between Organizational Commitment and Job Characteristics, Job Satisfaction, Professional Behavior and Organizational Climate," *Human Relations* 34, no. 12, 1981, 1079–89.

APPENDIX: IMPLEMENTING A JOB DESIGN PROGRAM

The process involved in redesigning a job requires selecting one that needs enlargement or enrichment and then instituting the changes that will make it better and more stimulating for the employee performing it.

SELECTING THE JOB

A simple questionnaire can be used to assess the potential of a job for redesign.

Select a job that is giving you problems—absenteeism, turnover, poor performance—and answer each of these questions for it, on a scale of 1 to 6, where 1 equals a great deal and 6 equals very little. Place your answer in the appropriate space.

Skill Variety

1. How much variety is there on the job? To what extent does the employee performing the job have the chance to do different things?

    _____

2. Does the job offer the chance to develop new skills and to advance in the company?

    _____

Task Identity

3. To what extent does the job involve a whole and identifiable piece of work with a beginning and an end?

    _____

Task Significance

4. Does this job affect guest satisfaction?

    _____

5. How important is this job to other people? Does it affect others' lives?

    _____

Autonomy

6. Does the job enable a person to be creative and imaginative, to use initiative?

    _____

183

7. Are there different ways of doing the job? Is there flexibility in job performance?

_____

Feedback

8. To what extent are the supervisor and co-workers able and willing to let the employee know how well he or she is doing?

_____

9. How much does the job itself, or actually doing the job, let the employee know how well he or she is doing?

_____

Total score: _____

Analysis

Jobs that receive a total score of 45 to 54 are candidates for a job redesign program; they have high potential to be enlarged or enriched. Jobs that score between 9 and 18 rank low in job redesign potential.

CHANGING THE JOB

Once candidates for job redesign are identified, the problem and preferred option should be listed. For example:

Problem: skill variety. Option: Have two employees trade jobs for part of the day.

Problem: task identity. Option: Make employee responsible for one identifiable piece of work, such as a clean room, a salad, a banquet room setup.

Problem: task significance. Option: Show employees how their job affects guest satisfaction. Publicize the importance of the job to those in other departments and outside the property as well.

Problem: autonomy. Option: Actively solicit employee suggestions on how to perform the job better.

Problem: feedback. Option: Ensure that supervisors give positive as well as negative feedback on the employee's performance.

ANOTHER APPROACH

Consider the outside organizations that employees join and contribute to, such as the Boy Scouts, Rotary, and various charities. Why do they actively get involved in these organizations? Why do they seem to contribute time and effort to a greater extent than they do on the job? It may be that you are a contributing member of such an organization. Why do you get involved?

Answering for yourself or for your employees, you will probably respond with such things as:

- "A feeling of authority or power"
- "Challenge, responsibility, a sense of being wanted"
- "Recognition"
- "The chance to get away, to work out frustrations"
- "The feeling of contributing to society"

The problem, then, may not be that employees are unmotivated to perform; employees may show effort and dedication when performing for other types of organizations. The problem is to get them to perform equally well on the job. Is there some way jobs can be redesigned in order that the employees performing them get the same rewards as they do off the job?

This thought process can be carried out either alone, in a brainstorming format, or with an actual group of employees. Ask them what hobbies or outside activities they engage in and why. They can also be asked in what ways their jobs can be changed to provide them with the very things they seek in their outside activities.

9 | IMPROVING PRODUCTIVITY: POSITIVE REINFORCEMENT

When an organizational climate rates low on the element of recognition, it indicates that the company is one in which the employees feel they are critized and punished when they do something wrong, rather than praised and rewarded when they do something right. In many companies, this is a prevalent feeling among employees.

The basic premise behind a program of positive reinforcement is that people perform in a way that is most rewarding to them. Management can improve employees' performance by providing appropriate rewards.

The theory is based on learning principles that Edward Lee Thorndike and B. F. Skinner described. Thorndike's Law of Effect states that behavior that appears to lead to a positive consequence tends to be repeated, while behavior that appears to lead to a neutral or negative consequence tends not to be repeated. Skinner feels that by the time employees enter the workplace, they have been conditioned by parents and society to understand what is right and wrong. The only tool needed for employee motivation, he argues, is the presence or absence of positive reinforcement; punishment is not needed to control behavior. Most managers will find this hard to accept.

Research does seem to show clearly, however, that positive reinforcement works better than negative reinforcement in producing and maintaining behavior.

PUNISHMENT AND DISCIPLINE

Various forms of punishment remain a crucial tool for managers. They use discipline in order to apply sanctions against employees who do not perform in the manner the company desires.

Progressive Discipline

To be most effective, a system of *progressive discipline* is in order. This is a method of applying punishment to the individual in a way that is increasingly severe. For example, the first time an employee is late for work, he or she may get a verbal reprimand. The next time, a written warning may go into the employee's personnel file. On the third occurrence within a given time period, the employee may be suspended without pay for a certain number of days. If the infraction occurs a fourth time, the employee would be fired.

186

The idea is to apply punishment appropriate to the offense in a way that will influence or shape employee behavior.

For punishment to be effective, certain principles should be followed. The action management takes should be immediate. For it to be effective, the employee must see a relationship between the act—say, coming in late—and the consequence of that act—initially, a verbal reprimand.

It is also important that the action, not the personality, be penalized. It should not be, "You are lazy," but rather, "Your coming in late caused others to work overtime."

Discipline must be applied consistently over time and with people. Employees must perceive the consequences for certain actions to be fair, which means applying the same sanction for the same actions to everyone and in every situation.

To be effective, punishment also must be moderately severe. That is, the employee must feel its effect. A story is told of a ski area employee who, after a couple of reprimands, was told that after one more occurrence he would be suspended without pay for three days. The infraction occurred, the employee was reprimanded—and he went off to enjoy three days of skiing.

It is important to reprimand in a setting that the employee perceives as warm and supportive. This, at first, may seem contradictory. Are we not giving mixed signals to the employee? The point is that while punishing one action, we are also setting a climate for future interactions and performance. It is vital to deal with the situation, then set a positive tone as a basis for the future.

Potential Side Effects

Punishment seeks the elimination of negative behavior by the application of negative consequences to that behavior. An employee comes in late. The employee is told, "If you come in late again, you will be fired." The negative behavior is the lateness; the punishment is being fired; the objective is to reduce or eliminate the negative behavior—to stop the lateness.

There are several problems with an overreliance on punishment. It may eliminate the lateness, but it may instead result in avoidance behavior. Our tardy employee wakes up late. Instead of coming in late and being fired, the employee may call in sick and not come in at all. Or consider the chef who is told, "Don't let me catch you with your food cost this high again." On the way out the door, the chef may mutter, "Don't worry, you won't catch me." The result may be actions that suppress rather than eliminate the negative behavior.

There is also the problem of the kinds of communication employees get from management. Consider the last time you heard, "The manager wants to see you." What goes through your mind? Most people say, "What did I do wrong?" Unfortunately, the only time it seems employees hear from management is when they have done something wrong.

Part of this is explained by the concept of management by exception. Performance is set and as long as everything and everyone is going along as expected, no action is taken. Only when something goes wrong—a customer complains, sales targets are not met, food cost is too high—does management step in. While some employees prefer to be left alone to do their job, most need feedback. When the only feedback is negative, it creates a negative climate. One answer is a program of positive reinforcement.

TYPES OF REINFORCEMENT

Positive reinforcement seeks to increase the occurrence of positive behavior by providing desirable consequences for that behavior. Negative reinforcement also seeks to increase the occurrence of positive behavior, but by the termination of undesirable consequences—unlike punishment, which seeks to reduce the occurrence of negative behavior by providing undesirable consequences for that behavior. There are several related terms. Extinction means no consequences or feedback; it is more punishing to most employees than punishment. Learned responses must be reinforced to recur. Behavior that is not reinforced in any way will eventually decrease and disappear. This is often true, for example, of the child who swears in front of a parent. The reaction to the "naughty word" is what the child is seeking. If no reaction is forthcoming, the behavior ceases.

Let us return to our tardy employee. Punishment occurs when the employee is told that being late again will result in firing. While that may eliminate lateness, it may instead result in avoidance. With extinction, on the other hand, the employee receives no feedback from the manager whether early, on time, or late. Suddenly the employee may be fired for not performing—and may end up leaving without knowing what went wrong.

Negative reinforcement occurs when the employee is told, for example, that a written reprimand for lateness will be removed from the file if on-time performance is maintained for a month. The hope is that positive behavior will increase by having the employee work toward having a negative (the written warning) removed.

Positive reinforcement occurs when employees are told that at the end of the week, all employees who have a perfect attendance record will be eligible for a drawing; the winners will receive dinner for two at the hotel restaurant. Some critics call this bribery. After all, employees are paid to come in on time. Why should they be additionally rewarded for what they should do anyway? When a child is told, prior to Grandma's visit, "If you behave yourself, you can have some ice cream," is that bribery or positive reinforcement?

The point is, if management has a problem and punishment is not working, it may be necessary to provide consequences for desirable behavior in order to get it. In many operations, the accent is heavily on punishment to reduce negative behavior. A void is present unless there is also in place at the same time a system of incentives to encourage desired behavior.

APPLYING THE CONCEPT

Positive reinforcement is appropriate when employees feel there is too much reliance on punishment and threats rather than verbal or other rewards. In addition, behavioral objectives may be ambiguous or nonexistent. Often an employee will be told, "Do a good job," without being told what behavior constitutes a good job.

Motivational Assumptions

Positive reinforcement assumes that employees are motivated by extrinsic rewards. In order to be sustained, desired behavior must be positively reinforced.

Unlike motivational models that look at employee attitudes as a cause of behavior, this technique focuses on rewards as an influence on behavior. It is a results-oriented, not process-oriented, approach.

Applicability

This technique can be applied to all jobs, because the emphasis is on the relationship between a job and its consequences. In reality, it may be rather difficult to specify the behavior appropriate in higher management positions.

Reward distribution

The reward for the employee can come in several different ways and at several different times. Reinforcement can be continuous, intermittent, fixed, or variable, as will be examined.

Consequences

On the plus side, performance can be improved if the desired behavior is outlined and linked to consequences important to the employee.

On the negative side, it can be time-consuming and costly to identify and monitor employee behavior.

MANAGEMENT'S ROLE

There are six steps to the effective implementation of a positive reinforcement program: describe existing behavior, develop expectations, determine needed behavior, reinforce this behavior, create employee feedback, and develop supervisory feedback.

Describe Existing Behavior

The starting point is an audit of existing performance in behavioral terms. Let us take sales of rooms and other facilities at the front desk as an example. From detailed observation, we may note that front-desk clerks, when asked the price of rooms, quote only the cheapest one available. When asked to describe the difference between the most and least expensive rooms, they are unable to do so. They do not offer to make reservations for incoming guests at the hotel's dining facilities.

Develop Expectations

At this point, it is necessary to set objectives. Objectives should be reasonable, specific, and within a set time period. The ideas developed in the chapter on management by objectives can be incorporated into this process. The difference in approaches is that the emphasis here is on the behavior necessary to achieve the objectives, as well as the consequences of that behavior. Objectives without feedback and positive reinforcement are unlikely to work.

We may decide at this point that we wish to increase the average room rate each desk clerk books by ten dollars and require each clerk to make dinner reservations for twenty guests within the next month.

Determine Needed Behavior

The next step is to identify the behavior necessary to achieve the objectives. To increase the average rate of rooms booked, it is necessary when asked the price of available rooms to mention the most expensive rate first. If price resistance is met, the clerk can mention the next most expensive room. When asked the difference between the room rates, it is necessary to describe in attractive detail the advantages of the higher-priced room. To reserve tables in the hotel dining facility, it is necessary to offer to make reservations for each incoming party on arrival. If asked, it is necessary to be able to describe the type of cuisine offered and the price range of the hotel restaurant. By engaging in these actions, the front-desk clerk will increase his or her average booked room rate and will increase business in the dining room.

Reinforce the Behavior

The key to this program is the reinforcement of behavior. Several types of reinforcement are possible. *Continuous reinforcement* involves reacting to the behavior each and every time it occurs. This is the type of reinforcement received when we put coins in a soda machine. Every time the correct amount of money goes into the slot, a can of soda appears. Continuous reinforcement is necessary to establish a new behavior. If we want an employee to greet guests with a smile, every time we see that smile we must reinforce it, with praise or some other reward.

Intermittent reinforcement, on the other hand, involves reinforcing the behavior only sometimes. A common example is a slot machine. We may put coins in without getting a payoff.

Related to this is the idea of fixed and variable reinforcement. *Fixed reinforcement* involves getting feedback on a set schedule in terms of either time or number of actions. The most obvious example of fixed reinforcement is the weekly or biweekly paycheck. Because that check comes each week, it becomes expected and, as a consequence, can lose its effectiveness as a motivator. *Variable reinforcement* is given on an irregular basis.

In terms of motivation, variable or intermittent reinforcement is more effective in sustaining already established behavior. Consider the soda machine compared to the slot machine. If you put coins in the soda machine and nothing happens, you may give up and leave, muttering under your breath; or you may kick the machine; or, if you are thirsty enough, you may put more coins in the slot. But if nothing still happens, will you put more change in? Not likely. We are used to a continuous schedule of reinforcement. When we go from continuous reinforcement to no reinforcement, the behavior stops.

Managers will often work with employees to improve their behavior. After lots of work, lots of coaching, and lots of reinforcement, an employee's behavior begins to improve. But then the manager goes to work with another employee whose behavior needs to be improved. Getting no more reinforcement, the first employee's new behavior may disappear.

Consider now the slot machine. We put in some coins, but get no response. Do we put in more? Of course! The behavior is continued far longer than we would feed the soda machine because we know that sometime there will be a worthwhile payoff. The intermittent, variable response of the slot machine keeps the behavior going.

In fact, research on animals has shown that once developed, behavior will be repeated with relatively infrequent reinforcement. Continuous reinforcement is necessary to get a new behavior started; intermittent reinforcement is necessary to keep it going.

Employee Feedback

The fifth step is to allow employees to keep a record of their own work. This self-assessment is crucial in that it generates its own continuous reinforcement.

Every time the desk clerk makes a reservation in the hotel dining room, he or she makes a note of it. The reinforcement is immediate. In this way, the clerk sees the relationship between the behavior and the consequence. The success interval, or the distance between the behavior and the measurement, is shortened. It would be somewhat impractical, for example, to attempt to improve employee tardiness by having a monthly drawing for on-time workers. The success interval here is about thirty days. If an employee is late the second day, there is no positive incentive to participate further.

Another point is that the perceived difficulty of the objective can be reduced by shortening the success interval. Selling sixty bottles of wine a month may sound intimidating to a young server. Selling two bottles a night sounds easier to accomplish.

Supervisory Feedback

In this sixth step, the supervisor looks at the performance of the employee and praises the positive aspects. Following Skinner's work, it would be unnecessary to comment on the negative aspects of performance. Neglecting them will encourage the employee to improve in order to receive more positive feedback. In fact, drawing attention to negative behavior may give the employee the attention desired. Teachers and managers are aware of the person who does something wrong in order to get attention. The punishment that results is better than the neglect the employee, student, or child usually gets. *The One Minute Manager* talks about catching the employee doing something right.

For reinforcement to work, the employee has to see the relationship between the behavior and the consequence. With continuous reinforcement, it has to be as immediate as possible. It also has to be meaningful to the employee. A waitress struggling as a single parent to raise two children has different priorities than the college student working part-time for "fun money."

Praise is not enough. When employees perform the way management wants and sales and profits increase, employees rightfully expect to share in the results of their efforts. People can handle only so many "Attaboys." The smart manager realizes that the welfare of the company is intertwined with the welfare of the employees. By distributing the fruits of the employee's labor in the form of higher wages and fringe benefits, the manager ensures that everyone benefits.

CRITICISMS

Various criticisms have been leveled at the positive reinforcement approach to employee motivation. These include conflicts between individual and group behavior, difficulties in finding the right rewards, the problem of overreliance on feedback, and concern that the approach is too manipulative.

Individual versus Group

It has been pointed out that positive reinforcement is a tool of management for individualized feedback, but many work situations involve group cooperation. Different things motivate each person within a group, yet the output of the group depends on the contributions of every individual. The behavior of each must be considered individually as well as in terms of the group. Each person's behavior as it contributes toward the group effort can be defined, observed, and rewarded accordingly.

Individualized Rewards

Associated with this is the problem of developing rewards appropriate to each employee. What one worker finds rewarding, another may not. While management may reward an employee's effort, that same effort may draw negative reaction from other employees who feel threatened by the individual's greater performance.

The key is in the design of the reward system. It is necessary to find out what works for each employee. This is very time-consuming. But then good management is very time-consuming. Management, it is said, is just one thing after another.

The Limits of Feedback

It has been pointed out repeatedly that feedback alone is insufficient to produce productive employees. A feedback system should have the dual objectives of getting the work done and making the job more enjoyable. This requires improved physical working conditions, equitable pay, and promotion opportunities, in addition to verbal praise.

Is It Manipulative?

The major philosophical argument against positive reinforcement is that it is manipulative. It does involve the manipulation and control of human behavior through a system of rewards and punishment. While we may feel comfortable about attempts to control the movement of rats through a maze, we like to think that humans operate at a somewhat higher level.

It may be argued, however, that an overreliance on punishment also controls behavior, and positive reinforcement is just an attempt to balance positively those management methods that are detrimental to the employee.

We might also ask rhetorically: if managers spend their nights thinking of the needs of the employees and how best to provide for these needs, whose behavior is being manipulated by whom?

MONEY AS POSITIVE REINFORCEMENT

Money is an extrinsic reward, as opposed to an intrinsic one such as job satisfaction. Does it motivate?

Herzberg's widely accepted view is that the absence of an equitable paycheck will cause employee morale to do down, but its presence will not cause an increase in morale. Of course, Herzberg believes that in the long run, intrinsic factors motivate.

Viewed in extrinsic terms, reinforcement is effective if given on an intermittent basis. Thus, the biweekly paycheck ceases to be an effective reinforcement. When employees expect to be paid every two weeks, the absence of that money would be viewed negatively. Its presence has little or no positive impact. Even a pay increase has only a short-term effect. The first time an employee receives the increase, there may be a rise in motivation. By the next pay period, the increased amount is expected, the employee's standard of living probably will have risen to meet or even exceed the increase in pay, and the motivating effect is gone. However, there are ways to extend the effect of the motivation.

Designing a Motivating Pay Plan

A pay scale must be developed that is sufficiently high that employees perceive it as equitable. This is necessary to prevent a reduction in motivation. At the same time, it is possible to build into that plan several elements that will take into consideration the positive aspects of reinforcement.

The pay scale for a job must have *internal equity* and *external competitiveness*. Internal equity means that a system should be established that identifies the relative worth of each job within the property in such a way that, for example, the desk clerk feels fairly compensated compared to the room attendant. It is a truism that equitable pay to the employee means not only the absolute amount of the paycheck but also how much it is relative to those of other people doing different jobs within the property.

Techniques for job evaluation described in chapter 8 can be used to establish internal equity. Having grouped jobs of similar value together, a salary range is established. The salary range has a minimum, midpoint, and maximum. The minimum is the amount paid to hire an employee with limited experience in that job. No one will be hired to do this job and be paid a wage lower than the minimum. The maximum is the highest rate to be paid for jobs in that particular salary range. If an employee is not promoted before reaching the maximum for the job, any increase in pay will come about only if and when the salary range is increased. The midpoint falls halfway between these two. Typically, it is the amount paid in the external labor market for someone performing a similar job.

Internal equity also means paying employees equitable amounts relative to other employees performing the same job in their unit. The introduction of a merit pay plan permits employee raises based on performance. If employees perceive the process of setting and measuring performance is fair, they will readily accept a merit plan. For it to have any motivational impact, employees must see a significant difference given for different performance levels. An example of a performance-based system is illustrated in table 9–1. For example, George is hired as a front-desk clerk low in the third quartile of the salary range, based on his significant experience. If his future performance is outstanding, he can expect a 12 percent increase in salary after nine to twelve months on the job. If George's performance did no more than meet the standards for the job, no raise would be given.

The development of a merit pay plan will have a more beneficial effect on motivation and productivity than either a flat rate or step rate plan. A flat rate plan is one in which everyone performing a particular job is paid the same

TABLE 9–1: PERFORMANCE-BASED PAY INCREASE GUIDELINES

Performance Level	Position in the Salary Range Before the Raise			
	1st	*2d*	*3d*	*4th Quartile*
Outstanding	16% 6–9 mo.	14% 9–12 mo.	12% 12 mo.	To maximum 12 mo.
Exceeds standards	14% 6–9 mo.	12% 10–12 mo.	10% 12 mo.	No raise
Meets standards	12% 9–12 mo.	10% 12 mo.	No raise No raise	No raise No raise

Source: Slade, Clifford, "How to Design a Pay Plan For Hotel Employees," *Lodging,* November 1981, 45–50.

rate, irrespective of time in the job or performance. A step rate plan allows for pay increases only on the basis of seniority in the job. The only times such a plan should be applied is when there is little opportunity for different levels of performance within the job.

External competitiveness refers to the relationship between how much an employee is paid and what others performing similar jobs in other properties receive. Employees must perceive that the amount paid is fair compared to what others in the marketplace are receiving. An unsatisfied employee can always leave. And if that is not possible, dissatisfaction will surely result. As noted above, the midpoint in the salary range is usually fixed at this external rate.

The timing of raises has implications for profitability and motivation. Giving a raise on the anniversary of employment is effective if seniority is important to the company. A raise at this time emphasizes another year of service. It also has the effect of spreading the expense throughout the year.

A calendar date plan gives raises on the same day to all employees. This makes budgeting much easier. Room or food and beverage rates can be adjusted to take pay increases into account. If this method is chosen, it is important also to take into account the effect of Social Security contributions. If the maximum was reached prior to the end of the year, an increase on January 1 will go unnoticed; the employee will be comparing a December paycheck with no deduction and a January paycheck with a deduction. The effect of the raise will be diluted. Obviously, this is important only to higher-paid employees, as they are the ones who will meet the maximum contribution by year's end.

To maximize the motivational impact of money, it would be wise to give several smaller raises over the year rather than a large one, as long as the smaller raises were noticeable in their impact on the employee. If we assume that the motivating effect of a raise lasts several weeks, more motivating weeks per year can be gained through multiple raises than through one.

Employees expect a paycheck. It is possible, however, to structure periodic awards of money to induce more motivated employees and productivity. Where a link can be shown between individual effort and unit profitability, profit sharing can be effective. Amounts awarded usually are based on a percentage of base salary and vary as profits vary.

Employees also could be awarded a production bonus. This could occur, for example, when the housekeeping staff is reduced by one person. If the remaining room attendants maintain the same level of quality in covering all the rooms, the salary of the employee who left can be divided among those who remain. This would provide more money to each of the employees while reducing fringe benefits for management. This can result in a considerable savings, as benefits can add one-third to the labor bill.

It is also possible to arrange special cash awards of recognition to employees for suggestions that result in savings to the property.

CAREER DEVELOPMENT
AS POSITIVE REINFORCEMENT

For many employees, advancement is very important. In a 1982 survey of foodservice supervisors reported at the National Restaurant Show, the question was asked, "Where do you see yourself five years from now?" In response, 29 percent said they saw themselves in their boss's job, 48 percent said any higher-management job, and only 10 percent saw themselves remaining at the same job. It is clear that many employees desire upward mobility. A career development system is important in getting them motivated.

Assessing the Need

The need for a career development system can be seen in the following signals:

- Most vacancies above the lowest-level jobs are filled from outside the company.
- Employees are not promoted from within the organization or move up very slowly.
- Employee turnover is high.
- Employee productivity is low.
- Employee attitudes are poor and morale is low.

The starting point is the preparation of an *organizational chart*. This chart should list the number of employees in each job and the reporting relationships between positions, in addition to the wage range for each job. Figure 9–1 is a modified organizational chart, without salary ranges listed. Next, it is necessary to compare the salary ranges paid to those in the local community. Salary

FIGURE 9–1 MODEL ORGANIZATIONAL CHART.

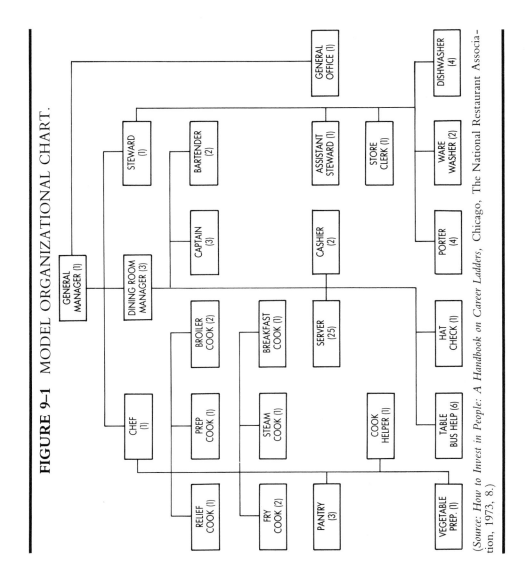

(*Source: How to Invest in People: A Handbook on Career Ladders*, Chicago, The National Restaurant Association, 1973, 8.)

ranges that are much higher suggest a drain on profits; substandard wages will likely lead to dissatisfaction and employee turnover. A final use of the organizational chart is to examine the number of employees in each position. Is it reasonable for an employee to expect a promotion soon? The fewer visible promotional opportunities there are, the greater the chance of employee dissatisfaction and turnover.

A *promotional pattern chart* shows how existing employees have been promoted within the organization. It shows the sequence of promotions and transfers, as well as the time intervals between each move. Such a chart can be constructed in one of two ways. Existing employees can be questioned to determine their sequence of jobs since they joined the company. It is also possible, if record keeping is sufficient, to establish a point in time and trace the movements of past and existing employees since.

In analyzing these charts, the manager is looking for several things. Charts with few ports of entry—jobs filled by hiring from outside the company— indicate good promotional opportunities. A large number of ports of entry suggests that too many employees are being hired from outside and that internal promotion opportunities are lacking. It should be noted that every port of entry above the lowest organizational level represents an opportunity for internal promotion. Ports of exit—positions from which employees leave the organization—suggest dead-end jobs that lead nowhere. The company that reduces ports of entry and exit can significantly increase internal promotional opportunities for its employees.

The organizational chart shows us where we are; the promotional pattern chart indicates how people have progressed through the company. From them we can identify opportunities for increasing promotional opportunities.

Designing the Structure

Typically, employees have been promoted on the basis of the lines of authority exhibited in a traditional organizational chart. A *career development ladder* links jobs based on the use of similar skills and knowledge (fig. 9–2). This clarifies the opportunities to move from one department to another or from the front of the house to the back of the house.

Creating a career development ladder requires analysis to develop job descriptions for each position on the organizational chart. Several steps are involved.

First, a job list is prepared of each and every separate function that the employee performing each job carries out. A server, for example, may be responsible for:

- Greeting and seating restaurant customers
- Serving water and lighting candles
- Taking beverage orders and serving drinks
- Presenting the food menu and beverage list
- Assisting customers in making food and beverage selections
- Placing orders in the kitchen

FIGURE 9-2 FUNCTIONALLY INTEGRATED CAREER PROGRESSION MODEL FOR A FOODSERVICE FACILITY

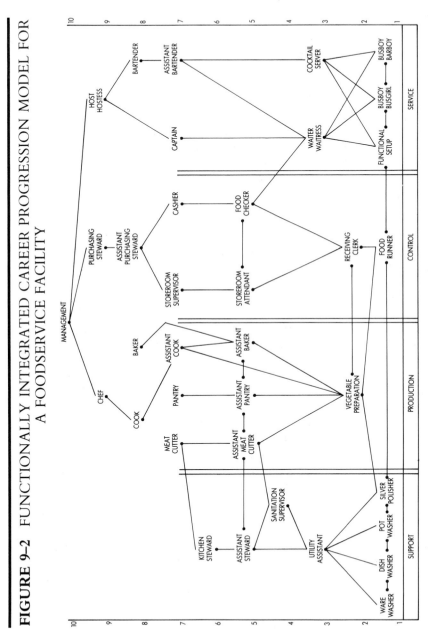

(*Source:* William P. Fisher and Paul L. Gaurnier, *Career Ladders in the Foodservice Industry*, Chicago, The National Restaurant Association, 1971, 25.)

- Serving food and clearing tables in between courses
- Serving wine
- Collecting money and making change
- Setting tables

From this, the supervisor and employee together complete a job breakdown, identifying for each function on the job list what has to be done, how it is to be done, and why it has to be done that way. This is a joint project because the employee is most familiar with what is done, while the supervisor is most familiar with how it should be done.

By comparing job descriptions on the basis of the skills and knowledge needed, the manager can construct the career ladder. Employees then can see that upward mobility is not restricted to traditional routes but is based on the acquisition of requisite skills and knowledge. They further see that the company is committed to a policy of promotion from within. Both of these points will increase employee motivation.

Designing the Process

Four activities are necessary to implement the above system of career development. Job vacancies must be predicted, employees informed of the vacancies, employee selection completed, and training undertaken.

By predicting job vacancies, employees can be prepared for promotions before vacancies occur. This is a delicate process. If management waits until a vacancy occurs before beginning the process of employee selection and training, production and service will suffer while the position is not fully staffed. On the other hand, if employees are trained and prepared for promotion but openings do not materialize, dissatisfaction is likely to result.

Job vacancies are best predicted on the basis of past records. A career ladder program, however, can eventually reduce past levels of employee turnover. Existing figures would have to be modified to take expected changes into account. Because turnover varies by position and possibly by time of year, monthly figures should be developed for each position. The formula is that the turnover rate equals the number of employees separated and replaced, divided by the average number of employees, multiplied by one hundred. The result is expressed as a percentage.

The turnover rate would be applied to the number of people in each job to determine the number of projected vacancies each month in each position. For example, if we have experienced a turnover rate of 20 percent during January in our servers and the number of servers during January is typically forty, then we would project eight vacancies (20 percent of forty) next January among servers. To this figure would be added additional vacancies if any expansion is predicted.

Assuming no expansion, a prediction is made that eight additional servers will be required next January. This serves as the basis for establishing training schedules. If twenty hours of training are necessary to prepare an employee for this position, eight employees should undergo one hour of training a day for twenty days to prepare for January's vacancies. Therefore, training should begin in December.

Successful Job Selection

To be successful, this system must be highly visible to employees and understood by them. This means employees must be aware that they can move upward if they want. They also must be told how to participate. This involves having access to a career ladder and information about both the skills required for each position and how to apply for it.

Selection can be accomplished through a *management-centered process* or an *employee bidding process*. In the management-centered process, employee records are scrutinized to identify suitably qualified individuals. Suitability is based on the various jobs held outside as well as within the organization, the sequence of jobs held, training for higher-level jobs already completed within or outside the company, and the length of time within each job and within the company. Management then interviews and selects qualified employees.

In the employee bidding process, employees decide for themselves whether they feel qualified to pursue promotion. Job opportunities are posted for all employees to see. In order to avoid legal challenges based on discrimination, it is far better to engage in an employee bidding process. In addition, management's task is reduced. There is no need to comb all employee files for suitable candidates. Third, employees are more likely to feel part of the system and, therefore, to support it. The primary disadvantage is that this method takes longer. Typically, there will be at least two weeks between the posting and the closing of bids. A management-centered process can identify employees in a matter of days. The files of those who apply are considered on the basis of the criteria noted above, interviews conducted, and employees selected.

Training can then begin following a time schedule as described above.

NONTRADITIONAL REWARDS

In the early 1980s, a White House Conference on Productivity was held to discuss the problem of declining productivity. The final report of that conference concluded that the major reward systems of the next few years will be:

- Sharing business information with employees
- Participative work practices
- Employment security
- Pay for performance

As a follow-up to this effort, the American Productivity Center and the American Compensation Association conducted a survey in 1986 to determine the extent to which companies were utilizing different reward systems. The 741 service companies that responded included 6 airlines, 119 hospitals, 3 hotel companies, and 11 restaurant organizations.

Over half of the respondents reported sharing business information with their employees on a frequent basis. This is most commonly done through the use of a newsletter or bulletin board.

Approximately half of all companies use participative work practices. The most widely used are small problem-solving groups and suggestion systems.

Almost one-third of the respondents use formal or informal strategies for employment security. These include such things as a written commitment to no layoffs and a guaranteed minimum number of work days or hours.

The most widely used nontraditional rewards were lump-sum bonuses, individual incentives, and profit sharing. Approximately 30 percent of service firms surveyed reported using one or more of these rewards. Two-thirds of all profit-sharing plans in the service sector have been adopted since the early 1980s.

Types of Profit Sharing

Profit-sharing plans can be deferred, cash, or a combination. The vast majority of profit-sharing plans are deferred. In a deferred plan, employees place contributions into a trust that is invested on their behalf. Payouts occur on termination, retirement, disability, or death. The advantage is that taxes on the profits are not paid until the employee withdraws them. In a cash plan, profits are usually paid out annually and taxes are paid on the income at that time. A combination plan pays some share of the profits regularly and defers some.

In a typical deferred plan, all employees over twenty-one years old who work at least one thousand hours a year and have been with the company a certain minimum period of time—one year, for example, in Marriott's plan—can participate. The company can choose to contribute to a share of the profits to the plan or may ask the employees to match the company's contribution. With the Marriott plan, the company puts in $1.50 for every $1.00 the employee puts in. Employees then can withdraw their money after a stated period of time. If the average length of service is three years, for example, the company may stipulate that employees wait four years before they can get the money. In this way, the plan acts as a device to encourage employees to stay. It is usual to specify a number of years—ten to fifteen—before the employee has the right to all the money in his or her account.

Other Rewards

The greatest growth in the past five years has been in the use of pay for knowledge, gain sharing, and small group incentives.

In a pay-for-knowledge plan, employees are paid on the basis of the number of jobs they can do rather than the number of tasks they actually perform on a given day.

Gain sharing refers to the idea of sharing increased profits or cost savings with all employees in a particular unit or department. If profit sharing is company-wide, it is known as a profit-sharing plan rather than gain sharing.

Small group incentives are similar to gain sharing. However, bonuses are paid on the basis of the performance of a group rather than on an individual formula. As such, the formula used can vary from group to group or department to department.

SUMMARY

If employees feel that management tends to threaten and criticize rather than praise and reward, a program of positive reinforcement is suggested. Many companies place an overemphasis on punishment to reduce unwanted behavior, without a program of positive reinforcement to increase desired behavior.

Behavioral expectations can be developed and a feedback system put into place that will reinforce the desired behavior, thus ensuring that it will be repeated.

Praise is not enough, however, to ensure desired behavior. Both money and career development can play an important part in producing motivated and productive employees.

SUGGESTED READINGS

Beatty, Richard W., and Craig Eric Schneier, "A Case for Positive Reinforcement," in *Personnel Administration Today,* Reading, Mass., Addison-Wesley Publishing Company, 1978, 467–78.

Blanchard, Kenneth, and Spencer Johnson, *The One Minute Manager,* New York, Berkley Books, 1983.

Eder, Robert W., and Douglas W. Naffziger, "Implementor's Manual" for *Personnel Administration: An Experiential/Skill-Building Approach,* Richard W. Beatty and Craig Eric Schneier (eds.), Reading, Mass., Addison-Wesley Publishing Company, 1981, 272–84.

Education Research, *Reinforcement,* Warren, N.J., 1979.

Hamner, W. Clay, "Worker Motivation Programs: The Importance of Climate, Structure, and Performance Consequences," in *Contemporary Problems in Personnel,* Kenneth Pearlman, Frank L. Schmidt, and W. Clay Hamner (eds.), New York, John Wiley & Sons, 1983, 285–312.

How to Invest in People: A Handbook on Career Ladders, National Restaurant Association, 1973.

Non-Traditional Reward Systems for Foodservice Employees, current issues report, National Restaurant Association, 1987.

Pavett, Cynthia M., "Evaluation of the Impact of Feedback on Performance and Motivation," *Human Relations* 36, no. 7, 1983, 641–54.

Slade, Clifford, "How to Design a Pay Plan for Hotel Employees," *Lodging,* November 1981, 45–50.

APPENDIX: IMPLEMENTING A POSITIVE REINFORCEMENT PROGRAM

The corporate sales office of an international hotel company has twenty salespeople who cover the domestic United States. Sales responsibilities are divided geographically and, in most cases, cover several states. Within the assigned geographic territory, each salesperson is responsible for selling all of the hotel products: midweek, weekend, meeting room, and convention space.

PROBLEMS

Geographic territories are unequal in terms of potential and actual sales volume. Originally they were divided up on the basis of seniority and past performance, the better and most senior employees getting the biggest potential and most important areas of the country.

Turnover is rather high among salespeople assigned to areas that produce the least amount of sales. Management feels that the potential from these geographic areas is about half of what is being produced at present.

Salespeople get commissions of 7 percent on gross sales, in addition to a set amount for monthly expenses. Neither the commission rate nor expenses vary for the salespeople. Bonus money is not available. All salespeople are offered a pension fund, a credit union, life insurance, and health insurance. The size of the pension fund and the life insurance benefits depends on the size of the salesperson's earnings.

One week of paid vacation is given after 1 year of service, 2 weeks after 3 years, 3 weeks after 6 years, and an additional week after each additional 10 years of service. The average length of service of salespeople in the high-producing areas is 12 years, in the lower-producing areas 1.6 years.

The newer salespeople have been complaining that their sales volume (and their earnings) is limited by the small number of potential accounts in their areas compared to those with the larger metropolitan areas such as New York, Chicago, and Washington, D.C.

Salespeople are in constant competition with employees of other hotel companies. Demand for the hotel's accommodation and meeting space is subject to the strength of the economy in the various regions of the United States.

The primary need is to design and implement a program of positive reinforcement that will result in increased sales for the company.

SOLUTIONS

The company takes a number of steps to eliminate its problems.

204

Quotas

Each salesperson will have a monthly quota of sales. The quota is set for each month for each of the sales areas. An analysis of past sales and trends must be done in order to determine the appropriate level of each quota. Monthly quotas deal with seasonal variations in sales. Adjustments can be made for external factors such as poor regional economic conditions, over which the company has no control.

The new program has to be announced in advance to give salespeople an opportunity to become familiar with the change. The beginning of the fiscal year is an obvious psychological time to change, as it gives the impression of a new start.

Sales Commission

Salespeople will receive a 7 percent commission on all sales up to their monthly quota, 10 percent commission on sales up to 10 percent above their quota, and 15 percent on all sales over the monthly quota if total sales are greater than 10 percent above the monthly quota. If the quota is exceeded by 25 percent, that salesperson will receive 12.5 commission on all sales for the month.

It was necessary to determine the appropriate rates through a feasibility study to ensure that the company could in fact afford such a scheme. The increasing rates suggested offer incentives to produce more. The greater the results, the greater the reward.

It is also important that salespeople know exactly what the consequences are of performing, or not performing.

Rewards are based on the amount of effort put into the job, and consequently on the results of those efforts. Rewards are given based on percentage increases in sales rather than total sales volume. This is more equitable to the salespeople in low-volume areas.

The commission structure is one of continuous reinforcement. Motivation occurs because salespeople will earn proportionately more from their increased effort. Low-quota salespeople do not have to sell as much to obtain their greater commission rates and will therefore have a greater incentive to sell.

Variable Vacation Time

The base vacation time will be one week a year. Additionally, each salesperson can earn up to three more weeks a year. The year is divided into three four-month periods. At the end of each four-month period, one month is chosen at random. All salespeople who surpass their sales quota for that month by 15 percent will receive an extra week of vacation.

The vacation plan offers both continuous and intermittent reinforcement. Reinforcement is continuous because the salesperson has a better chance of getting the reinforcement (one week's vacation) if the quota is exceeded by 15 percent. It is intermittent in that the salesperson has a chance to get the re-inforcement if the target is reached once, but he or she is not guaranteed the vacation unless the target is reached all four months. That is the reason the month is chosen randomly. The salesperson does not know which month will be selected and is therefore motivated to exceed the target in all four months.

The plan is equitable in that it is based on performance rather than seniority. Salespeople who have been with the company only a short period of time still can accumulate four weeks of paid vacation.

Promotion

Each of the sales districts will be ranked based on sales volume. When an opening arises in a particular district, each salesperson in an area that produced less volume than the one with the opening will be considered a candidate for the open position.

Promotion is based on merit. The company looks at the extent to which each salesperson, over the previous two years, exceeded or failed to meet his or her monthly quota. An increase of 10 percent over quota would rate a plus ten; failing to meet the quota by 8 percent would rate a negative eight. After the monthly ratings are added up, the salesperson with the highest positive figure will be offered the job.

If that person refuses the promotion, it will be offered to the next highest net producer. Thus, promotion is based not on seniority but on the ability to produce consistently over one's own quota. This adds incentive for the more junior salespeople.

Rewards here are intermittent in that they occur only as openings appear and are based on a sustained level of high performance over a two-year period.

Life Insurance and Pension Fund

The life insurance coverage for each salesperson will be the same. Pension benefits will vary depending on the individual's sales volume. A certain percentage of each person's commission will be deducted from the paycheck each month. This amount will be matched by the company and put into a pension fund account. The higher the salesperson's sales volume, the higher the pension benefits upon retirement.

Expense Accounts

All valid expenses will be paid. This will encourage salespeople who have to travel farther or work harder to build sales volume.

Demotion and Dismissal

Any salesperson who fails to meet his or her quota by more than 10 percent over any six-month period will be brought before a review board to explain the deficiency. If the board determines that the salesperson is not at fault, no action will be taken. If it is determined that it is the fault of the salesperson, that person is put on probation for six months.

At the end of the probation, the performance for the previous year is calculated.

If the sales generated are more than 5 percent below quota, the salesperson is demoted, switching positions with the employee who replaces him or her based on the promotion procedure already described.

At the end of the next year, if the performance of the demoted salesperson is more than 10 percent less than the quota for that year, the salesperson will be fired.

The review board is a punisher. It works on a fixed-ratio basis, as the salesperson must consistently underproduce for six months before he or she is called before it. The punishment consists of verbal reprimands in addition to the more serious embarrassment of having to explain his or her lack of performance. Salespeople the review board demotes are likely to resign rather than face the loss of income and prestige. The process also acts as a deterrent against poor performance.

COACHING POSITIVELY

One of your personable and bright salespeople looks as if he is headed for trouble. After a bad six-month period, Mark has been put on probation. As Mark's manager, you could either leave him to sink or swim over the next six months, or you could take an active role in trying to help him through positive reinforcement. You decide to try the latter.

What should your aim be in helping Mark? The overall objective is to ensure that his sales for the year are no worse than 5 percent below quota. However, this is too long-term an objective. By the time it is met, or not, the problem will be solved or Mark will be demoted. It is necessary to break this goal down into smaller facets. In this way, Mark's behavior can be shaped with small movements made on the way to achieving the goal.

Mark's target for the year was $150,000. During the first six months he produced $70,000 in confirmed bookings, $10,000 less than his target for that period. In order to avoid demotion, he must produce more than $142,500 ($150,000 less 5 percent) in annual sales. This means that in the next six months, Mark must produce another $72,500 to avoid demotion or $80,000 to meet the annual goal. The goal of $72,500 is an example of negative reinforcement: attempting to induce positive behavior through the avoidance of negative consequences—the demotion. Positive reinforcement—achieving positive behavior through the pursuit of positive consequences—would be working toward meeting or surpassing the annual goal and getting the appropriate commission.

At the moment, it probably would be better initially to go for the avoidance of demotion rather than anything higher. Realizing that this is not as powerful a motivator as the pursuit of a positive, you schedule a meeting with Mark. You express your desire to be of assistance. Together you break down the six-month, twenty-six-week goal of $72,500 into mini-goals of $12,100 a month and $2,789 a week.

At the end of the first week, Mark reports sales of $2,500. What do you do? Offering recognition of this subpar performance reinforces his not meeting the goal. The best thing is to keep quiet. By the second week, confirmed sales for the week are $2,800. Now what? Reinforce the movement, not the total. The total is still below the two-week target of $5,578. Emphasizing the total will freeze the number $2,800 in Mark's mind. You want to encourage the movement, however. Reinforce movement to get more movement; reinforce a level to maintain that level. A short note might do the trick: "Glad to see your sales figures are moving up. Keep up the good work!"

By the end of the first month, confirmed sales have risen to $12,000. Because Mark has missed the new goal by only $100, can we increase expectations to strive for the year-end target of $150,000, thereby ensuring all of Mark's commission? Probably not yet. One month of almost making it is not a good enough track record to suggest that the goal should be increased. Better to keep expectations at the same level.

Maintaining the positive feedback when the weekly objective has been achieved, and avoiding negatives when it is not, seems to be working. At the end of three months, confirmed sales are $40,000. You send Mark a $50 gift certificate for a local store. Another three months just like the last and Mark can make his quota and achieve his full commission. This would be a realistic time to sit down with him and raise the goal to that very thing. The monthly goal now becomes $13,334, the weekly objective $3,100.

For three weeks now, Mark has been passing his targets. What do you do? This is probably the time to cut back on the reinforcement. If you stop the reinforcement completely, chances are that Mark's results will drop off. The next time the weekly goal is met, make a mental note but do not get in touch with Mark. If it happens again, make note of the two-week target and let him know. In this way Mark does not know after which week the reinforcement, now intermittent, will come. He behaves, however, as if this next one will be the time for praise.

The end of the year is approaching. Mark's year-end confirmed sales are $147,500, $2,500 less than his quota. In view of his effort during these last six months—Mark's figures of $77,500 topped his previous six-month total of $70,000—should we waive the annual quota and reward Mark? (After all, think of the effort you also put in.) However, it would be a big mistake to reward Mark. It would reward him for not meeting his annual quota. The effect on the morale of the other salespeople also would be disastrous. But won't Mark be disappointed? Of course he will. Then what should you do? The key is to stress two things. First, that demotion was avoided and his record is clean. More important, focus on the second six months. If Mark can keep on producing at that level, he not only will meet his quota next time but also will get the bonus for surpassing the quota by more than 10 percent.

SUMMARY

Even with positive reinforcement, not every situation will work out perfectly. The point, however, is that by focusing on encouraging success, you will have a better chance of breeding success.

10 | IMPROVING PRODUCTIVITY: THE DEVELOPMENT OF TRUST

The last of the six dimensions of organizational climate to be considered is teamwork. This is the feeling of belonging to an organization, characterized by cohesion, mutual warmth and support, trust, and pride. Such employees trust and respect each other while feeling personal loyalty and a sense of belonging to the company.

When a survey of the climate indicates that teamwork is low, it is management's responsibility to instill a feeling of trust and loyalty.

MODELS OF ORGANIZATIONAL COMMITMENT

At this point, is it useful to examine three theories of organizational commitment to determine the factors that influence how and why employees are tuned in to the needs of a company.

Steers's Work Environment Model

Richard M. Steers hypothesized three major facets of the work environment that contribute to organizational commitment:

1. Personal characteristics: including age, education, and opportunities for advancement
2. Job characteristics: including job challenges, social interaction, and the amount of feedback
3. Work experience: involving organizational dependability and trust, perceptions of personal investments and rewards, and realization of expectations

A combination of these three elements determines the extent to which an employee is committed to the organization. The strength of this commitment manifests itself in the employee's desire and intention to remain, attendance and retention, and the level of job performance.

In his research, Steers identified six factors of prime importance:

1. The employee's need for achievement
2. Group attitudes toward the organization
3. The educational level of the employee

209

4. The extent to which employees can depend on the organization
5. The extent to which the employee is made to feel important to the organization
6. The extent to which the job the employee is doing can be related to the work of the organization (task identity)

Lewicki's Satisfaction of Personal Needs Model

Roy J. Lewicki saw commitment as an opportunity for the employee to satisfy the personal needs of security, self-esteem, and self-actualization. The more the employee's needs are met, the greater the commitment.

He presented four major managerial strategies to meet these needs:

1. Ideologically match the goals and philosophy of the organization with those of the employee.
2. Provide formal promotion opportunities with a formal reward system.
3. Provide challenging, involving work.
4. Create a pleasant work environment.

Salancik's Binding Force Model

Gerald R. Salancik explained commitment as a force that binds one to one's actions. An organization, he feels, can strengthen the cohesion between company and individual by applying three ideas: visibility, attachment, and volition.

Visibility is utilized by giving employees recognition for their work. If management informs all employees of what each is doing, visibility is heightened and employees are more likely to show commitment and less likely to show dissonance. Without this recognition, the motivation toward commitment is weakened.

Second, firms can bind employees to organizations by developing attachments that make it more difficult for them to leave. This can be accomplished through nontransferable benefits, team-building efforts, family approaches, and the development of employee skills that might not be valuable in other organizations.

The third concept is outside the control of the manager but is essential to a binding relationship. An employee must choose of his or her own volition to accept personal responsibility for involvement in the firm. This internal choice maintains a behavioral direction during fluctuations within the organizational climate.

Important to Salancik's explanation of commitment is the concept of *ideological myths*. In the myth-making process, employees act as if their actions are valuable. As they act, they renew that belief. Without realizing it, they have created a myth. The myth sustains the action, the action the myth. Myths give meanings to actions, sustain involvement, and make sense of sacrifices. Myths bind an individual to an organization by strengthening the belief that the work experience has value.

Common Concepts

The models contain several common ideas. The main factors that influence an individual's commitment are investments, reciprocity, lack of alternatives, and identification.

As individuals invest more in an organization in time, energy, and commitment, the less likely they are to leave as they accept future rewards—promotions, for example—for their contribution. If they leave the company, their investments will not be recovered.

The idea of reciprocity is based on the assumption that if employees feel they are getting more than they deserve—that the rewards of the job are more than expected—they will remain with the organization in order to repay this debt through future performance.

Lack of alternatives, in line with Salancik's idea of attachment, means that the more specific skills become to a particular organization, the less opportunity is available to use those skills outside the organization. This is not very important, however, in the hospitality industry, where the job in one hotel differs little from that in another.

Identification is defined as the linking of one's social identity to one's work. As identification increases, change becomes harder and commitment is strengthened.

MANAGEMENT'S ROLE

Management's task is to integrate the employee with the organization in such a way that there is evidence of mutual warmth and support. In a climate where trust and respect is found, employee feelings of belonging and loyalty will result.

Management Style

Contemporary managers have idealized models in their imagination akin to the *heroic manager*—the conquering leader who rescues helpless, disorganized employees from all problems and who leaves only when all has been accomplished by his or her own courage, intelligence, and skill. The helpless subordinates continue with their mundane tasks until another problem arises and the hero returns.

It is the feeling of control over themselves, but primarily over others, that creates this vision. When crises arise at work and tough decisions are called for, many managers feel responsible for knowing what the problem is, developing the solution, and exerting control over the situation.

When managers perceive their employees as being helpless and incapable and take full control, they elicit reciprocal behavior from their employees. Subordinates retreat to a defense of their narrow interests as managers exert complete control. The key is for managers to act as *developers*. Developers have a stronger employee-centered image. They earn how to have impact without exerting total control, to be helpful without having all the answers, and to be powerful without needing to dominate.

The developer-manager model consists of three components that must be nurtured to achieve productive excellence: interdependence, interpersonal skills, and commitment to an overriding departmental goal.

Within the organization there is a high degree of interdependence among departments and a constant stream of changes, both internal and external. This is especially true in the hospitality industry, where the satisfaction of the customer depends on the performance of many departments. Managers must develop a method to handle this interdependence and increased change.

The solution is to build a team that shares the responsibility of managing departments. It is a joint responsibility group that shares in making the core decisions and influences each member to ensure a high level of performance. Building such a team leads to greater subordinate commitment and motivation. Joint responsibility increases individual challenge and potential learning and growth. Development occurs in technical and managerial skills. Research has indicated that groups make better decisions than individuals when the problem is complex.

The second component in being a developer-manager is the importance of interpersonal skills. Daily interaction can be used to encourage and enhance growth in subordinates. Coaching from the developer-manager helps build competence. In this way, behavioral problems can be turned into an opportunity for growth.

The third component is getting the employees committed to the overriding goal of the department. The goal unites workers because it is a vision they can share and work toward. Employees do not work for money alone; the goal generates reasons that make the work worthwhile. It is the achievement toward the goal and appreciation of the extra effort that become rewarding to the employee. The goal gives the employee a sense of value. It inspires the employee to a level of performance beyond adequate. There is the potential for the goal to fulfill a core need within the individual: the need to belong to the organization.

Each component builds on the other. Working together, and encouraging employees by showing them that their productivity benefits all, is what is to be achieved. Integrating the components is the task of the developer-manager.

QUALITY CIRCLES

One method of developing employee trust and commitment is through the implementation of *quality circles*. Originally sold as a cure-all for employee problems, the idea has been criticized lately. This is unfortunate, because its reduced popularity results most from the fact that it was oversold, not ineffective.

Definition

A quality circle consists of a group of employees from the same area who meet, usually for an hour a week, to discuss any problems they are having, investigate the causes of these problems, recommend solutions, and take corrective action when they have the authority to do so.[1] As the concept developed, groups have also been formed of employees from different areas.

The general feeling of those who have participated in quality circles is that they should meet for one hour once a week, consist of five to ten people, and make presentations to top management on the results of their activities. There is general agreement that participating in circles makes their jobs more enjoyable. About half of these questioned indicate that they spend their own time on circle activities. They feel that the quality of work and productivity have improved, while the relationship with others in their own units as well as others has not changed.

Process

The quality circle methodology does not leave decision making in the hands of employees. It does allow for the involvement of employees in the development of proposed solutions to departmental problems:

A problem that affects the group can be identified by any member of it.

The group chooses the problems to be discussed.

The members of the group analyze the chosen problem with the outside provision of data from specialists, if necessary.

A recommendation is made to management.

Management reviews the recommendation.

Management makes the decision whether to implement the group's recommendation.

The problems the group identifies are usually of no interest to anyone else but affect their own work. Housekeeping may be getting inadequate service from an outside laundry, for example. The large inter-organizational problems are not ones with which the group can or should deal.

Brainstorming, a technique that stresses the creative development of ideas in a group setting and initially involving no criticism of the ideas, has been found to be the most useful way of developing problems to be studied. It is appropriate that the group members themselves identify the problems, because they are the employees who do the job and are therefore most familiar with the things that prevent them from accomplishing their tasks.

During the analysis stage, it is important that the leader of the group avoid attempting to solve the problem on his or her own. The satisfaction for the members, from which develops feelings of trust and loyalty, comes from being involved in the problem-solving process.

Similarly, when data is requested from outside specialists, it is important that they do not take over dealing with the problems. Once they have given the information the group wants, they must step aside and allow the members to continue.

Solutions are recommended to management by means of oral presentations. Typically, the presentation takes place on the employees' own time. For employees, the formal presentation offers recognition for them and their efforts that a written memo would not.

It is unusual for groups to recommend solutions to management that entail great deals of money. In fact, management has accepted anywhere from 85 to 100 percent of group recommendations from quality circles in existence. A thorough explanation, delivered in a timely fashion, is necessary if the idea has to be turned down. This is needed to prevent feelings of discouragement to enter the group.

Successful Implementation

Several factors must be present for a quality circle program to succeed.

First, management support is crucial. The kind of support is important. It must be within or under the control of the organization that is using the quality circle. It is necessary that line people believe in and control the activities, rather than a staff department interested in quality control, for example. That support should also be at the highest possible level of management. Depth of management support is also a consideration. The more people support the idea, the better its chances will be. Management support also must be visible. This can be done through management attendance at the weekly meetings—not to control, but to support. Presentations to management also offer the opportunity to express the support of top management.

Second, participation in circles must be voluntary. The percentage of employees who volunteer varies from 30 to 100 percent, with 70 percent being the average. The group will not work if employees feel they have to be there. A twist on this is to make everyone a member of the group, then suggest that after training, if they do not like the idea they can drop out. The advantage is that many who would not have tried it are exposed to the concept and find that they like it.

The attitude must be one of people building rather than people using. While employee ideas are being used, the rationale for this must be the development of employees. If employees are developed, their ideas will come. People building comes from such things as giving assignments to group members, involving everyone in meetings, giving training in problem solving, and allowing members to participate in presentations to management.

Training is appropriate for management, the group leader, and its members alike. Management training, extending over several hours, focuses on information to allow the necessary coordination and support. Leader training is much more intensive. Leaders are exposed over three days to the various techniques of quality circles. Additionally, they study the dynamics of groups, what motivates individuals, and how to encourage communication in a group setting. Member training occurs within the first few meeting sessions. They receive instruction on problem-solving techniques.

It is vital that teamwork be encouraged. While human beings are by nature competitive, the success of circles comes from their working as a team. To help establish this, circles will typically develop a code of conduct to guide behavior at meetings. Examples of such items would be:

- Attend all meetings and be on time.
- Criticize ideas, not people.
- Every member is responsible for the team's progress.
- Everyone is equal during meetings.

Employee recognition is another necessary element of the process. We all want to be recognized for our efforts. There are several ways of providing that employee recognition. The presentation to management is the most obvious and the one with the most impact. For the first time for many employees, this is their chance to present their ideas to management. The potential impact of this as a motivational tool cannot be overemphasized. Recognition can also be given in company newsletters, through photos on bulletin boards, and by management attendance at meetings.

Members must restrict the selection of problems to those over which they have some degree of expertise. Because they know something about the problem and its causes, they will have a greater chance of recommending a solution that will be successful. Success breeds more success. From this will come the confidence to attempt solving other problems.

Circle members must solve problems, not just identify them. It is all too easy to identify a problem and pass it off to someone else. The circle then becomes no more than a gripe session. When members are responsible for solving the problems they identify, they tend to select problem areas that are more manageable and that affect them more directly.

Quality circles by themselves will not solve all of management's woes. Properly implemented, however, they can result in employee feelings of trust and loyalty. These feelings come from the confidence management has placed in them by asking their opinion. In other words, they feel like part of the team.

MANAGEMENT BEHAVIOR

The day-to-day behavior of managers nurtures or destroys a climate of trust and loyalty. Employees are constantly looking to determine the extent to which they should be on their guard in dealing with management. The more they perceive management as being threatening, the more time they will spend on their own emotional defenses. The more they perceive an atmosphere in which they can grow, the more they can devote emotionally to the job at hand.

Behavior That Encourages Trust

To develop feelings of trust, employees must feel that their supervisor is sincerely interested in their welfare, that their well-being will be taken into account as management strives to meet the objectives of the company, and that managers have the necessary skills and authority to meet these objectives.

Several types of managerial behavior can inspire that level of confidence on the part of the employees.

Encourage employees to express doubts, feelings, and concerns. In some companies, expressing doubt about a management course of action is liable to have that person labeled a traitor to the organization. In such an atmosphere, creative ideas are stifled.

Tell employees the reasons behind requests. When people understand why they are being asked to perform, rather than just told what to do, they feel that management has a greater respect for them as individuals. Consequently, they respect management more and perform better.

When something goes wrong, be more concerned about what happened and how to prevent it than finding and punishing the guilty party. This does not mean permitting or encouraging slackness. It does mean that the focus is on problem solving—including the participation of affected parties—rather than on assigning blame.

Encourage employees to come to you for assistance, while at the same time developing independent judgment on their part.

Be candid about the person to whom you are talking, but never gossip about anyone else. Managers are never off the record.

SUMMARY

When employees feel that a low level of teamwork exists within the company, managers must move to increase feelings of trust and loyalty on the part of workers.

This means getting employees to invest emotionally in the company. As a developer-manager, a superior seeks to build team responsibility and interpersonal goals while increasing goal commitment on the part of subordinates. Quality circles are one way to encourage these things. The day-to-day behavior of management is also important to develop feelings of trust within employees.

NOTES

[1]Dewar, Donald L., *The Quality Circle Guide to Participative Management,* Englewood Cliffs, N.J., Prentice-Hall Inc., 1980, 2.

SUGGESTED READINGS

Buchanan, Bruce B., "To Walk an Extra Mile: The Whats, Whens, and Whys of Organizational Commitment," *Organizational Dynamics* 3, no. 4, 1975, 67–80.

Dewar, Donald L., *The Quality Circle Guide to Participative Management,* Englewood Cliffs, N.J., Prentice-Hall Inc., 1980.

Feinberg, Mortimer R., "Trust Is a Trade-Off," *Executive Housekeeper,* September 1977, 62–64.

Lewicki, Roy J., "Organizational Seduction: Building Commitment to Organizations," *Organizational Dynamics* 10, no. 2, 1982, 5–21.

Salancik, Gerald R., "Commitment Is Too Easy," *Organizational Dynamics* 6, no. 1, 1977, 62–80.

Scholl, Richard W., "Differentiating Organizational Commitment from Expectancy as a Motivating Force," *Academy of Management Review* 6, no. 4, 1981, 589–99.

Sheldon, Mary E., "Investments and Involvements as Mechanisms Producing Commitment to the Organization," *Administrative Science Quarterly* 16, 1971, 143–50.

Steers, R. M., "Antecedents and Outcomes of Organizational Commitment," *Administrative Science Quarterly* 22, no. 1, 1977, 46–56.

Stevens, John M., Beyer, Daniel M., and Trice, Harrison M., "Assessing Personal, Role, and Organizational Predictors of Managerial Commitment," *Academy of Management Journal* 21, no. 3, 1978, 380–96.

University Associates, Inc., "Developing Trust: A Leadership Skill," San Diego, 1981.

APPENDIX: IMPLEMENTING A CLIMATE OF TRUST

The manager's task is to increase feelings of loyalty and trust on the part of others. The easiest place to begin is with himself or herself. Group trust can be encouraged if the manager takes risks, disclosing some personal information to other members of the group. It is likely that in such a situation, the rest of the work group will respond in kind.

This exercise will help the manager understand the behavior associated with a climate of trust and will assist the manager in developing goals to encourage such behavior within himself or herself.

BEHAVIOR

Behavior associated with creating a climate of trust includes:

Sharing: the sharing of personal events

Vulnerability: the extent to which the manager is perceived as capable of being fallible

Loyalty: showing commitment to the goals of the company

Acceptance: accepting the unique behavior of others

Involvement: encouraging the input of others

Valuing: willingness to exchange ideas and ideals with others

Awareness: sensitivity to the needs of others

Communication: giving clear oral and written information

Openness: willingness to explore new ideas, opinions, and options

Honesty: avoidance of deceit

EVALUATING BEHAVIOR

To what extent do you exhibit these types of behavior in your dealings with your employees? Give an example of each.

Score as follows:

C: The behavior is exhibited *consistently* or most of the time.

F: The behavior is exhibited *frequently* (much of the time).

I: The behavior is exhibited *infrequently* (sometimes).

S: The behavior is *seldom* exhibited (very little).

Behavior	Score (C,F,I, or S)	Example
Sharing		
Vulnerability		
Involving others		
Valuing		
Awareness		
Communicating		
Openness		
Honesty		

DEVELOPMENT GOALS

For each of these types of behavior, develop goals for yourself. Commit yourself to specific behavior that will increase your effectiveness in establishing trust among your employees. Complete these sentences:

In the area of sharing, I will: _____

_____

In the area of vulnerability, I will: _____

_____

In the area of loyalty, I will: _____

_____

In the area of accepting others, I will: _____

_____

In the area of involving others, I will: _____

_____

In the area of valuing, I will: _____

_____

In the area of awareness, I will: _____

_____

In the area of communicating, I will: _____

_____

In the area of openness, I will: _____

_____

In the area of honesty, I will: _____

_____

INDEX

Date Due

DEC – 2 1992	
SEP 2 8 1994	
MAR 2 9 1999	